THE **BIGGER** BOOK OF APPS

● ●

Your Nerdy BFF's Guide to (Almost) Every App in the Universe

THE BIGGER
BOOK OF APPS

Your Nerdy BFF's Guide to
(Almost) Every App in the Universe

by Beth Ziesenis
Your Nerdy Best Friend

The Bigger Book of Apps

Your Nerdy BFFs Guide to (Almost) Every App in the Universe

Library of Congress Control Number:

ISBN: 978-1-7341834-0-5

Printed in the United States of America

Your Nerdy Best Friend Ink
Avenue Z, Inc.
11205 Lebanon Road #212
Mt. Juliet, TN 37122
yournerdybestfriend.com

When I was first learning to use computers,
I could use my father's modem to dial into his system to say hi
on the computer when I got home from school.

One day I hooked into the modem as usual, expecting to get
the "Hi, Biffy," greeting from him like I always did.

Instead, what flashed across the screen was

"YOU HAVE TRIGGERED THE EMERGENCY SYSTEM.
THE ENTIRE COMPUTER NETWORK
IS NOW SHUTTING DOWN
FOR THE ENTIRE COMPANY."

My eyes got as big as my face,
and I slowly backed away from the monitor.

Papa called a few minutes later.

"Ha ha!" he said. "My little trick scared you!"

To Scott Ziesenis, my papa,
a brilliant computer programmer
and one of the first computer pranksters

Thanks to the NerdHerd

The NerdHerd is the community of supporters who pre-purchase my books and provide advice and contributions along the way. This book had a record number of NerdHerders. Thanks to them all! Look for the NerdHerd Approved symbol to see their favorite apps throughout the book

Addison & Ashley Simon

Alicia Vincent

Allyson Pahmer

Amanda Glass

Amanda Jones

Andrea Hilyard

Andrew Rucker

Ann Hutchison

Anne Campbell

Anne DarConte

Anne Lupkoski

Another Nerdy Best Friend

April Tanner

Arlene Sarte

Barbara Hamilton

Barbara L. Rambow

Beth Bridges, The Networking Motivator

Beth Camero

Beth Surmont

Beth Tutwiler-McGuire

Betty Brock

Bianca M. Constance, CAP, OM

Bill Grubb

Blair Brown

Blue Ridge Association of REALTORS®

Bobby Wood

Bonnie Jo Davis

Brandie Fontenot

Breeda Miller

Brenda Garza

Bret Schanzenbach

Brett M. Hanft, CBA

Brian J. Owen

Bridgette Bienacker

Brook Dilworth

Brooke Silva, N.E.R.D.

Burton Dicht

Calvina King

Candi Rawlins

Candy Joyce

Carla the Crabby One

Carol C. Seal, RCE

Carol Campbell

Carol Hamilton

Carol Lane

Carol Zingelmann

Carolina Wilson, CAP OM / CEOE

Carolyn House, AE

Carolyn Parkin

Carolyn Phillips

Carrie S. Holt

Carrie Speer

Cathi Eifert Horner, CAE

Celia Fritz-Watson, IOM

Chad Hainline

Cheryl Smith

Chris Cavanaugh

Chris Champion

Chris Christensen

Chris Lyles

Christina Newton

Christine Guise

Christine Hokans

Cindy Camargo, CAP

Cindy L. Maggio

Clark Jones

Claudette Berwin

Coleen Curtis

Colleen Neill

Craig Borner

Crissy Hancock

Cristle Bray

Dana Frankland

Dara B.

Darcy Burnett

David "Captain Awesome" Crain

David Kirby, N.E.R.D.

David Littleton

DeAna Miller

Debbie Lowenthal

Deborah Hudson

Deborah Key

Debra Jason

Debra Strange

Debra Weidert

Debra Whalen

Denise M. Smith

Denise Merlino

Denise Morton

Dianne Richards

Donna Olewinski

Dot Raulston

Doyle Huggins

Duane Washkowiak

Ed Weaver

Eileen Blake

Eileen Schuster

Elizabeth Bartz

Ellen Wodiuk, CCE, ICCE

Emily Arrowsmith

Emily Garner

Eric Sutton

Erica Sturkie

Fran Rickenbach

Francine Butler

Gail Stanley

Garry Wicker

Gary Rifkin

Gay Wilson

Gayle Quedens

George Breeden

Gil Savage

Gina Sutherland

Gloria Rossiter

Greg Hummel

Gregory McLaren

Heather Blanchard

Heather Smith

Helen Hurst

Holly Cormier

Jackie Barry

Jackie Humphrey

Jackie Rakers

James B Martin

Jamie Buck

Jamie Rice, CMP

Jamison & Ashton Barcelona
(my adorable nephews)

Janet Jordan, CAE

Janet McEwen, M.A., CAE

Jeanette Alston-Watkins

Jeanne L. McAuliffe, cHAP

Jeffrey Horn

Jennie Dean

Jennifer Franco

Jennifer L. Van Ort, MA

Jeri Hendrie, CMP

Jerrica Dodd

Jerry Huffman, CCE

Jewels Doughty

Jill Rasco

Joanne Campbell

Joanne St-Pierre

Joe Ferri

Joe Lattimore

Joel Heffner

John & Kerry Harris

John Gann

John Gronewold

John Zink

Jon Petz, CSP

Joseph Webbe

Joy Potter

Joyce Pleva

Juan Lorenzo Martinez Colon

Judi Kadela

Judith Briles, The Book Shepherd

Judy Oiler

Julie Holmes

Julie Kellman

Julie Larson

Julie Lynch

Julie Perrine

Karen Butler

Karen Lowe

Karen Smith

Karla J. Thompson

Karyn Buxman & Greg Godek

Kathleen Fitzpatrick

Kathleen O'Regan

Kathy Hooten

Kay Babylon-West

Kay Snyder

Kerri Mertz

Kerri Wilson

Kevan Lyons

Kim Becking

Kim Haase

Kim Mangum

Kim Mydland

Kim Williams

Kimberly Joyce

Kimberly Lilley

Kitty Collins

Kristin Clarke, CAE

Kristine Spreigl

Kyla Kimball

L. Williams

Landa Pennington

LaRee Pearson

Laura Featherston

Laura Keasling

Laura Troyer

Lauran Star

Laurie Burney

Laurie Houston

Lena Wilson

Leslie Davidson

Leslie Whittet

Linda Richards

Lindsey Haley

Lisa Farquharson

Lisa Perry

Lisa Pinkston

Lisa Priepot

Lisa Weitzel, IOM, CAE

Liz Viall

Lois Creamer

Loretta Mingram

Loretta Peskin

Lori Ropa

Louise Smith, CAP, OM

Lousanne Lofgren

Lowell Aplebaum

Lynda Layer

Lynette vonAllmen

Maddie Williams

Malcolm Sweet

Marcia Clarke,
    Member, Brooklyn Board of
    REALTORS®

Marcia L. Turner, PDMM, CSA

Marcia Pecjak, AAB, CAP, OM,
    PACE

Margaret Martin

Mariko Lanicek

Marilyn Sherman, CSP

Mark Figg

Marlene LaMoure Urbach

Marquesa Pettway,
    The Speakerpreneur™ & Zoom
    Queen

Marti Kramer

Marti L. Wangen, CAE

McKinleyville Chamber of
    Commerce

Megan Mueller

Melissa Camp

Melissa Heeke

Melissa Hull

Michael F. Brown

Michele Huber

Michelle B. Grachek, M.Ed, CAE

Micki Novak

Misty Dawn Seidel

Ms. H. Montgomery

Nanci Saucier

Nancy Deichert

Nancy McCulley

Nell Withers McCauley

Nick Wallpe

Nicole Abbott

Nicole Sheets

Nora Y. Onishi, CAP, MEP, OM, PM

Pam Auld

Pam Donahoo

Pamela Brown

Pamela Whalen

Patricia Galligan

Paul Anderson

Paula Costa Bravo

Pete Todd

Phil Gerbyshak

Priscilla Bosco

RaDonna Hessel

Raquel Ortiz

Ray Atteberry

Rena Cotsones, Ph.D.

Renae Hinchey

Rhonda Ross, LBR Home Selling Team

Rhonda Zunker

Rita Tayenaka

Robert Kornegay

Robert Newman

Robert Tindell

Robin Hinders

Robin Wedewer

Robyn Turney

Roger Nelson

Ron Sarver, CAE

Ross G. Saunders

Samantha Ryan-Smith

Sandie Shea-Crabb

Sandy Lex

Sarah Luebbert

Scott Weaver

Scott Ziesenis (That's my dad!)

Shala Bible, IOM

Shannon Carroll, CAP, OM, TA

Sharon D'Arcey

Sharon Dawes

Sharon NeSmith, GM, Hampton Inn & Suites

Sharon Telles

Sheryl Robinson

Sidney Rothenburger

Skip Koski, Florida Panhandle REALTOR®

Sonja Morgan

Stacey Morris

Stephanie Butler

Stephanie Shapiro

Steve Snyder

Susan Armbrester

Susan Briley

Susan Mahnke

Susan Motley

Susan Panzica

Susan Valle

Suzanne Green

Sydney Isaac, CAE, MBA

Sylvia Ayers

Tami DuBose

Tammy Bruestle

Terry Eichel

Terry Murphy

The Dalles Area
Chamber of Commerce

The Diving Equipment &
Marketing Association
(DEMA.org)

Thomas Williams

Tim & Jamie Buckley

Tim & Shana Teehan

Tim Holt

Tim Zielenbach

Tina Litteral

Todd Crow

Tom O'Rourke

Tom Wright

Toni Fanelli

Tonja Money

Traci Brown

Tracy Taraski

Tracy Wilson

Trevor Mitchell

Trudy Bounds

UF Conference Department

Valinda & Bill Lessin

Vickie Lester

Victor Goodpasture,
Mr. San Diego

W. Craig Henry PRP, CPP-T

Wade Koehler, CAE

Wayne King

Yvonne A. Hersh, CAE

Table of Contents

Utilities   179

Security   201

Travel   231

Finance   261

How to Use This Book

Dear Readers,

The BIGGER Book of Apps is an updated version of *The Big Book of Apps*, which came out in 2018. This version has almost 600 apps, all of which are either brand new or completely updated.

When you read this book, keep these thoughts in mind:

Read This Book at Your Own Risk

In both 2017 and 2019, an app called FaceApp freaked everyone out. The app used facial mapping to apply weird and disturbing filters, such as making faces look old or trying on feminine and masculine characteristics. Once about forty-eleven million people had tried it out in a matter of hours, security experts sounded the alarm. The app was accused of things like using everyone's face for facial recognition in Russia and selling images and downloading whole camera rolls and all kinds of stuff.

I've vetted the tools in this book to the best of my ability. These are apps and sites I use and download. But I can't swear that they're safe. And even if I could swear they're safe today, I can't swear they'll be safe tomorrow. They may be hacked. They may be sold to dishonest people. They may have been lying to all of us all along. I just can't promise you anything.

Thus, I urge you to vet these recommendations on your own before you trust them. And if you find anything suspicious or hear of a problem, please let me know right away.

We should all strive to double check a tool's credentials before using and sharing, just like we need to fact check an outrageous-sounding story before posting. I have a few guidelines to protect myself from malware, harmful apps and other infected technology.

- I research whatever I find on reputable sites like TechCrunch, Mashable, C I Net and more. If a tool seems too obscure or unknown, I'll wait until it has a little more web history.

- I use safeguards to protect my identity like the ones on Pages 218–219 to not sign up for new things unless I'm sure that they're safe.

- I am very careful about the place I download a tool. Apple's App Store has very rigorous requirements for app approval, so apps from there are *rarely* inherently evil. Android is a different story. Be super, super, super careful about installing any Android app from outside the Google Play Store—and use common sense about apps within the store as well.

Get the Other Books

I can no longer write one book that includes everything I want to share with people, so I am adding supplemental information in companion volumes. Look for *The Little Book of Apps*, a quick reference guide with all the apps from this book. Then check out *The Little Book of Video Tools*, which contains in-depth tips for creating videos and graphics for marketing and social media.

This Book Is a Starting Point

The BIGGER Book of Apps is organized by common tasks and the apps that help you complete them. For each task, you'll find a couple of main recommendations plus several alternates. But the tasks and the tools that I've chosen to complete them are by no means exhaustive. My goal is to get you started in the right direction so you can find what you need.

These Tools Are a Starting Point

For the most part, each tool is just one option in a very crowded and competitive category. I included alternatives to each, but that list is just a starting place for a plethora of competitors.

These Tools Are Awesome

I chose these particular tools for their dependability, multiplatform availability, popularity and ease of use. If you've attended any of my presentations, this book serves as the missing manual for the tools I talk about.

I started this volume by examining the 460+ tools in the first book, I was happily surprised to find that less than 8 percent of the tools I chose had disappeared completely.

I'm very proud of that fact. It means that the vetting process I use to find the best apps is effective. I choose tools that have staying power, even in today's incredibly fast-changing tech world.

This Book Is Out of Date

We triple checked the pricing, platforms and functionality of the tools in this book right up until we pushed the print button, but the next week, the descriptions will be out of date. The good news is that most of the changes you'll see will probably be growth in availability and functionality.

Look for changes in these areas:

- Platform availability (access via new operating systems, etc.)
- Pricing (up and down)

- Extra-special features (groundbreaking, oh-my-gosh functionality with big announcements)
- Integrations and partnerships (increasing every day)
- Incorporation into the Internet of Things, like IFTTT (Page 33) logging how many times your smart dishwasher runs or Evernote (Page 15) automatically sending new recipes to your smart stove

Despite these inevitable changes and advancements, you can be confident that this book will serve as the starting place for putting this technology into action for your work, home and life.

Organization

●●●

In This Chapter...

Manage Lists

My secret shame: my "high-tech" task list manager is a pen and a spiral-bound notebook. I can't use an electronic list maker because I'm too easily distracted online. I have to have a physical list in front of me and the absolute joy of crossing things off.

But other folks are more advanced than I. Here are the best recommendations for to-do lists.

Start with...

Todoist
My Manager's Favorite Productivity Tool
todoist.com

I'm putting **Todoist** at the top of my list of list tools based on the masterful way my sales manager uses it to keep Nerd HQ on track. Molly Veydovec uses Todoist for every part of her life, from our short-term projects to our long-term ideas to the home projects she'll get to someday.

Like many of the top task list tools, Todoist lets you sync your lists on any device. When Molly forces me to use it, I find the integration with Gmail (Page 106) very helpful, because I can turn emails into tasks and throw them back on her plate with a couple of clicks. I never needed more than the free version, but Molly finds the extra features in premium very helpful, such as more projects, location-based reminders and the capability to work with more collaborators.

Todoist gets extra points for its natural-language task skills (such as "remind me to make my car payment on the first of every month starting in October"), as well as its integrations with automation tools like IFTTT and Zapier (Page 33).

Like Molly, several NerdHerders love Todoist, and at least one loves it *because* of Molly.

From Gary Rifkin...

> *We fell in love with this tool after Molly Veydovec (who is also AWESOME, by the way) recommended it. My colleague Bekah Selking and I wouldn't dream of getting on a conference call without our shared Todoist projects open on our screen. We can add comments to tasks, create sub-tasks and repeating tasks and ultimately get so much more done. They've even gamified the application with a personalized "karma score," which recognizes when you get a lot done and meet productivity goals. WE LOVE TODOIST! (And Beth Z and Molly for their brilliance!!!)*

Although they didn't use as many exclamation points, Barbara Rambow, Kathy Hooten and Thomas Williams also gave it thumbs up.

Then Try...

Plan
Task Manager and Planning Tool
getplan.co

One of my problems with task lists is that they're just lists. Sure, I can add a deadline to most of them, but that doesn't help me plan out when to get them done. The list just sits there and grows, and the traditional task list tools don't really help me plan to be more productive. That's why I was thrilled to discover **Plan**, a time-management tool that integrates task lists with calendars with time-boxing (Page 31).

This is the time-boxing tool I've been looking for. Not only does it allow me to keep track of the things I need to do, it also lets me put the tasks on the calendar so I can block off the time to get things done. I can also link tasks to documents in Google Drive (Page 64) and Box (Page 11).

The bummer thing is that Plan doesn't integrate with many other tools, so I can't take another task list and pull it in. I also can't turn a task I get via Gmail into a task like I can with Todoist. But when I'm trying to plan on how to get my tasks finished, this is a winner.

BONUS: Plan focuses on time management, and a handy dashboard lets you see how well you're doing.

Also Check Out...

Microsoft To Do
The App that Is Eating Award-Winning Wunderlist
todo.microsoft.com

Wunderlist
The Award-Winning Task Manager with a Rabid Fanbase
wunderlist.com

When I wrote the first edition of *The Big Book of Apps*, I was sure that **Wunderlist** would be gone by the time the book hit the shelves, absorbed by Microsoft's **To Do** app. But the Wunderlist fans rebelled, and, to paraphrase author Mark Twain, the reports of its death have been greatly exaggerated. So I jumped the gun. #NerdFail

By the time you read this, Wunderlist may or may not be around. Microsoft is slowly backing away from the tool in favor of To Do. In the spring of 2019, Wunderlist lost its integration with Microsoft's Cortana and other skills. Although the app is still being updated, Microsoft released a statement that said, "We're not currently working on new features for Wunderlist as we're concentrating on our new app, Microsoft To Do."

Another sign of the times: In the last book, Wunderlist was listed as the favorite app by four NerdHerders. This time Paula Costa Bravo was the only one who mentioned it. But she shows the typical love people feel for it: "Wunderlist is a simple to-do list and task manager to get stuff done!"

NerdHerd Thumbs Up: More Task Tools

BZ Reminder
Reminder Tool with Missed Call Alerts
bzreminder.com

Pocket Lists
NerdHerd Favorite Simple To-Do List
pocketlists.com

Our NerdHerd community has a couple more secret to-do list tools. Chris D. says the free version of **Pocket Lists** is an excellent tool for your task lists, and Tim Holt likes the simplicity of **BZ Reminder.** BZ Reminder bonus: When you miss a call, the app reminds you so you don't forget.

Hot Topic:
Integrate Your Personal
Tasks with Work Projects

The apps in this section are time-tested tools that can help with individual productivity. But because the line between work and home is often zigzagged, you might consider using a project management tool like those starting on Page 58 to manage things you need to do both in and out of the office. That way you can see at a glance what your full day looks like, rather than having to pop in and out of different lists to get the big picture. You can also use a calendar that pulls your personal and work tasks into the same view.

Manage Schedules

• •

I bet that zero people reading this book can keep track of every commitment they have at every moment of every day. We all need calendars—and more—we all need calendars that we can see and update from any device at any time.

Start with...

Google Calendar

The Calendar to Rule Them All
google.com/calendar

Google Calendar is a free tool to create and share multiple calendars and import other calendar feeds so your whole schedule is available when and where you need it.

Few tools offer as much versatility as Google Calendar. You might want to consider using it as the building block of your time management system. The beauty of this relatively simple tool is its capability to import from, export to and integrate with an ever-increasing mountain of other apps and systems.

Then Try...

Any.do

Simple Task Manager with Day-by-Day Manager
any.do

People adore **Any.do** for its simplicity. I'm fond of the day planner feature that helps you prioritize the day's events. You can also use the gamification incentives with Any.do to make task management fun (kidding—to-do lists are not fun).

Also Check Out...

Business Calendar 2

Best Android Calendar App

appgenix-software.com

Fantastical 2 (iOS)

Best Apple Calendar App

flexibits.com

I'm not being honest with either app in this category because Google is really the best calendar for either. But if you don't like Google, these are pretty wonderful. And the good news is that if you use Google Calendar, you can pull the events in through either of these tools.

Fantastical 2 wins awards and has a loyal following. In addition to doing all the wonderful calendar-y things, it integrates into your contacts and Apple reminders to help you remember birthdays, and other things you don't want to forget.

The photo backgrounds in **Business Calendar 2** on Android make the app absolutely beautiful. It also offers widgets and customization options to tweak it to your heart's content. A bonus feature you don't find on other apps is the ability to see weather in your calendar.

Organize and Store Files

Cloud storage systems have been around for years. They've proven themselves to be an essential business tool for many professionals. At this point in the game, you're probably trying to decide among the top three: Dropbox, Google One (Google Drive) and Microsoft OneDrive.

Even though many of the leading tools offer the same types of services, you'll find small differences that may affect how you choose to use them.

Common Characteristics of Cloud Storage Systems

The cloud storage service field is very, very crowded; but a handful of companies lead the pack. In a nutshell, they serve as your hard drive—everywhere. When you sign up for an account, you download the software to your machine and install apps on your devices. The system creates a folder on your computer, and anything you place into that folder is available anywhere you need it.

Most of the major players in this field have many of the same characteristics and capabilities. Here's a summary of the features you'll find in most (if not all) of the top tools.

- Free storage of 2-16GB, including the capability to earn more when you spread the word
- Web and mobile apps to access your files from anywhere
- Real-time synchronization wherever the service is installed
- Two-factor authentication options for enhanced security
- Secure, encrypted storage with strong security measures to protect your files

ORGANIZATION

- Capability to restore deleted files and older versions
- Collaboration via shared folders or files, sometimes with different levels of permissions
- Instant file and folder sharing via links
- Integration with third-party apps for enhanced features and accessibility

Start with...

Dropbox
Arguably the Best Cloud Storage System
dropbox.com

Dropbox is perhaps the most well-known tool in this category, and it boasts the most third-party integrations. Dropbox gives 2GB of storage for free, and you can earn up to 16GB by inviting colleagues and through other tasks. Paid versions start at less than $10 a month for 2TB of storage, which is a helluva lot.

Dropbox is known for personal accounts—they're working on growing the business side. You can collaborate via Dropbox Paper (Page 66) inside apps in Microsoft Office 365. With the paid versions, the Smart Sync option makes access to files not stored on your hard drive a lot faster. Otherwise the synchronization can be kinda slow.

It's no surprise that Dropbox is a NerdHerd favorite. "Dropbox may be an 'oldie,' but it certainly is a 'goodie,'" says Robyn Turney. Anne DarConte calls it "so much better than Google Docs." Chris Cavanaugh likes that it's free and uses it to share large files like PowerPoint. And Vickie Lester says simply, "It changed my life, and the new rewind feature already has saved my bacon."

Then Try...

Google One
Google's Cloud Storage System
google.com/drive

Microsoft OneDrive
Microsoft's Cloud Storage System
onedrive.com

Google One gives you 15GB free for Google Drive and Gmail. Your slightly smaller images and videos can be stored for free in Google Photos (Page 19), but if you want to keep the original high resolution, you can store them in Google One.

I pay for the first tier, 100GB for $20 a year, and I use Google One to back up my most important files, which I also keep on an external drive and in Dropbox. On the paid levels, you can invite family members to share your storage, plus you get Google support (which is very hard to find if you're not paying them something). And you can upgrade to the Google business-level suite with G Suite (Page 12) starting at $5 a month.

As one might expect, Google One integrates seamlessly with all things Google. You also have built-in software for editing and creating.

An advantage of working in the Google One infrastructure is the real-time collaboration. If you have several committee members working on the same document at the same time, their words and changes appear on the screen, color-coded and even labeled with the users' names. Like Dropbox, Google One gives you the ability to revert to older versions of files.

Another excellent characteristic of Google One is its multimedia sharing capabilities, which make it easier to watch video online without having to download.

Unsurprisingly, Google One / Google Drive has NerdHerd admirers. Emily Garner shares the characteristic she loves best: "Storage, storage, storage!" Emily adds, "I have it set up just like my paper filing system. Just scan my documents to a file cabinet in the cloud and know they are protected. It is wonderful!"

Michelle Grachek loves it because of the collaboration capabilities:

> *Google Drive has made my life so much easier when it comes to collaborating with colleagues on documents. With Drive, multiple people can be in the same document without saving over each other's work. It is fabulous!*

OneDrive's primary purpose is to make it easy to store Microsoft documents when you have a Microsoft 365 subscription. Although anyone can get an account with 5GB of free storage or 100GB starting at $1.99 per month, if you're a subscriber, you get 1TB free.

OneDrive lets users communicate in real time when they're in Microsoft Office documents. For years this functionality kinda sucked, but my last test was a big success.

Also Check Out...

Box
Business-Focused Cloud Storage System
box.com

Sync
Extra-Secure Dropbox Alternative
sync.com

Box is focusing almost exclusively on the business market. For the personal level, Box gives you 10GB with the free plan, but you'll have to pay extra for version tracking and some of the other features Dropbox gives for free. The Personal Pro plan is $10 a month, but instead of 2TB of data like you get with Dropbox, you get a measly 100GB.

Starting at $5 per user on the business plans, you can start collaborating (but just between paid users). For $15 per user per month, you can enable project management with tasks and deadlines.

A cool feature with Box is the built-in editing software. Box has its own software that lets you edit and create documents within the system, as well as through outside software such as Microsoft Office and Google.

While there is no shortage of Dropbox alternatives, **Sync** bills itself as a super-duper secure Dropbox alternative. The overall cost is less than Dropbox, but you have to pay yearly. Sync's security uses the "zero-knowledge principle," which means that, unlike Dropbox, the company has absolutely no access to your files.

NerdHerd Thumbs Up: G Suite

G Suite
Google's Professional Office Suite
gsuite.google.com

Many millions of us have learned to ignore the ads in Gmail and deal with the workarounds to be able to send and receive emails from different domains, but for many business owners, the free version of Google's tools is not enough.

According to NerdHerder Jill Rasco,

> Our company moved to Google (before there was **G Suite**) years ago, and I am totally spoiled by the way we can collaborate on documents, spreadsheets, presentations, etc. AND, good ole Google Search works to help me find things since I rarely remember the actual name of the file :).

G Suite is Google's answer to the full Microsoft Office suite. You can set up emails with personal domains, collaborate with co-workers, store and search for lots and lots of files and much more. Investing in G Suite starting at $5 a month also gets you an ad-free experience and access to online meeting services such as Google Hangouts.

Keep Track of Ideas: Solo Edition

Think about all the little things you research and collect daily: Photos, websites, documents, recipes, notes....And many people keep these little pieces of digital references in several different places: photo albums, bookmarks, computer folders....

To get organized, we need a system that lets us access everything we need in a couple of seconds rather than having to search different systems or hunt hither and yon. That's where the note organization tools can help.

Note: Although all of these tools have sharing capabilities so you can share resources with teams, check out the tools for better resource sharing on Page 64.

Start with...

Apple Notes
Apple's Internal Note System
On Apple Devices

Google Keep
Google's Note-Taking Tool
google.com/keep

OneNote
Microsoft's Note-Taking Tool
onenote.com

Where do you hang out? That's where your notes can hang, too. I think using the tools native to your main platform may be the best place to find a tool for taking notes and storing all the digital files you need to find in a flash.

Though Microsoft's **OneNote** preceded the ever-popular Evernote by 5 years, people didn't really start using it until the free version of

Evernote took off and Microsoft made OneNote free. The two systems are relatively similar in that you can store anything and search for anything. OneNote obviously does a great job of integrating into the Microsoft suite of products, allowing users to throw bits of information into the system from any Microsoft program. NerdHerder Carolina Wilson gives it a thumbs up because OneNote is her "Post-It Notes" gathering place on the computer.

Google Keep is also easy to use within Google's infrastructure, but both OneNote and Keep can stand on their own as well. Google Keep has fewer features than the other two top note-taking tools, but NerdHerder Sydney Isaac loves it "because I don't have to have a thousand sticky notes!"

I live in the rarefied Apple air, so I use **Apple Notes**. It's nowhere near as robust as Evernote or OneNote, but it suits my needs perfectly. I take notes into the app on my phone, they're synchronized through iCloud to my Mac, and I can reach them on any browser. I can store photos, links, tasks, lists and regular old notes that are searchable from my device (not just inside the app). NerdHerder Deborah Key loves it, too. "I use Notes for grocery lists, special quotes I want to remember and things I want to do quickly and access easily," she says.

Then Try...

Simplenote
A Very Simple Note-Taking Tool
simplenote.com

If all you need to do with notes is to actually write notes (as opposed to saving multimedia, etc.), check out the lightweight tool **Simplenote**. It's very minimalistic, hence the "simple" name. But it's free, and people love it.

Also Check Out...

Evernote
The Past Champion Note-Taking Tool
evernote.com

Updating this section has been tough. On one hand, **Evernote** has been the undisputed champ in this category for years. But it's not what it used to be, and rumors have swirled amongst the nerdy folk that the grandfather is on its way out. But Evernote's insanely loyal user base is sticking with it, and CEO Ian Small says it is financially sound and making changes. In a blog post called "Looking Ahead: Evernote's Priorities for 2019," Small says:

> ...honesty requires us to state—straight out—that we can do better with the product you have today than we are currently doing. In fact, we can do better than we have been doing for some years.

So they're getting another mention, although not in the "Start with…" pole position. Though they've taken away some of the free features that we love, it's still a tool that stands out with the most features and integrations.

Evernote enables you to store pictures, documents, notes, webpages, snippets of text, handwritten doodles on napkins, emails and anything else you can possibly imagine. The search engine even combs through text in pictures (and in PDFs for Premium subscribers).

You can add your information to Evernote in every possible way as well—through browser plug-ins, email, web apps, desktop apps and mobile apps. When you have the information you want, you can tag it, organize it into folders, share it and search for it. The free version now limits you to two devices, but it's still feature-rich, and NerdHerders still love it.

NerdHerd members Doyle Huggins, Marcia Turner, Nancy McCulley and Patricia Galligan are all Evernote fans. "No more little scraps of info written and then tossed by mistake," Marcia says. And Nancy adds, "Text, images, reminders…it has everything I need!"

NerdHerd Thumbs Up: Going High-Tech with Handwritten Notes

Rocketbook
Smart Notebook to Save Handwritten
Notes to the Cloud
getrocketbook.com

I'm so glad NerdHerder Jackie Rakers shared **Rocketbook** as her favorite tech tool. Everyone needs to know about this tool that blends old school handwritten notes with modern technology. You take notes in the smart notebook just like you would in a steno pad. Then you can program the system so you can snap pictures of your notes and immediately send them to wherever you want: Evernote, Dropbox, email and many other options. Once you fill your notebook, you can erase the ink and use it again without losing any notes. What's more, handwriting recognition means your notes are transcribed into editable text.

Jackie is a huge fan. "Handwrite your notes on an erasable notebook and upload to the cloud! You get organized notes without hunting through your notebook!"

Create a Mind Map

I'm a linear thinker. Give me a traditional outline, and I'm good to go. But lots of you like to balloon one idea after another and connect them in creative ways. These tools are for you.

Start with...

Creately
Online Mind Map Tool
creately.com

Stormboard
Teamwork-Type Mind Maps
stormboard.com

Creately revamped its look in 2019 to create a colorful, intuitive online mind-mapping tool. You can start with all kinds of template and layout options, and within a few minutes, you can fill in the boxes to visualize your ideas. **Stormboard** has a similar colorful aesthetic, and both of them let you have a handful of projects for free.

Then Try...

Mindly
Mobile Mind Map Tool
mindlyapp.com

If you're sitting in a doctor's waiting room and get a grand idea, the **Mindly** app can help you get it all down. The interface is simple and clean, and you will love making the little circles swirl around. Unfortunately it's not on the web, but Mac owners can download the software.

Also Check Out...

MeisterTask
Task Management Tool with Mind Map Integration
meistertask.com

MindMeister
Mind Map Tool with Task Integration
mindmeister.com

I like the concept behind **MindMeister.** When you layout your ideas, you can convert them to actionable tasks by integrating **MeisterTask**, a favorite task management tool for teams.

Bonus: Very Basic Mind Map Tools

Bubbl.us
Super Simple, Super Free Mind Map Site
bubbl.us

Draw.io
Open-Source Diagramming Tool
draw.io

Mindmup
Free Mind Map Site
mindmup.com

Talk about easy...**Bubbl.us** and **Mindmup** are your instant gratification mind map sites with no registration required. Bubbl.us opens directly into a blank screen, and Mindmup just takes one click to get there. Neither site is very pretty, but they sure are fast.

Although **Draw.io** is not specifically a mind-mapping tool, it can undoubtedly help you layout your brainstorms. You can also create a flowchart, illustrate a timeline and visualize a concept with a Venn diagram. Use this free tool online or download the software and integrations for Google Drive, Microsoft Office and more.

Organize and Store Photos and Video

The shoebox full of old photos has been replaced by a data-hogging digital folder of images and video clips documenting soccer games, breakfasts and selfies. And both are still just as unorganized as ever. These tools help you organize, store and identify your photo memories.

Start with...

Google Photos

Unlimited Photo/Video Storage with Image Recognition
google.com/photos

Even though Apple has gained some ground in the photo organization realm, **Google Photos** is still the best by far. In 2016 Google Photos offered a great gift to the internet universe: free, unlimited photo storage for all. Besides the awesomeness of the free/unlimited feature, Google includes some positively eerie (creepy?) functionality that will forever change how you organize and find images.

Google groups photos by timelines and geography first, so you can look back to the pictures you took last April or just click on the New Orleans category to see your vacation photos from 2010. As NerdHerder Karen Butler says, the search features can save time and sanity. "I Love Google Photos!! Especially searching by subject or month!! It is a lifesaver!!"

Then it starts getting creepy. The service uses artificial intelligence through your photos and can identify faces and objects. Without any help from me, Google identified all the pictures of my nephew Ashton from a couple of months old through his teen years, even though he changed height, weight, location and even hair color.

When you click on the Assistant button, you'll discover a host of videos, collages and timelines that Google Photos created for you. You can also use their templates and search features to choose photos and videos to make creations of your own.

Then Try...

Amazon Drive

Amazon's Cloud Storage System
amazon.com/clouddrive

Amazon Prime Photos

Amazon's Answer to Google Photos
amazon.com/photos

If you have an Amazon Prime membership, the mega-seller offers a Google Photo-like storage and image recognition functionality.

Amazon Prime Photos stores your photos for sharing and accessing on your Amazon devices. You can use your photos as a screensaver for your Amazon Fire TV, for example.

Amazon Drive is definitely more of a personal storage solution than a tool you'd use for work, although you can still share files from the drive. You get 5GB free plus unlimited storage for photos if you're a member of Amazon Prime. Unlike Google Photos (Page 19), Amazon lets you upload the images in full resolution but limits your video uploads to 5GB. Like Google Drive, Amazon Drive is great for watching movies from your media collection.

Also Check Out...

ACDSee

Image Organizer and Editor with the Best Name
acdsee.com

Forever

Image Storage Tool Designed for Family Legacies
forever.com

Mylio
Image Organizer with Facial Recognition and More
mylio.com

Google Photos is my absolute top choice for image organization, but not everyone loves Google. These three tools provide advanced image organization capabilities at a price.

ACDSee's name makes me the most nostalgic, but its functionality is top notch. Although it's primarily made for professionals, ACDSee has a plan for individuals that lets you store, manage and edit images and video. It will pull all your images together to help you find duplicates, plus let you batch convert images from one format to another and much more. **Mylio** has similar functionality, and they both use facial recognition and other advanced-search features to help you categorize and sort your images.

Forever goes a bit further...ok, a lot further. The image storage site promises to "Save, Organize and Share Memories" for "Your Lifetime +100 Years Guaranteed." You'll pay a one-time fee of $199 for 10GB, but remember, that's for your lifetime plus 100 years, so I guess it's a pretty good deal. The site also comes with all kinds of memory-making add-ons, such as book printing and scrapbooking tools.

One More...

Slidebox
Mobile Photo Album Organizer
slidebox.co

As I write this, I have 10,758 images and videos on my iPhone's camera roll. That's insane! Most of them are completely worthless, like the screenshots or the accidental photos of my thumb or the 75 selfies I snapped in order to get one that hid my double chin.

Slidebox is a lightweight little photo sorter that lets you swipe through your images Tinder-style to delete or categorize.

Scan Your Old Photos

Wouldn't it be nice to dig through your old photo albums to find the great pics of you in middle school so you will win the #TBT hashtag on Throwback Thursdays? These apps and services help you manage your hard-copy pictures and old video reels.

For a Handful of Pictures, Try...

Photomyne
Photo-Scanning App for Photo Albums
photomyne.com

PhotoScan
Google's Mobile Photo Scanner App
google.com/photos/scan

Photomyne lets you snap a picture of multiple photos at once, like photos in a photo album. Then it automatically separates the photos into individual images for fine-tuning and sharing. Google's **PhotoScan** does the same thing, although I liked the results from Photomyne a little better.

For Photo Collections, Try...

DigMyPics
Service for Photo Scanning and Video Transfer
digmypics.com

Forever (Page 20)

If you have more than a handful of photos to scan, consider a service that does it for you. My sister and I digitized boxes of old photos for my dad with **DigMyPics**, and that remains the best present we ever gave him, he says. DigMyPics converts photos for $.39 each. We sent them hundreds of photos through the mail. Within a few days, they were online, and we could delete the awful ones and just pay for the ones we wanted to keep. Then they touched them up, organized them and even printed soft-cover thumbnail books as a guide. The money we spent was totally worth it.

The **Forever** site (Page 20) also offers these services.

> How many ears does
> Mr. Spock have?
> Three! ...The right ear, the left
> ear... and the final front ear!

Get Your Affairs in Order

· ·

When Mom died, she had emails in her inbox that went unanswered because we didn't have any passwords. No one likes to talk about passwords before we pass away, but these tools can help make things easier for your loved ones to manage your digital life.

Start with...

Everplans
End-of-Life Document and Information Organizer
everplans.com

SecureSafe
Super-Secure Online Storage Platform with "Data Inheritance"
securesafe.com

You'll be doing your family members a favor if you take the time to assemble the information that **Everplans** recommends. The site will help you create a personalized list of tasks and resources that you own in all kinds of corners of the internet and beyond, such as financial information, medical records, online accounts and legal documents. Everplans also lets you write letters to loved ones that will be sent after, well, you know.

If you'd rather think about this process as creating an online safe instead of creating a death plan, check out **SecureSafe.** It's a password manager and online storage system with extra secure protection. Many individuals and businesses choose SecureSafe over regular file backup tools (Page 180) because of the data inheritance capabilities.

Then Try...

Platform System Settings

Password Managers (Page 212)

Everyone has heard stories of battles with social media companies and cloud-based services to get access to a deceased family member's device or account. Because of the outcry, almost every name-brand digital company has tools in place to handle the handover of accounts to a loved one following a death. You'll have to dig around on each platform to find the settings. Facebook lets you appoint a legacy contact, or people can provide proof of a Facebook account holder's death to memorialize the page. You can also request that your page be deleted after death.

Google lets you set preferences for inactive accounts. Mine says that if Google doesn't see any activity from me for three months, the company will notify my husband that I seem to be dead. He will probably already know, but still. You can also tell Google to delete everything on your account if you are officially declared inactive.

Password management tools are useful for more than keeping your passwords safe. LastPass (Page 212), for example, lets you designate someone who can access your vault after your passing. And if you keep every single login safe in the LastPass vault (like you should), your trusted designee can access bank accounts, email and social media sites to take care of what needs to be taken care of. And if you've been backing up your social media assets with Digi.me (Page 182), your loved ones can collect your pictures and posts and memories.

Also Check Out...

Giving Docs

Online Will Creation for Charity Planned Giving Campaigns
givingdocs.com

About 10 minutes ago, I paused my book writing to craft my very first Last Will and Testament. It took me two minutes. The tool I used was **Giving Docs,** a charitable endeavor I discovered via AppSumo (Page 148). Note: If you go to their website, you'll be greeted with info for charities and fundraisers. You'll have to find a charity that is doing it in order to use it.

Giving Docs partners with charities that benefit from bequests. The charities offer the free will generator to their followers. When someone creates a will through the charity's link, the user will be provided a chance to leave a percentage of the estate to the charity that sent you the link—or any other charity you designate.

I was able to name my hubby the heir (you get the cats, honey!) and my sister the secondary beneficiary. You can get as precise as you want to with your possessions and riches. Then the site generates an official-looking document that it encourages you to run by an estate attorney before getting it notarized.

Once you create an account on Giving Docs, you can go back and complete other official forms, such as Advance Health Care Directives, Power of Attorney and more stuff you're supposed to do.

Giving Docs told the success story of Chive Charities. Of the 4,400 people who activated a Giving Docs account within 48 hours of getting the link, 42 percent left a bequest to Chive Charities. The users can go back in and modify anything at any time, but chances are Chive Charities will get donations from their efforts for years to come.

When I proudly presented my lawyer husband with my very first Last Will and Testament, he spent several minutes explaining to me that online wills may not hold up if contested. "Well, you're getting everything, so don't contest the will," I said. Then I came back here to write this review. #LawyersWillBeLawyers

Productivity

· ·

In This Chapter...

Focus and Get Things Done

When we are deep into a task and get interrupted, research says it takes about 23 minutes to get back on track. That means by the end of the day we have more work to do than we began with.

We need systems to block out the craziness of our digital world so we can get stuff done. Start here.

Start with...

Marinara Timer
Online Pomodoro Timer for Groups
marinaratimer.com

PomoDoneApp
Pomodoro-Type Task Management App
pomodoneapp.com

Pomodoro.cc
Simple Online Pomodoro Timer
pomodoro.cc

The Pomodoro Technique®
Kitchen Timer Productivity Technique
cirillocompany.de/pages/pomodoro-technique

Hands down **The Pomodoro Technique**® is the very best tool in my focus toolbox. The technique was created by an Italian guy named Francesco Cirillo with a tomato-shaped kitchen timer ("pomodoro" is Italian for "tomato"). He'd set the timer for 25 minutes and focus on ONE TASK . . . just ONE . . . for the entire 25 minutes. He'd block out calls, emails, dings, dongs and doorbells. When the timer went off, he'd take a 5-minute break to catch up on other things, then dive back into another 25-minute stretch.

The cool thing about the Pomodoro Technique is that you can do it with a kitchen timer, a fancy app or just the stopwatch on your phone. I have a couple of timers on my Mac. You don't have to complicate things...just set a timer and go.

But if you do want a little more structure, try **PomoDoneApp.** This tool connects with your favorite tools for tasks and projects. The most flexible plan will cost you about $50 a year, but your peace of mind and productivity are worth it.

And if everyone in your office has the same productivity problems, have a #PomodoroParty! Go to the **Marinara Timer** site and start a Pomodoro session. The site will create a link you can share with others. Everyone with the link will hear the same timers and be on the same productivity schedule. Every once in a while, I host an online #PomodoroParty. Participants are amazed about how much they can get done in a morning without interruptions. NerdHerder Eric Sutton says Marinara Timer is his favorite.

And finally, if you just want a site with a timer for Pomodoros, go to the no-frills **Pomodoro.cc.**

Then Try...

RescueTime
Software that Tracks Where the Time Goes
rescuetime.com

Toggl
Time-Tracking Tool for Clients and Projects
toggl.com

If you're constantly wondering "Where did today go?" you might be ready for **RescueTime**. This software runs on your computer and keeps track of every second you spend on your device and every place you spend it. You'll see time reports for how long it took you to finish a document in Microsoft Word and how many minutes you spent surfing cool cupcake pictures on Pinterest. The free version is quite robust.

If you're not good at keeping track of time yourself, give **Toggl** a try. Just click the timer once when you start a project and once when you finish. Toggl keeps track of your work hours to help with hourly billing and time management. And if it senses you're working without tracking or you stopped and forgot to turn off the timer, Toggl gently reminds you.

"Beloved" is how NerdHerder Jackie Barry refers to Toggl. "In an environment where we're not billing clients but want to be able to know where we're spending our time, it can be tough to convince some staff members to use a time tracker," Jackie says. "Three clicks and you've switched from your last project to your next project, and a desktop widget makes it even faster."

Also Check Out...

Be Focused

Apple Focus App
**xwavesoft.com/
be-focused-pro-for-iphone-ipad-mac-os-x.html**

StayFocusd

Chrome Plugin for Site Blocking
nerdybff.com/stayfocusd-app

StayFocusd is the site-blocking app that kept me out of my email and off Facebook so I could write this book. This simple Chrome browser plugin that lets you set rules to restrict yourself from going to time-sucking sites.

Be Focused is a Pomodoro-type Apple app that NerdHerder Stacey Morris loves. It's also one of the top-rated apps for focusing and tracking goals, but I excluded it from my list because it's Apple only. So thanks to Stacey, we can share it!

Hot Topic:
My Three Favorite Focus Tips

One of my most popular new sessions is called "Productivity Brain Break: A Facilitated White Space." In the session, I share the easiest, fastest, best ways to be more productive and efficient, according to an analysis from a company called Filtered Technologies.

They analyzed 100 productivity tips that were listed in all kinds of blogs to rank them by type, usability and difficulty. It's one of the best lists I've seen: nerdybff.com/100productivitytools

Here are my top three techniques.

One: Time-Boxing

Time-Boxing is Filtered's #1 pick for productivity, with good reason. It's easy to do, free and very helpful. Just use your calendar to schedule specific tasks and block off that time. This technique not only helps you get through your to-do list...it also enables you to realize how long you actually spend on tasks. And when you set aside a certain amount of time for a task, you can trick your brain into better focus because of the deadline.

You don't have to use any specialized apps, but the to-do list app Plan (Page 3) will let you create tasks and place them on a calendar to set aside enough time to get them done

Two: Control Social Media

No surprise that this tip made it into the top ten on their list of 100. We all know that it's easy to get lost in your social media accounts, from watching what your friends are doing without you on Facebook to obsessing over political jabs on Twitter.

I use the following techniques to help.

- **Add "Mess around on Facebook" to your to-do list**
  If I don't have a paper list of tasks in front of me at my computer, I flounder. And I am easily distracted by Facebook, especially since I use it for both work and personal. So I add a task on my list and give myself a time limit, such as 30 minutes to scroll aimlessly. Then when I reach my limit, I cross off the task and move on. It really works.

- **StayFocusd (Page 30)**
  StayFocusd is a Chrome plugin that lets you set limits on certain sites. I have used it for social media and news sites since I can get lost in both.

- **Use your phone's tools**
  On some newer phones, you can set limits for your device use for free.

Three: Take Short Breaks

This is my favorite, favorite! I can't really get real work done (like writing my book) without focusing on ONE thing for a short interval and then taking a short break. If I don't use The Pomodoro Technique™ (Page 28), I can burn out from working too hard for too long, or I can easily get distracted.

• •

Automate Tasks

Without even realizing it, you probably do the same tasks over and over, such as checking the weather, saving attachments from emails, tweeting your latest blog post on Twitter.

Though it takes just a few minutes to complete each task, these little jobs add up fast, and you probably have better uses of your time in today's crazy-busy lifestyle.

Start with...

IFTTT
Free Multi-App Automator
ifttt.com

Zapier
Extensive Multi-App Automator with Paid Levels
zapier.com

Zapier and **IFTTT**, which stands for "if this then that," are two of the tools that will help you automate some of these little tasks so you don't have to think about them. Just connect your cloud-based services, social media accounts, phones and more, and create little recipes ("Zaps" with Zapier and "Applets" in IFTTT) that trigger under your rules.

They both work with several devices and gadgets, venturing into the world we know as "The Internet of Things." You can automate tasks with smart thermostats, Philips Hue light bulbs and many fitness trackers. You can also create opportunities to use specific iOS and Android features, such as location tracking and selfies.

IFTTT is free for thousands of connections. Zapier has lots of free options but also has paid levels for multi-step automations. We just upgraded here at Nerd HQ so that several integrations trigger when a contract is signed. The automations will save us at least two hours of labor a month, which more than justifies the upgrade. IFTTT revamped some things in 2019 but struggled to keep up with Google's changes to access to its products.

You can browse through the thousands of applets that other IFTTT and Zapier users have shared or use the wizard to walk through setting up your own. As NerdHerder Kevan Lyons says, "IFTTT is one of those apps that I see the potential and just have to experiment with it. It's sort of like a productivity game that isn't a waster of time!"

My favorite party trick: Set up an IFTTT applet to ring your phone with a touch of a button to get you out of a boring meeting. See Page 33 for more of the best IFTTT automations.

Then Try...

Shortcuts
Apple Device Automator
In the App Store

Tasker
Android Device Automator
In the Google Play Store

Tasker and **Shortcuts** are automators that make your mobile devices more efficient. You can set up little automations to run for common phone tasks, such as reading the news (have Siri read it to you), posting to Facebook, combining photos into a GIF, letting meeting attendees know you're running late, and much, much more.

Tasker fans have become a little cranky in the reviews lately, with a common complaint about how complicated it can be to set up a task. Shortcuts has glowing praise and lots of pre-set templates.

Also Check Out...

Pushbullet

Notification and Sharing Center for Texts, Files and More

pushbullet.com

Have you ever had to go through all kinds of strange iterations to get something from your phone to your computer? **Pushbullet** links multiple devices and services so you can minimize the number of places you have to go to perform everyday tasks. You can hook up your favorite messaging apps so you can text from your computer, or instantly share a picture from your phone with your computer and other devices.

Hot Topic:
Nine Reasons I Love Alexa

For several years, Amazon's Alexa has been a member of our household. I've gone all-in with Alexa, purchasing teeny tiny Echo Dots for different rooms plus an adorable little Echo Spot with a touchscreen face for my nightstand.

By the way, just because I love what Alexa can do doesn't mean I trust it entirely. It's always listening, and, with the video-enabled versions, always watching. We all know that can't be good. But if you're like me and willing to risk privacy for some cool conveniences, read on.

1. Our House Is Filled with Music

Before we got Alexa, we lived life without a soundtrack. We had an old stereo in the garage that D.J. would use when he was working on his bikes. But if we wanted a little music at dinner, we'd have to turn on the TV and surf to one of those music channels. Now every meal has a musical theme. On Valentine's Day, we have romantic concertos. While packing up the holiday gifts, Alexa fills the house with Christmas music. When I found myself missing Mom on her birthday this month, I asked Alexa to play a little Waylon Jennings. It's just SO EASY. I just ask her to play a genre, give her an artist's name or simply say, "Alexa, play something I might like." (Of course, I just did that to test it out, and she played "The Merry Old Land of Oz." So….)

In addition, a podcast addict like myself is in heaven with Alexa. Just ask her to play Radiolab, and the latest episode starts playing. (See more podcasts I love on Page 142.)

2. Alexa Helps Me at Work

"Alexa, what's my next appointment?"

The integration with my work calendar has made staying on task so much easier. At any moment, I can check what's coming up and any tasks on my list. I can also set a timer to help me practice the Pomodoro Technique, where I work on ONE task (and only one task) for 25 minutes or so, then take a break for email, Facebook, etc. (See Pomodoro apps on Page 28.)

Have an Android device? Alexa will even let you dictate a text message. Apple is stingy with its SMS access, so I can't do this yet. But the integrations just keep getting better. Amazon is hoping to move more into the workplace with more uses.

3. Alexa Finds My Phone

I can't tell you how often I wander around the house looking for my phone. I used to grab D.J.'s phone to call myself, but now I just ask Alexa to make it ring. Alexa also will remind me of tasks and appointments.

4. Alexa Finds My Husband

Speaking of phones, the Alexa system is basically a messaging app as well. You have the ability to call and message individual devices or even phones associated with those devices.

D.J. often turns off his ringer when he's in court (he's a lawyer, not a criminal). And he forgets to turn it back on at home. So when I track his location (via Apple) and see that he's at home but not answering his phone, I just "drop in" to the living room Alexa device. It chimes into the room, and all D.J. has to do is say, "Hello" to connect the call.

I think it annoys him a little, but I'm good with that.

5. I Always Know the Weather

In the last 60 days I've visited ten cities in two countries. I've experienced a snowstorm in Toronto, a deluge in Houston and an exquisite day in New Orleans. Packing for the weather is a total pain.

Rather than looking up each city, I can keep packing and simply ask Alexa about the weather in Detroit on Tuesday and Atlanta on Wednesday. My husband laughs at me when I check the weather here in Tennessee by asking Alexa instead of just looking outside. But I bet I'm not the only one who does that.

Another really cool (but very basic) feature makes me happier than it should…I love being able to ask Alexa what time it is. The Echo Spot in the bedroom has a clock face so I can see it at night, but during the day, I often lose track of time.

Asking for the time is easier than looking at a device. It's just so annoying to have to find my phone, pick it up, push a button… whew. I'm tired just thinking of it.

6. I've Solved a 10-Year Marital Issue

My husband has a super-human ability to see well in very low-light conditions. So he can flip off the bedroom light and tuck himself safely in our bed while I grope, cuss and shuffle in the dark. So I set up Alexa with some smart plugs so that I can say, "Alexa, turn on Beth's side" or "Alexa, turn on the bedroom" so I have the lights I need to get to my side.

I adore this solution because we no longer have to coordinate our bedtimes, and I don't have to wake him up to turn off/on the light so I can get to my side safely.

7. Alexa Lets Me Show Off a Little

I don't use Alexa for shopping very much because if you say, "Alexa, order Nerds Candies," you will get annoyed by Alexa's reading the first couple of results on the search page to you. But sometimes D.J. will ask me to buy him something on Amazon, and I'll show off a little. Every six months, he'll say we need a new refrigerator water filter, and I'll just say, "Alexa, order the water filter," and it shows up the next day. Then I get to give D.J. the look that says, "Yes, I CAN do everything."

8. Alexa Integrates with My Other Devices

Alexa devices now serve as hubs for lots of gadgets that live in the IoT (Internet of Things) world. I can ask Alexa to change the temperature upstairs, turn the light on in the den, tune to "Buffy the Vampire Slayer" on Hulu…. Basically I don't really need to leave the couch ever again.

9. Alexa Helps Me Reach You Guys

As soon as I finish this manuscript, I'm going to take all the tools in this book and create an Alexa "Skill" that will let my followers get a tech tool tip on Alexa on demand. Ain't that cool?

Hot Topic:
Getting Started with Automation

As I reflected on the progress of technology since the first *The Big Book of Apps* came out, I realized that we don't necessarily need more apps and downloads to move ahead…we need to create workflows so that the tech we have will work better.

Tools like IFTTT and Zapier (Page 33) are the keys. These services connect cloud tools and web-connected devices to automate simple tasks to free up your time. In one session, a woman shared that she nerded out on automations that start her workdays. When she says, "Alexa, I'm going to work," here's what happens:

- Her garage door opens.
- Her car starts.
- Her thermostat sets to an energy-efficient mode.
- The lights and TVs turn off around the house.
- And her favorite Starbucks receives an order for her favorite drink.

That's some advanced nerdin' right? I don't even have things set up that well (maybe my excuse is I don't have a garage?). It's easier to start small with some little automations that take just a couple of minutes to set up but can save you time every day.

IFTTT Automations for Newbies

Keep Track of the Weather

Stop wasting time checking the forecast…have news about the weather delivered to you when you need it. Several weather apps (see a list starting on Page 161) let you set up automatic notifications.

Track Your Whereabouts in Google Sheets

If getting fit is your goal, you can set up a geotag that records your visits to the gym automatically every time you pull into the parking lot. Of course, all bets are off on the efficacy if the shopping center also houses a cupcake bakery.

This is also a great way to log hours in the office.

Have Alexa Find Your Phone

I love this one! With this Applet, I just have to say, "Alexa, trigger find my phone," and usually less than 15 seconds later, I hear a faint jingle from the phone under the couch.

Synchronize Your Favorite Playlists

IFTTT does all kinds of fun things with music. Start with synchronizing your favorite songs among multiple music services and perhaps keeping a list of favorites automatically.

Have the Coolest Superbowl Party Atmosphere Ever

IFTTT works with connected lightbulbs like Phillips Hue. You can create an automation to turn the lights in your house to a team color when someone scores. Going back to the weather connections, you can also change the lights if there's an emergency weather announcement in your area.

Save Your Favorite Tweet "Notes" for Reference

So you're at a convention in a dull breakout session. You check Twitter, and the feed is blowing up with valuable tips from attendees in other sessions. Don't fret! You can create an automation that will save tweets for you into a Google spreadsheet. Just create a little recipe that says if I favorite a tweet or if someone tweets with a certain hashtag, save it in a document.

And Finally… My Favorite IFTTT Recipe

Now you're having a boring conversation with the boring instructor from the boring session you just attended. Life's too short. IFTTT lets you create a trigger that will make your phone ring on command. So the speaker is droning on, and RINGGG! Then you say, "Oh, gosh. I have to take this. It's important. And I'll be back…ummm, never!"

Outsource Work Tasks

One of the best things I've done for my business is to recognize that I can't do it all. I regularly outsource tasks and projects rather than trying to do them myself. It's not as expensive as you might think with these services.

Start with...

Fancy Hands

U.S.-Based Virtual Assistants for Small Tasks

fancyhands.com

As I am writing this section, a **Fancy Hands** assistant is checking details for some tools in the first chapter of this book. She's going through a long list of sites to gather the most recent prices and levels and the latest features.

This task would take me a couple of hours, and I just don't have the time. By outsourcing that one data-gathering task, I can focus on evaluating the thousands of tools I'm reviewing for this book.

If there's one tool a busy professional needs, it's an extra set of hands. Fancy Hands employs a stable of U.S.-based virtual assistants who take annoying little tasks off your list so you can concentrate on getting work done. Fancy Hands helps me set appointments, track down lost mail, transcribe business cards, create cool graphics, research tech tools—you name it—all kinds of little 20-minute tasks that can take me out of work mode and make me lose more time.

Fancy Hands is fast! I've submitted tasks on weekends and holidays, and almost all of them are completed and back to me within the hour. It doesn't promise to make any type of deadline, but you can indicate that a task is time-sensitive when you send it in.

Prices start at $30 a month for up to five tasks.

Then Try...

Fiverr

Freelance Marketplace for Small Jobs Starting at Five Bucks
fiverr.com

Upwork

Freelance Community for Larger Projects
upwork.com

Need to build a new website? Or create a fancy intro video that makes your logo dance? Or revamp your marketing material? Help is on the way.

When I need something done, my first thought is always **Fiverr**. Fiverr is a marketplace of thousands of people who do all kinds of stuff—starting at five bucks (a fiver, get it?). The site presents the engagements in an attractive format and gives you plenty of ways to search for the right freelancer. If you can't find a gig you want, you can write a description of your project and request bids.

Hot tip: It's smart to choose three to five designers for the same project to see which one gives you a better product. You're still not out very much money, and you'll get a variety of results that you can build on.

Fiverr gigs will often cost you more than five bucks because of the add-ons. You may pay extra for a rush job or for the addition of color or a background to a graphic. You're still paying very little for someone's hard work, so the upgrades are easily worth it.

Although Fiverr is incredible, you're not always going to get away with a $5 project to advance your business. For larger projects, you can find any number of freelancer marketplaces; and on each site, you can find thousands and thousands of proven experts who can help you with every imaginable task. I think of these types of sites as

Craigslist on steroids where you can find potential contractors, evaluate their ratings, keep track of their work and control the payment.

When I need to outsource a large project, I head to **Upwork**. You describe your project and set the parameters: your budget, your timeline, your hopes and dreams for a successful project. Then you open your project for bids to the marketplace. To find the right person, you might want to search the providers and invite your favorites to bid. If you're commissioning an illustration, for example, hop around in their portfolios to find a designer with a style you like.

After you declare a winner on Upwork, the site serves as a super-efficient project management tool. You and your new contractor agree on the project terms. On larger projects, you can divide up payments with milestones. As you work, the system acts like your own Basecamp site (Page 60). Every email you send is cataloged in the system. Every file you exchange is kept in the workroom. Every milestone is tracked. The system even has communication tools for collaboration with your contractor.

Also Check Out...

Thumbtack

Freelancer Marketplace for Projects and Experts
thumbtack.com

Need to mount your flat-screen TV? Or maybe assemble a new foosball table? There's an app for that. A number of services keep handy people in your area on speed dial, making it easy for you to arrange for a plumber, painter, yard person or general fix-it guy. **Thumbtack** was one of the early services. Like many of the services in the sharing economy, these companies let you read profiles, skills and recommendations of service providers before you hire them to come into your home.

I have used it for videographers and hair/makeup experts on the road with great success. It's a little weird, though. Thumbtack connects you with the experts, but you're not confirming or paying through Thumbtack. They basically just get you in touch with experts, and when you choose a provider, you two negotiate and figure stuff out.

As much as I was puzzled by the negotiations that take place outside the platform, I definitely liked it better than TaskRabbit. I only tried TaskRabbit once to help me put shelves in my office closet, but I had a really hard time working with one of their experts. He and I went back and forth so much that it got annoying (he got annoying), and I decided to cancel and do the job myself. And then TaskRabbit charged me a $50 fee for canceling late. Bleh!

> Dear cool people…
> they didn't name a candy
> after you, did they?
> Sincerely, Nerds.

Keep Your Environment Peaceful

Chances are at some point in your career you've glared over a cubicle at a co-worker because the phone conversation he's having with his best friend from college is driving you batty. With these tools, you can take control of the sound level of your environment to find the best background noise for working, relaxing and sleeping.

Start with...

Noisli
Background Noise Tool
noisli.com

I have a very tough time working in complete silence—something has to be on in the background. These days I usually have a small tablet tuned to reruns of "Law & Order" (it's always on somewhere). But if you don't have that option, just pull up the **Noisli** site for sounds that will help you get stuff done. You can click on a pre-programmed Productivity button to hear birds chirping and a gentle creek flowing, or you can fine-tune the sounds by clicking around the icons. I like the sounds of a coffee shop mixed with the rain.

Then Try...

Brain.fm
Music Productivity Tool
brain.fm

Focus@Will
Personality-Based Music Productivity Tool
focusatwill.com

It's 4 A.M., and I'm up working during my writing retreat because I can't sleep. It's pretty funny/not funny that I'm now writing about two tools that claim to be scientifically proven to help with focus, productivity, relaxation...and sleep.

Both **Brain.fm** and **Focus@Will** offer custom background music soundtracks that they claim are scientifically proven to change your brain state to help in different areas of your life. Focus@Will gives you a little personality test before recommending a music category for optimal efficiency. My result: "Your focus personality predicts the ADHD Type 1 channel can increase your work productivity up to 4x."

Brain.fm received a $225k grant from the National Science Foundation to study inattention and ADHD. Both sites have white papers and research results to support their claims of science-based success. As for price, both have very limited free trials. You'll pay $47.40 a year for Brain.fm and about $99 a year for Focus@Will, though it looks like you can sometimes find significant discounts on both.

Also Check Out...

SoundPrint
App to Find Your Quiet Place
soundprint.co

A romantic date with the one you love deserves a quiet atmosphere so you can hear the words of love. And an afternoon of work in a coffee shop can't be so loud you can't hear the productivity music (Page 45) in your headphones. Download the **SoundPrint** app to discover public places you can hear yourself think. The app asks you to help grow the databases by recording 15 seconds of sound at the places you visit. And it lets you search for spots that have already been tested.

Stay Healthy at Your Desk

• •

Today I've been sitting at the computer working on the book for about nine hours so far. My shoulders are slumped; my eyes are dry; my butt is numb.

This is not good, but this is how many of us work, hour after hour, staring at our computer screens without good posture or healthy breaks. These tools can help us maintain a healthy routine of breaks and self-checks at the desk.

Start with...

Regular Breaks

Site that Traps Your Cursor Until You Take a Break
regularbreaks.com

We should be taking a break every hour. **Regular Breaks** is a site that forces you to take breaks while you're working away. You have to register and keep your Chrome or Firefox browser open to the page to activate the system. My favorite feature is that it will trap your cursor until the break is over.

Then Try...

Healthy Browsing

Chrome Extension for Health Reminders
In the Chrome Web Store

PostureMinder

Chrome Extension to Encourage Better Posture
In the Chrome Web Store

You'll find multiple extensions like **PostureMinder** and **Healthy Browsing.** They all do the same kinds of things. You'll get reminders at regular intervals to drink water, sit up straight, blink, walk around. If you would rather not use the tech tools, my husband is available to rent.

Also Check Out...

Duet Display

App that Turns Your iOS Device into a Second Screen
duetdisplay.com

F.lux

Computer Lighting Adjustment Tool
justgetflux.com

I have two monitors on my desk, so that's three screens with my laptop. I miss the extra space when I'm on the go. NerdHerder Ross G. Saunders shared the answer. "For years I lugged around a clunky 'portable' display to use as a dual monitor on my laptop. With **Duet** I can use my iPad—which follows me everywhere anyway—as my dual-display on the run!"

Whether you're sitting in front of one screen or three, your eyes can get tired. More computers and smartphones are offering settings that adjust brightness and hue throughout the day, but **f.lux** is still my favorite. F.lux is a download that adapts the lighting level of your computer's display to the time of day, such as warm at night and like sunlight during the day. After staring 8 hours at your screen, you'll appreciate the mellow and adjusting light.

Change a Habit

Want to stop smoking? Exercise more? Break your smartphone addiction? These tools might be the best place to start your New Year's Resolutions.

Start with...

Habitica
Gamified Habit-Forming Tool
habitica.com

HabitShare
Social Habit-Forming Tool
habitshareapp.com

If you're motivated by gold stars and "winning," **Habitica** may be for you. The system is set up like a video game where you conquer little monsters to meet daily goals and establish better habits. Along the way, you can earn "sweet gear" like an invaluable 8-bit sword or pixelated horned helmet. While the idea is clever, I think I'd be more motivated by earning digital cupcakes. Habitica lets you join forces with friends to hold each other accountable.

HabitShare takes social accountability to another level. You invite your friends to join you on the app, and you all work together to achieve all the things. You get to choose which goals you want to share with which friends, so you don't have to let your co-worker know your goal of getting a new job. This tool is great for social groups like running clubs when you're all motivating each other to do better.

Then Try...

Way of Life
Simple Habit Maker with Easy Updates
wayoflifeapp.com

Don't want to turn your goals into a game or tell someone else you want to lose 15 pounds? People love the simple interface and easy update capabilities of **Way of Life**. I like the name because it reminds us that a new habit should be part of our daily lives.

Also Check Out...

Fabulous
Science-Based Habit-Forming Tool
thefabulous.co

Fabulous' roots are connected to the Duke University Behavioral Economics Lab, and they take on helping you with habits to improve your health, such as sleeping better, drinking more water and becoming more mindful. From the home page, the app claims to help you "build healthy rituals into your life, just like an elite athlete."

Fabulous has almost 5 stars with a quarter-million reviewers, and it won a Google award for "Most Charming Engagement." Both Google and Apple have named it an Editor's Choice.

My grumpypants impression: As "fabulous" as the Fabulous app looks, I'm kind of turned off by the cheery "fix everything" approach. I would unfriend a friend who tried "charming engagement" to get me to drink more water, but millions and millions of people have downloaded it, so what do I know?

Manage Your Stress

Even if you're not in crisis, you may be struggling with depression, anxiety or any number of mental health issues. Give these highly recommended tools a try.

Start with...

Calm
Award-Winning App Designed to Aid Sleep, Boost Confidence and Reduce Stress
calm.com

Headspace
Meditation and Stress Relief App
headspace.com

Calm and **Headspace** are the two tools that come out on top over and over again when people talk about meditation and anxiety/stress relief. They're both available on a variety of platforms, and both have basic free versions and worth-the-price paid subscriptions.

Then Try...

Sanvello
Mental Health Tool with Clinically Validated Techniques
sanvello.com

Sanvello (formerly Pacifica) helps you manage stress, anxiety and depression with Cognitive Behavioral Therapy techniques, mindfulness, meditation, relaxation and mood tracking.

Also Check Out...

Stop, Breathe & Think
Meditation App with Custom Solutions
stopbreathethink.com

Stop, Breathe & Think starts with surveys to find out what kind of help you need. Then it tailors the meditation and self-help tools toward your biggest challenges with programs such as "Relax, Ground and Clear" and "Lion Mind."

Motorola executive
Martin Cooper made
the first consumer mobile
phone call in 1973.

Seek Resources for People in Crisis

Robin Williams. Anthony Bourdain. Kate Spade.

We hear the names of well-known people who died by suicide, and we are instantly sad. They seemed to have it all: wealth, fame, wonderful families. Why in the world would they have wanted to end their lives? And, more importantly, why didn't anyone KNOW? Why didn't anyone HELP?

After Anthony Bourdain's death, I asked my community if it was appropriate to gather apps for suicide prevention and mental health. The response (my most commented on post ever) was overwhelmingly positive. Naively I thought I could quickly compose a list of apps and dash out an article easy breezy like usual.

The Bad News: There's Not Really an App for That

In 2016, researchers analyzed 123 apps that referred to suicide. About 50 of those included at least one suicide prevention feature. But therein lies the problem . . . one prevention technique doesn't suffice. "Many suicide prevention apps are available, some of which provide elements of best practice, but none that provide comprehensive evidence-based support," the paper states.

My "No Kidding" Statement: Suicide Is Complicated

Take a look at the risk factors for suicide from #BeThe1To, a site from the National Suicide Prevention Lifeline for resources to prevent suicide. There's a bunch of them. It's not always about a lack of a community, or mental health issues or any one of the factors that might come to mind. So apps that address any one of these factors may not be enough.

I'd love to be able to offer you a list of perfect apps that you can simply install and be healthy. But as the researchers found, one tool doesn't do everything. So here are some of the best resources I've seen.

Start with...

#BeThe1To

Resources for You to Help People in Need
bethe1to.com

Crisis Text Line

Free, 24/7 Text Chat When You Need It
Text HOME to 741741

National Suicide Prevention Lifeline

Site for Resources, Crisis Lines, Chat and More
suicidepreventionlifeline.org

The **National Suicide Prevention Lifeline** (1-800-273-8255) links to centers around the U.S. I used to work on a crisis line — the 12am–3am shift in Dallas. Volunteers are trained to help. Really. And you can even call if you're worried about someone else. If you're online, you can also visit the site to chat with someone who can help.

If you're a veteran, a disaster survivor, a kid or someone who has suffered a loss, the National Suicide Prevention Lifeline has specific help for you and other communities who may need specialized resources.

You can also text the **Crisis Text Line** for 24/7 connections.

The #**BeThe1To** site's goal is to support people who are trying to help others in pain. It has warning signs, resources, community awareness resources and grassroots movements.

Then Try...

BetterHelp
Online Counseling Service
betterhelp.com

We're all busy these days, and it's tough to find a therapist and make weekly in-person appointments. **BetterHelp** charges $40–70 a week for counseling sessions through messaging, chat, phone and/or video.

Also Check Out...

MoodTools Apps
System of Apps to Address Suicidal Thoughts and Depression
moodtools.org

The 2016 study liked the resources in apps that focused on safety plans. You download the app when you know you're struggling, and it helps you assess and organize your coping strategies. The kicker, though, is that you have to be in a place where you're willing to take steps.

MoodTools has several apps that focus on helping people lift themselves out of a downward spiral: Suicide Safety Plan, Depression Test and Mood Diary. The researchers singled out MoodTools as a resource with the most features that could really support a person in a suicidal state.

Hot Topic:
What to Do When You See
an Alarming Post on Social Media

If you see warning signs of self-harm on social media posts, many platforms have a way to report it to get help for the person.

- **Facebook**
  Not only does Facebook have a reporting system in the help area, but it's also using artificial intelligence to identify self-harming behavior automatically. You can read all about the resources at facebook.com/safety/wellbeing/suicideprevention.

- **Twitter**
  Twitter lets people report tweets through a form: help.twitter.com/forms/report_self_harm.

- **Instagram**
  To report threats of suicide or self-harm on Instagram, tap the three dots below the post. Tap "Report," then choose "Inappropriate>Self injury."

- **Snapchat**
  Snapchat's reporting tool is in the Snapchat Support area.

- **YouTube**
  To report threats of suicide or self-harm, click "More." Highlight and click "Report" in the drop-down menu. Click "Harmful dangerous acts," then "Suicide or self-injury." YouTube will review the video and may send a message to the uploader with the Lifeline number.

Collaboration

· ·

In This Chapter...

Manage Projects

The project management world is a crowded space, but a few companies stand out. These tools are the most recommended by audience members in my sessions, and those guys are way smarter than I am.

Like the cloud storage tools, you'll find many of the same characteristics in the top contenders. In general, here are the features these tools contain:

- Capability to set up projects with tasks, goals and milestones
- Collaboration tools for teams
- Feeds and dashboards for latest activity and status updates
- Ability to assign tasks to team members
- Shareable file library
- Notification system via email or third-party tools
- Multi-device access to cloud-based data
- Free or low-cost basic features with upgrades for larger teams and projects

Beyond these common characteristics, you'll find variety in the look and feel of the most popular tools.

Note: Check out Page 73 to read about PATboard, a really cool physical tool to help with visualizing projects on a whiteboard.

Start with...

Trello
Project Management Tool Good for Personal
Task Management
trello.com

After all these years of reviewing project management tools, I'm still enamored with **Trello.** Trello offers an interesting take on project management by organizing your projects into "cards" that lay out like a deck across your screen. You can click on any card to flip it over and see the details, including tasks, collaborators and due dates.

Trello organizes all your projects into boards, allowing both personal and shared boards. Your account lets you have as many boards as you want, and you can manage the permissions for each for everything from read-only access to full privileges. You create lists and deadlines for each board, and you can assign tasks to others. It's easy to reprioritize and assign list items with a quick click and drag.

Trello gets bonus points because it has personality: a sense of playfulness as well as serious business features. You can choose bright, fun backgrounds for your projects, and a "Power-Up" feature (that doesn't even cost more money) lets your older cards show their age. Plus, the Pirate View is what you need in your life.

I'm not sure if they've ever tried out the Pirate View, but NerdHerders Janet Jordan and Raquel Ortiz both love Trello. Raquel says...

As my projects multiply and my task list gets longer, I'm finding them easier to manage from a visual tool. I keep Trello open as I work and always know what's my next step. Adding deadlines, checklists and recurring tasks help ensure that I don't miss something when I get deep into a project.

Then Try...

Asana
Favorite Project Management Tool with Robust Free Version
asana.com

Smartsheet
Spreadsheet-Based Project Management Tool
smartsheet.com

Asana and **Smartsheet** are crowd favorites at my sessions. Many teams report that Asana gives small teams everything they need at no cost for up to 15 users. And although Smartsheet isn't free, its users adore the fact that the system has templates for almost any type of project, and the layout is the familiar spreadsheet format.

Also Check Out...

Basecamp
Classic Project Management System
basecamp.com

Freedcamp
(Almost) Free Project Management System
freedcamp.com

Basecamp was probably the first online project management system, and it's undoubtedly one of the most popular. Basecamp also has the most integrations, including social networks, mobile phones and invoicing software. All the systems update each other and keep everyone on track. The company has changed its pricing structure multiple times since I started using it, but it looks like they've settled on $99 a month flat rate. One seriously cool benefit of Basecamp is that it's completely free for teachers and half price for nonprofits.

In case you missed that last paragraph, Basecamp charges almost $100 a month! That's kind of insane since so many other tools are way less. So if you want the basic structure of Basecamp without the crazy price, try **Freedcamp.** Unlimited users. Unlimited projects. Unlimited storage. What's not to love? Freedcamp gives away much more than many of the other top project management systems in this section. They start charging for integrations with Google Drive, larger file uploads, CRMs, invoices and issue tracking.

NerdHerd Thumbs Up: More Phenomenal Project Management Tools

monday.com
Flexible Project Management and Team Collaboration Tool
monday.com

Teamwork
Project Management Tool that Gets Team Member Buy-In
teamwork.com

Wrike
Project Management Tool with Gantt Charts
wrike.com

I haven't used **monday.com** or **Wrike,** but it's hard to argue with the enthusiastic love from some of my trusted nerd friends. Taylor Hageman, who was on our team at Nerd HQ. She has tried out Trello, Asana and many other project management tools, but her favorite by far is monday.com.

> *I use monday.com for just about everything. From personal to nonprofit work and professional work, I try to keep all ongoing projects and ideas in there. It helps me toss ideas back and forth with people, and keeps me organized and on task. I find it robust but user-friendly, which makes it easier to bridge the gap between professional projects and personal projects.*

Julie Perrine loves **Teamwork,** which we at Nerd HQ just started using. Julie says the ease of use means that teams are more likely to stay with it.

> *I love Teamwork! You can test it out with two free projects indefinitely, but even the starting packages for multiple projects are super reasonable. It's the first project management tool I've used that is intuitively designed, quick and easy to set up, and my entire team will consistently use it!*

And finally, Wrike receives a similarly glowing review from NerdHerder Beth Bridges.

> *Gannt Charts are almost as nerdy as Venn Diagrams! Wrike, a project management tool, has them so you can see how long parts of your project should take, what depends on other tasks and who is involved, all at a glance.*

> *Plus it's got a super-customizable dashboard so you can manage tasks, to-dos and projects in as fine a detail as you want.*

Hot Topic: Kanban Boards

KanbanFlow
Project Management Tool with
Pomodoro Timer
kanbanflow.com

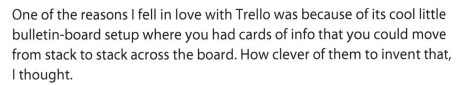

One of the reasons I fell in love with Trello was because of its cool little bulletin-board setup where you had cards of info that you could move from stack to stack across the board. How clever of them to invent that, I thought.

Uh. Turns out Trello didn't invent the concept. The arrangement is a Kanban board, based on a Japanese system for process management and improvement. I didn't hear the term until maybe 2015, and when I asked my Facebook Page community, about 80 percent hadn't heard of it either.

On a Kanban board you might organize your columns into categories such as *to-do, in progress, waiting for approval* and *done*. It's a way to visualize a whole project to track progress. Many project management systems, including Trello and Asana, lay projects out on Kanban boards.

NerdHerder Sarah Luebbert's favorite tool, **KanbanFlow,** is—unsurprisingly—a Kanban board. And it's so much more. Sarah says, "It's a Pomodoro timer, to-do list and time tracker all in one." Sarah creates her task lists and moves the tasks she wants to accomplish for the day into one column. Once they're done, she moves them into the done column, "so I can see what I have accomplished that day." Not only does KanbanFlow have a great free version…the paid level is only $5 a month.

Collaborate on Files

• •

Remember the days when you sent everyone a copy of a document for feedback, then you had to read each version and compile the feedback into one file? Yeah, I've blocked out those dark times, too. These tools offer real-time collaboration and sharing for teams and committees.

Start with...

Google Drive

Real-Time Collaboration in a Robust Office Suite
google.com/drive

Oh, the glory that is **Google Drive**. It's hands down the best and easiest free tool for document collaboration out there. You can create or upload word docs, spreadsheets and slides, then invite collaborators to edit and comment. The best feature is that you can see the updates made by any contributor in real time. Collaborators can participate even if they're not Google users, though if they are, the system will identify them by name.

Although Google Drive doesn't have the most features or the best interface, the free collaboration features earn my thumbs up for this category.

Then Try...

Microsoft Office 365

Office Suite with Collaboration Features

microsoft.com/office365

Microsoft Office 365 is much improved from the original *The Big Book of Apps*. The only reason it's not my first choice in this category is because you're going to have to pay for a 365 subscription to get all the goodies. The upgrade is so worth the price for the incredible features (Page 99), but Google Drive is a great alternative if you just don't want to pay.

Like Google Drive, you can collaborate with colleagues in real time using the Office 365 files you store in Microsoft's cloud-storage system, OneDrive (Page 10). Although the online versions of Word, Excel and the like are not as full-bodied as the computer versions, you'll find similar interfaces and functionality. I like that collaborators don't have to sign in, but if they do use their Microsoft login account, you can see who is in the "room," and participants can even Skype (audio, video and chat).

You can even collaborate if you're on a phone, though you'll have to go through the extra steps of requesting the desktop site instead of the mobile version, and then clicking "Edit in browser." And BONUS: this collaboration tool works really well in Microsoft Teams (Page 67).

Also Check Out...

Dropbox Paper
Dropbox's Document Collaboration Tool
dropbox.com/paper

You definitely want to choose Google Docs or Office 365 when you and your teammates are writing a document together. But if you want to get online to brainstorm or plan together, give **Dropbox Paper** a try. I don't think you'd use this to create a formal document, but it would be great for meeting minutes, project planning and other in-house projects you want to think through with a team.

I love that you can connect your calendar with Dropbox. Your appointments will show up on the Paper homepage, and you can click on them to create an agenda. You can also @mention colleagues for tasks, notes and input. The platform also lets you insert a timeline, which adds a handy guide to deadlines and project progress while you're collaborating.

You can pull in your existing Dropbox files to review and comment on, but you're not going to be editing them in real time. The ability to quickly add emojis and GIFs kind of puts me off. I can imagine that my team and I could waste a lot of time throwing reaction GIFs into our collaborative document instead of getting stuff done. You should see our text message threads. We have a GIF problem.

Communicate with Internal Teams

At times in the world of technology, we see giant leaps and dramatically new ways of doing things. Smartphones forever changed the center of our computing universe from a desktop machine to devices that are with us all the time. Cloud storage tools (Page 8) transformed the way we store and share files. Social media platforms altered the very way we live our lives and interact with others. And tools like these internal communication systems have the potential of weaning us off email in the office.

The Only Real Players in the Business Chat Game

Microsoft Teams
Slack Competitor for Microsoft Business Users
teams.microsoft.com

Slack
Simple Chat System with Monumental Capabilities
slack.com

Perhaps the biggest mover up the ladder from the last version of *The Big Book of Apps* is this one: **Microsoft Teams** is poised to surpass **Slack,** the pioneering team chat and collaboration system that started a movement.

In the simplest terms, Slack is instant messaging. The system connects teams and allows them to send quick messages on almost any platform, avoiding the annoying email strings that we've all learned to ignore. The chats can be tagged for different topics and created for different groups inside the same network. It's basically a social network for the workplace, as well as the perfect setup for sports teams, volunteer committees, church groups and community discussions.

But Slack is really so much more with hundreds of apps and integrations that exponentially expand its capabilities. Teams can use Slack for...

- Project management (who is supposed to do what and when?)
- Employee recognition (award your favorite team members virtual tacos when they do something awesome)
- Lunch coordination (who wants what from the Thai place?)
- IT system monitoring (IT guys love to monitor stuff)
- Videoconferencing (don't just type to your team...see them)
- Weather (let Poncho the Cat tell you when to bring an umbrella)
- Transportation (order a Lyft)

There's even an integration to create a group Swear Jar.

Slack has a free version to let you try it out. A couple of challenges to a successful Slack rollout for your team: You'll have to get buy-in from your whole team, and convincing some people to step away from email can be tough. You may also be annoyed by all the notifications. But the benefits may outweigh the drawbacks when you see your email inbox shrink to a manageable size and notice that your teams are finally working together better to get stuff done.

Microsoft introduced Teams in 2017, and the buzz is that Teams would eventually replace Skype for Business. I'm not going to predict yes or no here (remember how I thought for sure that Microsoft was killing Wunderlist [Page 4] and it didn't and then my book was wrong?), but the two tools are definitely similar, with Teams being better for project management and collaboration. Teams integrates video and audio conferencing using Skype technology, and the free version lets up to 80 people conference. But again, I am not predicting anything.

Here's why Microsoft Teams has the advantage over the innovative Slack platform.

- **Teams Has a Bigger Market Share Already**
  IT community Spiceworks surveyed businesses about their use of chat apps in 2016 and 2018. Skype for Business had 44 percent of the market, up from 36 percent. Slack had seen a modest rise from 13 percent in 2016 to 15 percent. And Microsoft Teams had moved from 3 percent to 21 percent in two years, scooting past Slack.

- **Teams Is Very, Very Free**
  Slack's free version is adequate, but Teams' is amazing. You don't even have to have a subscription to Microsoft Office 365. You get lots of free space for documents and assets, plus very generous user allowances.

- **Microsoft Teams Has Microsoft**
  Slack wins the integration battle for its enormous number of third-party addons. But Teams is smack in the middle of all of Microsoft Office's popular apps: Word, Excel, Outlook, OneDrive and more. And since the MS platform is by far the leader in business software, the easy integration with tools they use already is a big selling point for users.

- **44 Percent Plus 21 Percent Is a Whole Bunch of Users**
  If Microsoft can transition the Skype for Business users to Teams, Microsoft wins.

NerdHerd member Beth Camero has seen Teams raise the bar drastically in just a year.

This software has improved so much over the last year. It does EVERYTHING. You can host online meetings, take notes, use the Slack-like messaging piece, store files and create channels for different teams. The online meeting component is replacing the deprecated Skype, which is going away in 2021, I think. Inside Teams we have an IT team, a legislative group, an admin group and lots of others!

To be fair, though, Slack received more thumbs ups from the NerdHerd. Tim Teehan and Pam Donahoo love Slack. And Bret Schanzenbach adores it.

> *Slack is great for all our Boards, committees and initiatives. It so much more efficient than "group emails." It allows us to post resources, links and more, and keep a running dialogue going that is searchable. And it eliminates the dreaded "reply all" that results in tons of useless emails.*

The Also Ran...

Workplace by Facebook

Facebook's Answer to Slack
workplace.fb.com

To be honest, Google Hangouts came in behind Slack in the 2018 survey, but Google is changing it to Google Meet and Google Chat or something. I don't really know. At any rate, I don't really consider Google a player in this particular competition.

Workplace by Facebook had a tiny share of the users in the surveys, holding steady at 1 percent in both. Facebook is counting on the fact that millions of us sneak peeks at Facebook during the workday, so Workplace is integrated into our lives already.

We at Nerd HQ tried Workplace. Our team was growing, and we were all using different systems to keep track of things. I thought Workplace would be an excellent solution for communication and project updates.

I was the first one to jump on, and I kept tagging team members and teasing them about how fun it was on the Workplace page. It drove everyone nuts. We were all trying to stay away from Facebook and get work done during the day, and having to go in to see the stuff on Workplace was just too distracting. Plus the Workplace login is actually different than your personal one, so that was a pain as well.

Facebook kept sending me messages trying to entice me to check in on the site, but I didn't see the value. It just wasn't the right solution for us. At last Facebook warned me it was going to shut down my page. I'm good with that.

NerdHerd Thumbs Up: Standardize Your Inspection Procedures

iAuditor
Inspection and Checklist Tool
safetyculture.com

NerdHerder Julie Lynch pointed me to **iAuditor**, a tool that helps you standardize your inspections, checklists and compliance reports. You can create as many templates as you want, even on the free plan. You can go through your checklist, add photos and notes and track corrective actions. The Premium level is $19 per user per month and includes more inspection storage and team/role management.

Julie says, "The app is sooooo easy to set up, especially since you can convert already established checklists in just minutes."

Keep Track of Ideas: Team Edition

Tools like Evernote, OneNote and others (Page 13) were built for individual productivity. The following tools create more of a company wiki repository for notes, documents, resources and more.

Note: Tools like these serve double- and triple-duty as project management (Page 58), communication (Page 67) and collaboration tools (Page 64). These days we just don't have dividing lines among them.

Start with...

Notion

Nerds' New Choice for Note Taking and More

notion.so

When I asked tech gurus from Product Hunt (Page 148) about their favorite replacements for Evernote (Page 15), **Notion** took the crown. The company describes the platform as an all-in-one workspace for notetaking, as well as project and task management. Use it alone to organize your information snippets and work life, or set it up for your team to bring all the pieces and parts together.

Notion is going head-to-head with Evernote to win over disgruntled users. The first paid level of Notion is cheaper than Evernote, and they've made it easy for you to switch with a handy Evernote importer.

Then Try...

Notejoy
Evernote-Like Note and Document Organizer for Teams
notejoy.com

Notejoy is pretty much what you'd expect an Evernote competitor built for teams to be. You can drag documents to share, clip things from the web and add them to private or public notebooks. Team members can share and collaborate on notebook contents as well as leave comments. Pricing starts at free! Always a plus.

Also Check Out...

PATboard
Physical Board for Projects, Tasks and Group Notes
patboard.com

Ok, so maybe this tool belongs in the Manage Projects section (Page 58), but it's a great way to visualize notes and components for a team. It's a series of cards that you physically put on a whiteboard, chalkboard or glass board so you can see elements and move them around.

NerdHerder Kristine Spreigl says **PATboard** is for "the visual peeps who want to see their goals, tasks and progress visually."

> *This is great for keeping the big rocks (uh hum, goals) front and center and keeps you accountable for moving forward with them. It allows others on your team to also quickly size up where things are at vs. the many email exchanges ... AND it forces you to get up and move occasionally.*

Share Large Files

• •

The day before I wrote this section, my husband's teenage niece surprised me with a FaceTime call. "How do I share some video clips with my friends? They're too big to text."

Oh joy! I'm a Nerdy BFF for teenagers as well! I was happy she asked and thrilled that I had the answer.

Her solution was easy: I told her to select the videos on her iPhone and create an album. Then she could make the album public and send her friends the link to her iCloud folder.

But not all large files are that easy to send. And though Dropbox and other cloud-based storage systems (Page 9) make it pretty easy to share links to large files, you may need other choices from time to time.

Start with...

WeTransfer
Easy File-Sharing Service
wetransfer.com

There's nothing fancy about **WeTransfer's** services, and there doesn't have to be. You choose a file to upload (up to 2GB free) and drag it to the screen. Then it uploads. And then you share it. You don't even have to register. Another thing I love is that on the upload/download pages, WeTransfer showcases some of their favorite artists and special projects.

Then Try...

Send Anywhere
Instant File Transfer
send-anywhere.com

If you're standing next to your boss who wants a file immediately (as bosses do), **Send Anywhere** might be perfect. When you upload your files, you have the option of a direct transfer. Send Anywhere displays a 6-digit code. The recipient just needs to enter the code on the site on the receiving device within 10 minutes. Then the file is streamed from one device to the other without being stored in the cloud.

You only have to register on the site if you want to create or email a link. But then you could just use WeTransfer.

Also Check Out...

7-Zip
Free Windows File Compression Utility
7-zip.org

The Unarchiver
Free Mac File Uncompression Utility
theunarchiver.com

WinZip
Classic File Compression Utility
winzip.com

Compressing or zipping files together can significantly reduce file size and ease transfer issues. Operating systems these days have built-in zipping tools, but specific utilities have more features and can further reduce the sizes.

WinZip is an oldie but a goodie. It continues to stand out as a handy utility for both Mac and PC. If you don't want to pay $30 for WinZip, **7-Zip** is a worthy free alternative for Windows devices. **The Unarchiver** is good to have on Macs because some zipped files won't open with standard Mac tools.

Create Surveys and Polls

Many of us check the temperature of a topic via social media, but for an actual information-gathering exercise, we still need to use survey software. Although one company more or less rules this space, you have other choices.

Start with...

Google Forms
Google's Free Survey Tool
google.com/forms

Microsoft Forms for Excel
Simple Form Maker for Excel Online
forms.office.com

Let me make my opinion clear: I adore **Google Forms**. Within minutes you can create a simple form online and get a link to share. I use it all the time to survey my readers, attendees and anyone else I want to hear from. It's 100 percent free for as many questions and responses as you want.

So why is this not my first recommendation? Well, it's just plain ugly. It's blocky, simplistic and kinda clunky. It is free and looks free, and it has Google branding at the bottom to tell everyone that it is free. So it's wonderful, but it may be too simple and unprofessional for business needs.

When I was researching other free survey tools, I was surprised to come across **Microsoft Forms for Excel.** This decidedly non-fancy tool can help you gather info into your spreadsheet. The kicker is that you can only make them through OneDrive (Page 10) online.

Then Try...

Cognito Forms
Molly's Favorite Form Tool
cognitoforms.com

Typeform
Wizard-Format Online Forms
typeform.com

Funny story: When I was looking for a better survey tool in 2018, I remembered that Manager Molly loved **Typeform** and encouraged me to check it out, so I upgraded to the $300+ a year level. Gulp.

And I didn't like it a whole bunch. The user experience is pretty cool because instead of showing a form with a whole bunch of questions, you can step the user through one question at a time, making it more of a chatty conversation. For example, your "Name" field could be, "And what should we call you?"

But I wasn't really happy with the templates and never really spent time to make it do what I wanted. Flash forward to the pre-order period for *The BIGGER Book of Apps* (that's this book), and I was looking for a way to take the orders online. Because I had paid the big bucks for the service, I used their e-commerce template. And again, I didn't like it. It took way too long to set up the logic trees, and I couldn't get the receipts to work right.

Anyway, here I am updating this section from the last edition, and I look at the notes for **Cognito Forms,** another survey tool.

From *The Big Book of Apps:*

> *Molly Veydovec, my manager, often sends along standout tech tools for my consideration. And she sent me a short note about Cognito Forms: "One of our clients just used this and I like it." I have to agree that Cognito Forms looks awesome. Not only does it have a beefy free version for forms, but it also can handle registrations and proposals, including payment options. The paid versions are very reasonable as well.*

Molly liked Cognito. Not Typeform. Oops.

Also Check Out...

Survey Anyplace
Interactive Questionnaires for Increased Engagement
surveyanyplace.com

SurveyGizmo
Multi-Platform Survey Tool
surveygizmo.com

SurveyMonkey
Biggest Online Survey Tool
surveymonkey.com

I think it's safe to say that **SurveyMonkey** is the leader in the online survey field. The company was founded in 1999 and has dominated the market for quite some time, gobbling up rivals and related companies along the way, such as Wufoo, Zoomerang and Precision Polling.

Even though SurveyMonkey is the powerhouse, you have plenty of options. I'm in love with the interactive features of **Survey Anyplace**. I can't wait to try the "scratch-off" screen capabilities.

SurveyGizmo is suitable for respondents who use many different platforms. For all these tools, you'll find various levels of survey, question and response limits before you get to the paid levels.

Meetings

In This Chapter...

Schedule Meetings with Individuals

Going back and forth with a contact to find a time to meet is a waste of her time and yours. Book your appointments without the hassle using a little tech touch.

Start with...

Evie
Virtual Scheduling Assistant with 5 Free Meetings a Month
evie.ai

X.ai
Virtual Scheduling Assistant with Booking Page
x.ai

For several years now, we've had a plethora of AI-powered scheduling assistants. **X.ai** has been around the longest, and I still like it the best. X.ai's virtual scheduling assistant is Amy Ingram (for *AI*, get it?). Amy has a brother named Andrew, if you'd rather have a male assistant. To schedule a meeting with a contact or small group, copy Amy on your emails. Amy will email your contacts directly to find a time to meet. She "reads" meeting requests and responses as you write them in natural language. After people settle on a good time, she sends an invite to everyone. I put Amy to the test with a week's worth of meetings, and she worked so well (for the most part) that many of my invitees forgot that she wasn't real even though I told them.

Because it's nice to have the flexibility to offer email-back-and-forth or choose-your-own-time options, X.ai includes a booking page in its $8 a month level. I paid for a year of service and realized that I only used Amy twice. So I'm switching to **Evie,** a similar service that gives me five free scheduling sessions a month. Evie's company is aiming to use its AI power for recruitment and sales.

Then Try...

Appointlet
Almost Free Do-It-Themselves Scheduling Tool
appointlet.com

Assistant.to
Gmail Schedule Picker
assistant.to

Calendly
Do-It-Themselves Scheduling Tool
calendly.com

Sometimes it's just easier to send your calendar to someone and have her pick her preferred appointment time.

When my fellow speakers start chatting about scheduling and calendar tools, the fans of **Calendly** go wild with exclamation points. The system connects to your online calendar (like Google or iCloud) and shows open slots available for meetings. Your meeting partner can choose the slot she wants, then she adds her name and email for automatic reminders and a downloadable confirmation. She can use the confirmation link to update or cancel the appointment as well.

The pricing, features and functionality resemble many other calendar meeting tools, with the added benefit of a plethora of integrations with other apps and tools. The free version is pretty good, but **Appointlet's** free version is a favorite.

Rather than making the attendee visit another page to pick a time, **Assistant.to** lets you select a few time frames to insert into the email, err, I mean Gmail. Assistant.to is one component of the sales and scheduling tools from Cirrus Insight, but it's 100 percent free.

Also Check Out...

MeetWays
Site to Find a Place to Meet
meetways.com

WhatsHalfway.com
Google Map-Powered Site to Find a Place to Meet
whatshalfway.com

A speaker colleague says she uses **MeetWays** to find a place to meet clients for coffee between their two addresses. You visit the site and put in your address and your client's address, then choose what kind of place where you'd like to meet. You'll be instantly presented with all the coffee shops, restaurants or whatever at halfway meeting points, complete with Google and Yelp reviews. It's very, very handy.

I'm a little concerned about the health of this site. The front page where you put in the addresses works perfectly and looks very professional, but none of the other pages were working. You don't have to put in any personal info, so there's no harm in using it. I just don't know if the company (which I couldn't find) is still supporting the site.

A similar site, **Whatshalfway.com,** looks a little dated on the home page, but I like that it uses Google Maps (Page 236) to search. When you're typing your locations, Google Maps options will show up so you can choose the exact place. Then when you search, you're taken straight into Google Maps, which is super legit.

Hot Topic: You Can Automate Your Scheduling... But Should You?

In the original *Big Book of Apps*, I wrote this sad tale:

> *Once upon a time, I had an immediate need for a freelancer. A colleague gave me a recommendation. I tried to call the freelancer for a quick chat and left a message, followed by a detailed email.*
>
> *She wrote me back and asked me to fill out an intake sheet, which asked for the same details I had already emailed.*
>
> *I pasted the answers into her form then asked again for a quick call.*
>
> *Instead she sent yet another link to a scheduling calendar, and the first timeslot that would work with my schedule was 3 weeks out.*
>
> *So, I called another freelancer. And Molly answered the phone. And I hired her. And she is still with me.*
>
> *Although automated scheduling tools can be handy, putting up with a little inconvenience by personally booking your appointments may pay off in the end.*

At that time, I was convinced that everyone would prefer to go back and forth with a real person. Giving someone a link to put in an appointment was an annoyance and an inconvenience.

And then I started reading about different generations and work cultures. There are whole groups of people who absolutely hate email (ok, this could be everyone in the world). They don't want to have to interact with people. They don't answer their phones. I realized that for many, the ability to just pop over and choose a time is a relief, not an insult. So now we give people the choice of picking their own meeting time or working with us to find a time to meet.

Schedule Meetings with Groups

How many emails does it take to set up a committee meeting? One, if you use one of these cool tools that help you find a time to meet.

Start with...

Doodle

Everybody's Favorite Scheduling Tool

doodle.com

Every time I ask for favorite apps in my presentations, **Doodle** comes up. NerdHerd member Ron Sarver even named it his favorite tool. Besides having an adorable name, it's dead simple to use. Without ever entering your email address or any personal information (making it commitment free), you can propose several dates and times for a meeting. Then Doodle generates a link for both your admin view and the participants' responses. You send the link to your participants, and everyone responds with availability, allowing you to use the admin view to find the perfect time.

Doodle also lets you use the apps to check on your schedules and propose more meetings. Plus, you can create a MeetMe page that gives you a private URL you can send to colleagues to let them suggest a time to meet based on your availability, like the tools on Page 80.

Then Try...

LettuceMeet
Block-Style Scheduling Tool
lettucemeet.com

When Is Good
Horrible-Looking Scheduling Tool
whenisgood.net

Yes, Doodle is wonderful, but it has its limitations. You have to pick specific times for people to vote on, and sometimes they're just arbitrary. That's why I love the block-style scheduling options from **LettuceMeet** and **When Is Good.**

As the organizer you pick out a few days and time ranges for a potential meeting. Then you paint in your actual availability before sharing the link with others. When all attendees have filled in the times they have available, the tools will show the overlaps for the best time.

Both of these recommendations make me cringe, and if I could find alternatives with the same simple concept, I would replace these. LettuceMeet hasn't updated its social media for a while. But come on. The name is awesome.

And When Is Good, bless its heart, is hands-down the ugliest site in this book. But it still works.

Also Check Out...

SignUpGenius
Volunteer Organizer
signupgenius.com

SignUpGenius' primary purpose is to help groups organize who is doing what and when, letting volunteers sign up for tasks and time slots. It's free for smaller projects and very handy for group meetings.

NerdHerd Thumbs Up: An App for Events

Yapp
Event App for Organizations
yapp.us

At a price point of $400 a year, **Yapp** is not a typical tool for my book of bargains. But NerdHerder Nicole Abbott says it's super affordable for cost-conscious event organizers. Yapp lets you turn a conference program into a handheld guide, organizing session schedules, attendee lists, sponsor pages and more on a mobile app. Nicole says Yapp is easy to use and set up and that even the most basic level has excellent features. "It's a great intro app for newbies," she says.

Take Meeting Notes

Just because you have a great way to conduct a meeting doesn't mean your meeting is going to be productive. But you can make use of a couple of free tools to keep you and your meeting organized, on track and effective.

Start with...

Voicea

AI-Powered Meeting Recording and Notes
voicea.com

I run across dozens of new apps a week that I kind of tuck into my toolbox for later examination. But every once in a while, a tool like **Voicea** comes along, and I put it to use immediately.

In a word...wow!

Voicea is the company that created "Eva," an artificial intelligence meeting recorder that will change how you're meeting with people. At its core, Eva is a voice recorder. You can invite her to dial into teleconferences or simply call her during a meeting, and she will record the audio. But with the addition of artificial intelligence speech recognition tools, Eva "listens" for keywords during your meeting, such as words related to action items, follow up tasks, numbers, people, etc. After your meeting is over, the AI tools scan the recording for those words and pull out the audio highlights.

You can also invite Eva to your online meetings via email or just by including her in the meeting participants. The free version limits the length of the recordings, but the unlimited level starts at just $7.99 a month.

My favorite feature is the ability to see your meeting in the form of a word cloud. I love to capture the spirit of a discussion by reviewing the most common topics to see what rises to the top.

Then Try...

Otter.ai
AI-Powered Meeting Recording and Notes
otter.ai

If I hadn't fallen in love with Voicea first, I'd probably use **Otter** like my nerdy buddy and NerdHerd member Phil Gerbyshak does. Like Voicea, Otter uses artificial intelligence to record and transcribe meetings. The emphasis with Otter is on the transcription, which it can do in real-time. The tool is not as set up for meeting notes as Voicea, but the transcription is hard to beat, especially since you get 10 hours a month for free.

Phil loves it for his face-to-face meetings.

> *I especially love that the app on my phone transcribes (at 95 percent accuracy) the in-person meetings I have, as it picks up what I say and what the others in the meeting say. When I remember to add people to my calendar appointments, after I do an Otter recording, the platform also prompts me to share the recording AND the transcript with my meeting attendees. I can't live without this tool.*

> What do you say to
>
> comfort a grammar nerd?
>
> There, their, they're.

Also Check Out...

AudioNote
Voice Recorder with Synchronized Written Notes
luminantsoftware.com

Samepage
Meeting Management with Videoconferencing
samepage.io

Although this tool might really belong in the videoconferencing section (Page 90), I'm sharing it here because of its focus on teamwork and remote meetings. **Samepage** is made for cooperation and online meetings, from its real-time collaboration to the task management. Samepage is an excellent tool to use to keep your remote team on, well, the same page. Sorry. I couldn't help myself.

Even if you take notes as fast as you can, it's easy to miss important points. **AudioNote** is a note-taking app that simultaneously records what's happening in the meeting. When you review your notes, you can play the audio from that moment in the meeting. The big, big bummer about AudioNote is that it hasn't been updated since 2014. But the reviews are current, so people are still finding it helpful, and I haven't found anything I like more.

Meet Virtually

Phone calls are so 2007. These days we feel more connected with teams when we hear, see and participate in our remote meetings. Here are five scenarios for meeting with people from afar that brings them closer together.

"Let's plow into this project together."

Skype
Perhaps the Original Online Meeting/Chat Tool—Now with Instant Translation
skype.com

Microsoft Teams (Page 67) and Microsoft Office 365 (Page 65) have come a long way in the real-time collaboration world. They will let you use the old favorite **Skype** while you're writing and reviewing a document in real time.

"Let me take a look at that whosiewhatsit."

FaceTime
Apple's Videoconferencing Tool
apple.com/facetime

Google Duo
Google's Video-Calling Tool
google.com/duo

Messenger
Facebook's Videoconferencing Tool
messenger.com

You sell whosiewhatsits. You're out running errands, and one of your team members texts you. She is having a problem installing the thingamabobby switch to make the whosiewhatsit jiggle for a new client. No problem, you text back. And you tap your screen a couple of times to start a video call with **Google Duo**. Google Duo acts a lot like Apple's **Facetime** and Facebook's **Messenger**. The three tools are not just for connecting the kids with Grandma: They can help you connect with colleagues one on one or extend your view to troubleshoot projects in the field.

"We need a face-to-face meeting."

Zoom
HD Videoconferencing Tool
zoom.us

My favorite professional HD videoconferencing tool is **Zoom.** It's free/affordable, fast, flawless and fantastic. The first two levels let you pull in up to 100 HD video streams at the same time. Meetings have a time limit for the free version, but you can look at this as a benefit. Imagine saying, "We're trying to save the organization money, so we're using the free version, which means that this meeting must last less than 40 minutes!" Everyone will love you.

Zoom started out as the best-kept secret in the videoconference world, but now it's the top choice for almost everyone, including the NerdHerd. Lindsey Haley says Zoom has been "instrumental in boosting volunteer participation" because it allows her members to participate in professional activities from afar. And Marquesa Pettway has earned her nickname of the "Zoom Queen."

> *Zoom is my favorite app. The app version does everything from recording important conversations (video, audio, transcript) to giving me a green screen background without any tools needed. I can help someone meet me on the app with just one word (my brand of course). And I can live stream to several social media platforms right from this app AND access the recording afterward. I guess that's why they call me the Zoom Queen!!!*

"The last time we had a video conference, Jim forgot to wear pants. We're going back to teleconferences."

FreeConferenceCall.com
Free Conference Calling
freeconferencecall.com

StartMeeting
FreeConferenceCall's Upgraded Conference Platform
startmeeting.com

UberConference
Conference Call Tool with Hi-Tech Features
uberconference.com

I tried my best to leave teleconferencing out of this book, but I still find myself on a number of teleconferences when I get together with a committee to talk about an upcoming event. When will these disappear?

Since they haven't gone away, here are some options. You can use several of the videoconferencing tools for audio-only calls, but they'll still use the apps, and logging into them is more complicated than just dialing a phone number.

FreeConferenceCall.com is just that . . . free conference calls, plus a whole lot more these days. They make money from the calls because the phone companies pay them a small fee when the calls route through certain centers. They also offer free video conferencing and screensharing for up to 1000 participants. Upgrades include a dedicated number for about $4 a month or a more professional setup for about $15 a month with their **StartMeeting** product.

For a different take on teleconferences, try **UberConference**. The differentiator here is the web interface during a call. The site pulls in social media profiles like LinkedIn to show the pictures of the people talking. It has a free version with unlimited calls for up to 10 participants, but the coolest feature is in the paid level ($120 a year): The system calls out to participants at the designated time, so no more pin numbers.

Then Try...

Appear.in
Instant Video Conferencing with Screensharing
appear.in

In the first version of *The Big Book of Apps*, I included **Appear.in** with my fingers crossed, worried that it would disappear. But the tool has matured and is a legit resource for instant video conferencing with screensharing.

You register, choose a custom link suffix then press a button. Instantly your window is transformed into a conference area, and your lovely face is broadcast on the screen (turn off the camera if you don't want to be startled like I was). Then you can use the free version to meet with up to three other people to share your screen. You can't record your meeting with the basic level, but this tool is perfect for super-quick online meetings.

Jazz Up Your Presentations

• •

For—I don't know, 200 years?—the standard for presentations has been Microsoft's PowerPoint. Ever since we dropped the overhead projector/transparency model, we've emphasized key points of our educational sessions with hard-to-read, badly designed bullet-point slides.

Although PowerPoint is still the most popular program, it has become the software we love to hate. That's why we're always looking for alternatives.

Start with...

Canva
Design Templates for Instant Social Media Posts, Flyers, Invitations and Much More
canva.com

PowToon
Whiteboard Video Tool
powtoon.com

Visme
Creative Presentations and Infographics
visme.co

What the what??? None of these tools are for presentations. I bet you're thinking, "Beth, have you gone mad?"

Nope—I'm not crazy at all. And I didn't list these tools here by mistake. Although all three of these tools are known for different functions, they each have the capability to create interesting, non-traditional presentation decks...the perfect alternative to boring PowerPoints.

Canva (Page 357) is known for having thousands (millions?) of templates for social media, invitations and more. But it also lets you create complete presentations that you can present online or post on a page for viewers to scroll through alone. You can also embed video in the presentations.

PowToon (Page 342) is primarily a tool to make animated and explainer videos. But you can also use their fun graphics to create a presentation.

And **Visme** (Page 361) is a favorite for infographics, but you can also create and present slide decks.

Then Try...

Prezi
Storytelling PowerPoint Alternative
prezi.com

Sway
Microsoft PowerPoint Alternative...Created by Microsoft
sway.com

Chances are you've seen a **Prezi.** The presentation is kind of like you have a giant whiteboard with all your information for your presentation. The presenter has a high-quality video camera. As she tells the story, the camera zooms in and out of relevant areas of the whiteboard, even rotating the camera into new areas to draw people's attention to the right elements, then pulling back to show the big picture.

As with PowerPoint, your content will be organized by slides even though the final Prezi looks nothing like a slide-based presentation. Each slide represents where your Prezi will move next.

#NerdConfession: I just don't like Prezi. So it zooms in and out and does a little twisting and turning. Big deal. It's kind of a one-hit wonder. And frankly, it makes me a little dizzy, all that zooming around. I can do so much more with PowerPoint.

The free version of Prezi lets you create public presentations and share them online. Starting at $7 a month, you can keep your Prezis private, and $19+ a month gets you the software to create Prezis without an Internet connection.

Believe it or not, one of the coolest PowerPoint alternatives comes from . . . the creator of PowerPoint. **Sway** is a sleek presentation tool that enables you to create a slide deck that's more like a flowing website, including dynamic content like embedded videos and social media posts. You can use it in place of traditional slides or let it stand alone.

Then Try...

Google Slides
Google's PowerPoint Alternative
slides.google.com

Haiku Deck
Presentation Tool for Presenters with Few Words
haikudeck.com

Although I'm still not in love with the **Google Slides** templates, the online tool is easy to use and can be convenient for presenting on the go. Tip: Check out Envato (Page 352) for presentation templates that don't suck.

Haiku Deck provides beautiful, easy-to-use templates for presentations on the iPad and the web. The clean look of the templates is perfect for the minimalist design trends we see in today's best presentations.

Also Check Out...

Beautiful.AI

Slide Designer Powered by AI with Robust Free Version
beautiful.ai

Slidebean

Slide Designer Powered by AI
slidebean.com

If you struggle with how to create a slide deck, these tools could help. They both claim to be powered by artificial intelligence, meaning they analyze what you're writing and how you're writing it to make real-time suggestions for layout, organization and design.

I don't know. I could never get either one of the slide design tools to predict what I needed. But like Haiku Deck, they create clean, sleek, modern presentations that you'll be proud to share. **Beautiful.AI** has a pretty good free version. You're going to have to pay at least $100 a year to make a finished product in **Slidebean**. You can play around with both of them before buying.

Hot Topic:
Interaction in the Classroom

Flipgrid
Social Video Platform for
Collaborative Projects
flipgrid.com

Kahoot
Trivia and Quiz Game for Audiences
kahoot.com

Quizziz
Self-Paced Quiz Games
quizizz.com

These three tools are #NerdHerdApproved and great for engaging students no matter what age.

School librarian and NerdHerder Amanda Jones loves **Flipgrid,** a tool that lets people create little videos to put on a discussion board. "I love to embed Flipgrids into my library website for students to share book talks, record videos of research findings and collaborate with their peers through videos."

My sister, Sarah Ziesenis, is a brilliant middle school science teacher. She loves to educate her students with **Kahoot**, a tool that lets presenters create quizzes that audience members can answer in a flash. Kahoot has a competitive component that makes it fun for participants to jump in to answer first. "I like it. Kids LOVE it!" Sarah says. "It makes trivia games easy for students to play, and that helps them stay engaged while answering academic questions."

Although Kahoot's primary focus has always been schools, they've been pushing the business and pro plans. Check them out for training, onboarding and corporate events.

The bad thing about Kahoot is that it's a competition, and Sarah says kids sometimes don't have time to absorb the information because the pace is too fast. That's why she started using **Quizziz** instead. Just like Kahoot, you can set up knowledge and trivia games, but the kids answer at their own pace.

Hot Topic:
PowerPoint Is Still Really Powerful

Microsoft Office 365
Office Subscription that Gets All the Goodies
office.com

PowerPoint has a bad reputation because people use it badly. One of my secret weapons for making beautiful slide decks is the Envato Marketplace, a gallery of easy-to-personalize templates for presentations, blogs and much, much more. See more about Envato on Page 352.

In addition, if you subscribe to **Microsoft Office 365** (which I consider one of the most valuable investments I make—I pay $99 a year for up to 6 users), you have all kinds of features that will help make your presentation interesting and awesome.

Here are two bonuses you get with Microsoft Office 365 and good old PowerPoint:

- **AI-Powered Design Suggestions**
  Office 365 subscribers can turn on the Design Ideas feature to see (non-boring) layout ideas for each slide. Microsoft uses artificial intelligence to figure out what's on your slide (title, photo, bullets, etc.) and suggest other ways to design that slide.

- **3D Objects with Animations**
  Oh joy! You'll have so much fun adding 3D emojis, animals, symbols and more that move and jump and spin. They add a literal 3D layer to your flat slides. My favorite is a little toaster that pops out toasts. I don't get out much.

And features you can use even if you don't have Office 365:

- **Live Closed-Captioning**
  Go to Slide Show >> Always use subtitles to show real-time closed-captioning while you're speaking (just make sure you are near the input microphone…I connect my AirPods so the sound goes directly to the computer wherever I am in the room).

- **Find Online Images**
  Go to Insert Pictures and choose Online Pictures. A menu will appear at the side with a Bing search engine. Search for the image you need, and Bing will return images that have been designated as being in the public realm. This also works in other Office apps.

  NOTE: The image may not truly be free to use. Read more about copyright issues with online images starting on Page 352.

Create Creative Online Documents

In this age of e-books and dynamic content, you don't want to represent your organization with a plain old downloadable Word document saved as a PDF. Luckily we have some great tools that can help us create online content that wows as well as informs.

Start with...

Designrr
eBook Maker and More
designrr.io

I. Love. This. Tool.

Designrr lets you take a blog post or other content and within a few clicks turn it into a beautiful formatted e-book-y thingy. I say "thingy" because it can be an official e-book or a white paper or a flippable online magazine like Issuu or let it live on the web or all kinds of things.

It's just so dang easy. Just paste the blog post URL into the online wizard, then choose a theme and press a button. Designrr will apply theme styles to the text and lay it out for you. I did it with an article I wrote about the dangers of public Wi-Fi (Page 209). In less than an hour, I had a very stylish white paper thingy. I wouldn't call it an e-book because it was short, but I will go back to the same document and add other privacy and security posts to make a real book.

You can even push a button to get a 3D mockup of your e-book-y thingy so you can promote it. Seriously. It's just so cool.

And that's not all! I haven't tried this yet, but you can upload audio or video to get a transcript that you can then turn into a document. The fun never ends!

I found Designrr because when I click around these sites, I end up getting a lot of ads for random tools like this one. Designrr's ad offered a $27 lifetime subscription to the Pro level, which they say is regularly hundreds a year or something. I signed up, and this basic, basic version is probably going to be adequate, at least for a while.

Then Try...

Issuu
Online Magazine Maker
issuu.com

Have you ever created a fantastic PowerPoint and saved it into that boring 4-slide-per-page handout? The mystical, magical site called **Issuu** transforms your boring handout into an interactive, dynamic, interesting online magazine, book or catalog that people can flip through. The graphics of the viewing interface will make you look like a pro, and it has built-in features that allow readers to share and download your files.

Transforming your boring document into an online magazine is embarrassingly simple. Just drag a file to the uploader, name your document, add a description and press a button. Issuu will process your file in no time and then provide you with everything you need to share your new magazine. It works with any PDF, but I've found that slide decks make great magazines.

Also Check Out...

Lumen5
AI-Powered Video Tool for Blog Posts
lumen5.com

I know this is officially a video tool and should be listed in the graphics section that starts on Page 323, but **Lumen5** has a place here. This online tool is another great way to repurpose your existing content. Like Designrr, you can paste a blog post link, choose a theme and push a button. Then Lumen5 uses artificial intelligence to analyze your content. It identifies key sentences and related royalty-free media to create one of those Buzzfeed-type videos with the headlines over graphics. You choose a soundtrack and publish, and you have a 60–90-second overview video of the major points of your content.

Like Designrr, you definitely have to tweak the first draft that the AI puts together. But most little videos won't take you any more than 5 minutes. You can also make those super-short, portrait-view videos favored in social media stories.

What does a Jedi use
to open a PDF file?

Adobe Wan Kenobi

Communication

COMMUNICATION

In This Chapter...

Manage Email

● ●

The best thing to happen to us as professionals is that we can get email wherever we go.

The worst thing to happen to us as professionals is that we can get email wherever we go.

Here are some of my favorite tools to make our email inboxes a little less horrible.

Most Versatile Email

Gmail
Versatile Email Platform
google.com/gmail

In my humble opinion, **Gmail** is the strongest tool in my fight against email madness. Wait, let me clarify . . . *Inbox by Google* was the best, but Google killed it because Google is mean.

But even with the regular Gmail platform, you can import all your email accounts into the Gmail system (and send them from the different accounts as well). One of the best features is that Gmail filters spam better than any tool I've used. In fact, as I played around with different apps to write this section, I was horrified at the spam emails that hit my inbox. I never saw them with Gmail.

In addition, Gmail's integration with about a kabillion tools means that I can extend the functionality to manage my travel, organize my to-dos, track my packages, research my contacts and much, much, much more.

Surprisingly Capable Email

Microsoft Outlook

Email Triage Tool
microsoft.com/outlook

Once upon a time, I was a Microsoft girl, and if there was any tool that would get me to return to Windows, it's **Microsoft Outlook**. Not only do I love the rules that helped me organize my inbox (Gmail's aren't as good), but I also adore the Microsoft Outlook app, which has extra characteristics beyond the desktop Outlook we've all come to know.

Like Gmail, you can consolidate all your other email accounts into the Outlook app. Then the fun begins. Use the app to schedule emails, find times to meet, attach files and swipe and scan your way through your inbox on the go. Best of all, the mobile app with all its advanced features is free, which means you can use it on the go while still keeping your main email system, such as Gmail or Yahoo.

Chat-Friendly Email

Spike

Conversational Email that Looks Like Texting
spikenow.com

Right now you have someone in your life who never responds to your email, but if you pop them a text, they write back in seconds. **Spike** email is perfect for those folks. The platform styles emails into windows that make it look like you're texting back and forth rather than working with the more formal email interface.

Here's a conversation between me and my designer in Gmail…

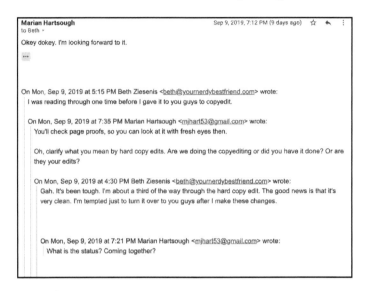

And here's how Spike displays the same conversation…

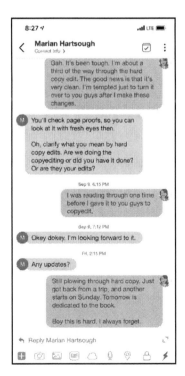

Spike identifies the actual conversation part and sets it up like text messages. I like Spike, but I'm a little iffy about its future. It might be too different to find an audience. But it is really cool.

#HelpfulButCreepy Email

Edison

Free Email with Advanced Assistant Help and Unnerving Tracking
mail.edison.tech

I'm kind of a hypocrite. I am willing to accept the receipt-tracking tools in Unroll.Me (Page 224) and Slice (Page 220), but **Edison** creeps me out. There's no doubt that the advanced features in Edison will help you get through your emails and tasks quickly. But it seems really invasive, and I just can't bring myself to use it.

Edison email searches your inbox for package receipts, unwanted subscriptions, travel confirmations and more. And then it alerts you for deliveries and flight updates, plus lets you unsubscribe with one click. Ummm. . . . Gmail does all that as well in exchange for letting Google track you all over the place. But again, Edison just creeps me out. But it has won all kinds of awards, so I guess you just have to choose which creepy email tool you want.

> Our society will never go
> entirely paperless. There's
> always the bathroom.

Super-Secure Email

ProtonMail

Encrypted Email Platform

protonmail.com

ProtonMail's servers are in Switzerland, so the company proudly states, "This means all user data is protected by strict Swiss privacy laws." The platform offers end-to-end encryption that keeps your privacy and data security top of mind. They don't keep IP logs, and you don't need personal information to create a secure email account. They have a free version and a strong plea of community support.

> *ProtonMail is community software, funded by the community, and open source. We do not show ads or make money by abusing your privacy. Instead, we depend on your support to keep the service running. Revenue from paid accounts is used to further develop ProtonMail and support free users such as democracy activists and dissidents who need privacy but can't necessarily afford it.*

Email for Collaboration

Spark

Email Platform with Team Features

sparkmailapp.com

Spark has smart features for categorization, quick replies and email triage, just like many of my top choices do. But where it gets interesting is with the team integration. Spark lets you and your team collaborate on responses and activities around emails.

For example, a client sends a salesperson a question about the contract. The salesperson would likely send separate emails to different team members to get answers or coordinate the response. Then the salesperson would aggregate the responses into an email back to the client.

With Spark, team members can chat quickly inside the app around any email instead of having to send more emails back and forth. Team members can also compose and edit emails together and keep a bank of email templates for consistency. And users can delegate emails to other team members without having to write intro emails "looping customer service in" with the clients.

Also Check Out...

FollowUpThen
Software-Free Email Reminders
followupthen.com

FollowUpThen is an email reminder tool for the app-phobic. Want to get something out of your inbox because you don't need to deal with it for a week? Send it to 1week@followupthen.com. Keep forgetting to finish your monthly report? Send a note to everymonth@followupthen.com. Checking the notes for your client review half an hour before your meeting? Forward them to Aug25.1030am@followupthen.

That's it. No app. No software. No plugin. Nothing to download or install. Just use @followupthen.com with a timeframe to manage your inbox. That's why it gets a thumbs up from NerdHerder Chris Champion.

The free version offers 50 reminders a month. Paid versions start at $2 a month and include features like automatic response detection to monitor whether you need to reach out again to someone who hasn't written back, and a calendar feed to keep track of your FollowUpThen pending notifications.

Send Video Emails

• •

Your first email: "Here's the proposal. As soon as you sign, we can get started!"

Their response: [nothing]

Your second email: "Hey, just checking in. Did you get a chance to review the proposal?"

Their response: [nothing]

Your third email: [you smiling in a short video and asking about the proposal]

Their response: "Yes! Thanks for getting in touch. We are ready to move forward!"

Sending an embedded video with a personal message in your emails will get you noticed, and several tools make it easy to stand out.

Start with...

BombBomb
Video Email System
bombbomb.com

Dubb
Video Tool for Email, Screencasts and More
dubb.com

Loom
Screencast Video Tool
loom.com

BombBomb is the industry standard, but it comes with a premium price tag. The attractive format creates a clean, inviting email for your contacts. Each video has a big play button and the video length listed. When the recipient clicks on the video, she is taken to the hosted page since right now many (most?) videos won't play inside email.

The Google Chrome plugin takes over your Gmail (Page 106) page but adds lots of helpful sales tools, such as email tracking. And you can click one button to dash off a quick, personal video. You can also create a bank of videos for automated replies (such as follow-up requests, etc.).

BombBomb starts at about $40 a month, a little on the pricey side compared to most tools in this book. But I'm going to put it into the category of worth the price for sales and customer service folks.

I was lucky to snag a lifetime subscription to **Dubb** through AppSumo (Page 148), but pricing starts at free. We like free. Dubb is similar to BombBomb with embedded video, landing pages, tracking and more. **Loom** is my favorite choice when I'm on someone's site and want to talk about an upcoming meeting or I want to demo from my screen. But since it has more features than most of the screen-capture tools on Page 184, I think it belongs here. Jennifer Van Ort says she loves Loom because it's free (we love free) and, "It provides a new way for me to walk members through our website."

Then Try...

CloudHQ Video Email
Video Email for Gmail
cloudhq.net

If the price of BombBomb scares you off, give this free Chrome plugin a try. CloudHQ has dozens of very specific Gmail tools, and many of them are free. It took me a few minutes to figure out how to sign up for **CloudHQ Video Email** while avoiding their other (paid) services. But after I installed it, I was able to send a video email in seconds.

The system lets you record a video from your Gmail (Page 106) compose screen. Then you choose upload options such as Google Drive, YouTube or your computer. Although I love the service, I've found it to work perfectly one day then not at all the next...usually when I'm trying to demo it to hundreds of people during a session.

Also Check Out...

Paperless Post
Deluxe Emails with a Real-Mail Look
paperlesspost.com

My husband proposed to me in August of 2010. After a negative experience with my practice husband, I wasn't about to let this good one get away. So we set the date a mere three months into the future. This gave me no time to get traditional invitations in the mail, so I chose the elegant email service **Paperless Post** to create what I thought were handsome replicas of a paper invitation.

Paperless Post sends emails that look like envelopes and open dramatically when you click. You can send invitations, thank-you notes, birthday cards and all kinds of greetings with these interactive emails. You will probably see an uptick in both your open rates and ROI because they're different, fun and interactive. Paperless Post has free and paid options. You can also use their colorful "flyer" pages for event invites.

One More Idea...

Although fancy emails are super cool, people still love to get personal notes in the mail. Check out my favorite snail mail options on Page 337.

Manage Calls

· ·

We text. We email. We message. We post. And sometimes we even still call. Here are a couple of tools that make your time on the phone a little less annoying.

Start with...

HulloMail
Voicemail Management System
hullomail.com

YouMail
Voicemail Management System with Spam-Stopping Tools
youmail.com

If you're in an industry that receives a lot of calls, check out **HulloMail.** The voicemail-in-the-cloud functionality gives you the ability to save, search and share voicemails, and even receive and catalog the transcriptions. Plus you can reply to the voicemails via text. NerdHerder Chris Christensen gives it a thumbs up for saving time.

After 10 years of an ad-supported free version, they started charging less than a buck a month for their lowest tier. The change made lots of people mad and led to negative reviews that drove down their excellent reviews. But gosh, folks, everything can't be free. ☺

My friend and fellow speaker Jessica Pettitt uses **YouMail,** and it's the coolest thing. Thanks to YouMail's "Smart Greetings," when I call her, the system says, "Hi, Beth. Jessica is currently unavailable. Please speak clearly. This voicemail is being transcribed by YouMail."

Like the voice says, YouMail then transcribes my message for Jess. And because YouMail connects with a caller before the call gets to you, YouMail claims it weeds out spammers and scammers. The company also manages The Robocall Index, which tracks the BILLIONS of robocalls a month—about half of which are scams.

Then Try...

Google Voice

Call Management System

voice.google.com

Have you ever had to write an email to someone that says, "If it's after 5 P.M., call on this line; or call the office during the weekdays, unless it's Tuesday, when you can reach me at the volunteer center"?

Google Voice gives you one phone number to text, call and check voicemail. You can reach it from any device, managing all your communications in one place wherever you are.

It's not a phone service; let's call it an advanced call management system. Most of the incredible features are free, and it can centralize (and revolutionize) your phone and text communications. My sales manager, Molly, uses a Google Voice number for calls to Nerd HQ so she can answer work calls on her personal phone without having to share her real number.

The truth is I've been worried about Google Voice for several years because they stopped updating it and it seemed forgotten. But in 2016, Google brought new features and energy to the service, and I'm thrilled to recommend it again.

Here's a partial list of Google Voice awesomeness:

- Custom vanity phone numbers
- One number that can route to all your phones
- Free and low-cost national and international calls
- Free text messaging
- Call screening and blocking
- Transcribed voicemails
- Personalized greetings for different incoming numbers
- Conference calls
- Call recording and archiving
- Mobile apps for multiple operating systems

Also Check Out...

Slydial

Phone Service that Goes Straight to Voicemail

slydial.com

Do you ever dial the phone with a grimace, hoping like heck the recipient doesn't pick up? NerdHerder Brian Owen calls **Slydial** "the perfect tool to call that customer who talks your ear off." Use Slydial to skip straight to voicemail so you can leave your message and get on with your life. Slydial only works with mobile numbers, but it's super handy. The free version makes you listen to their ad about the premium version, which is only about $30 a year.

So here's the deal about Slydial . . . everybody loves them, but I'm a little worried about their stability. As of this writing, the iOS app hasn't been updated since 2017. The Android app received an update in 2019, but a lot of the reviewers were unhappy. They also had a solid two years of quiet social media (never a good sign), and their last Slydial news was in 2011.

These are all warning signs, but when I tried out a few numbers using their phone service instead of the app, it worked fine. Just dial 267-SLYDIAL (267-759-3425). I decided to check in with Slydial to see if I'd get an update:

So . . . I guess that settles that.

Organize and Synchronize Contacts

• •

My contact list is a big honkin' mess, full of duplicates, sloppiness and overall chaos. Don't be like me. Use these tools to get your contact list in line.

Start with...

Contacts+

The Best Contact Management System on the Planet
contactsplus.com

Every time I have a discussion with attendees about contact management systems, **Contacts+** (formerly FullContact) is the top response. The system merges your duplicate contacts, even from different devices and platforms, keeping all your contact systems current no matter where they live. It also scans public data to keep you up to date with your contacts' latest photos, jobs and social profiles. When your contacts have a new signature line, Contacts+ updates the info in their profile.

A super feature of Contacts+ is its business card processing (see more business card tools on Page 197). Just snap pictures of cards, and Contacts+'s human people will transcribe them and add them to your list.

The free version gives you 1,000 contacts and the ability to sync with one other account. Plus, you get 10 business card transcriptions. The paid levels start with syncing to five accounts and 25,000 contacts.

Then Try...

Contactually
Contact Management with a Built-In Bucket Game
contactually.com

Nimble
Social Media-Connected Contact Management Tool
nimble.com

Although Contacts+ is mentioned most often by my community, **Contactually** and **Nimble** have special features that make them stand out. Contactually helps you sort your kabillion contacts into buckets by way of an amusing game of flicking them into literal buckets. And Nimble gets extra points because it not only connects your contacts via email, but it also searches out their social media posts to give you more of an idea of who they are and where they hang out online.

Also Check Out...

IXACT Contact
Real Estate Contact Management Platform
ixactcontact.com

Salesforce Essentials
Basic Level of a Very Robust CRM
salesforce.com

My real estate friends have some great industry-specific contact management solutions, and NerdHerder Craig Borner says **IXACT Contact** is the best. Craig says...

> *IXACT is an excellent cloud-based contact management program specifically for real estate to track contacts, escrows and listings. It also has tailored marketing follow-up emails to your database. It also provides integrated website design, plus a complete calendar with reminders and alarms, automated periodic mailings (either boilerplate or customizable) and much more.*

When I was in sales, I adored **Salesforce**. It's an incredibly robust customer relationship manager that can be customized to the 97th degree. NerdHerder Tonja Money named it as her favorite because of how customizable it is. At $25 per user per month, Salesforce Essentials level is the very, very cheapest entry point in a system that can add on features and plugins until it's quite the budget line item. At the Essential level, you can track contacts, customer communications, sales opportunities and more.

Hot Topic:
How to Stop Emails from Tracking You

We business professionals have a love/hate relationship with email tracking.

On one hand, we don't want anyone tracking whether we open or click on an email we receive. How dare they!

On the other hand, it's incredibly helpful when we know that a recipient looked at our email so we know whether we need to send it again.

Here are some helpful tools to both track the emails you send and make sure the emails you receive are not tracked.

Stop Emails from Tracking You

Block Auto-Loading Images
In Your Email Platform Settings

Ugly Email
Email Tracking Pixel Blocker for Gmail
uglyemail.com

Here's how most email trackers operate: The sender embeds a tiny image, usually just one pixel in size. When you open your email (or even show the preview), the pixel is downloaded, which lets the provider know when, where and how it was downloaded.

To stop the tracking, you need to prevent the pixel from being downloaded. In the settings for your email platform, such as Outlook, Gmail and more, you'll find switches regarding external images. You can choose to prevent the download of images or prompt for your permission.

If you use Gmail, you can also use an extension like **Ugly Email.** When an email with a tracking pixel shows up in your inbox, Ugly Email marks it with a creepy-looking eye. And when you open the email, Ugly Email will disable the tracking, even if other images are downloaded.

Track Emails You Send

MailChimp
Mass Email Platform with Free Version
mailchimp.com

Even though we hate that other people track us, we like to track people. Using an email-sending platform can not only help you track interest in your newsletters or promotions…it can also keep you in compliance with anti-spam regulations. **MailChimp** is one of the best-known email platforms around. Although MailChimp is pivoting toward an all-in-one marketing platform with advertising, landing pages and higher pricing levels, the company remains the top choice for email marketing and maintains a decent free version. NerdHerder Judy Oiler loves it, saying, "It's free. It's beautiful (received lots of compliments from my audience). It's customizable."

• •

Research Connections and Prospects

When you're meeting with a prospective client, employer or just a new contact, you should take a few minutes to read through the company profile, the LinkedIn facts, recent news mentions and other interesting tidbits that will show your contact that you're paying attention.

But if you're like me, you will run out of time before you do your homework. Wouldn't it be nice if you had help with your research? Stay tuned....

Start with...

Crystal
Contact Research Tool that Analyzes Personalities
crystalknows.com

Did you know that I respond well to emoticons in written communication?

Or that I'd like to chat a little about this and that before we get down to business?

Or that you should schedule a meeting with me around food and drink?

Although I haven't spent that much time on self-analysis, it was no surprise to me that when a service called **Crystal** analyzed my personality based on my online presence and writing, it declared that "Beth is social, creative, trusts feelings and gut instinct more than rules or logic, and loves talking about ideas."

For years I've been looking for a tool that does what Crystal does, but it just doesn't have any real competition. Crystal scours online profiles and returns recommendations for talking, writing and selling to our contacts. The system is set up to analyze online content and immediately categorize people using the DiSC® personality profiles. You can take a 10-question personality quiz to help it analyze your personality, and if you verify a relationship with someone, you can answer questions about others as well.

They've changed the pricing and the freebie offerings a few times, but as of this writing, you can analyze "friends and co-workers" for free, or lookup anyone for $29 a month. The paid version includes the very valuable Gmail plugin, which analyzes contacts as they come into your email inbox and guides your email correspondence as you type.

NerdHerder Beth Tutwiler-McGuire uses Crystal at her association. "It helps me connect with my members, even if we don't spend a lot of time together."

A tool named Emma was the closest idea to Crystal, but since Emma relied on LinkedIn and LinkedIn's API is a little selfish, Emma never really found its footing and closed shop in the fall of 2019 (about a week before we sent this book to the printer). I'm leaving the Emma comparison here to demonstrate the differences.

Emma used a Chrome plugin when you visited LinkedIn, whereas Crystal brings in more data points.

Here is my profile, according to both tools:

Emma said . . .

- Strength: "Organized, pragmatic and good at managing their time."
- What matters to them: "A culture where honest feedback is valued."
- Things to avoid: "A loose organizational structure."

Crystal says...

- What comes naturally to Beth: "Try to reduce or avoid structure and bureaucracy."
- What drains Beth: "When others nitpick details" and "Feeling micromanaged."
- In a meeting with Beth: "Send a reminder the day before" and "Be casual about scheduling a meeting."

These two lists of characteristics describe two different people. Emma said I'm organized and should avoid a loose organizational structure. Crystal says to avoid structure. Emma said I'm good with honest feedback. Crystal says others should back off. Emma said I'm good at managing my time. Crystal says I need reminders for meetings.

Crystal nailed it. Emma missed. And now Emma's gone.

Then Try...

Contacts+ (Page 118)

Hunter
Email Hunting Tool and More
hunter.io

Hunter Campaigns
Email Campaign Manager
hunter.io/campaigns

Contacts+ is really a contact management tool, but I love the way they help with researching connections. The system is always working to match your contacts with other points of information, such as blogs, LinkedIn profiles and more. Contacts+ also offers a "dossier" report on any people listed on a calendar event.

Let's say you'd like to find someone at my company. You'd go to **Hunter** and enter my URL, and every publicly listed email address for people at our company will show up along with the source of the info. You can also verify email addresses and search a couple of different ways, including with browser extensions. You get 50 searches a month for free.

In 2019 Hunter introduced **Campaigns** to help you compose, personalize and schedule follow-up connections with your new contacts. It's like a little secret mail merge site for your cold emails with systems for tracking whether they have opened, responded, called the cops, etc.

Also Check Out...

BatchGeo
Lead Mapping Tool
batchgeo.com

Google My Maps
Another Lead Mapping Tool
google.com/mymaps

Both **BatchGeo** and **Google My Maps** let you upload spreadsheets of your prospects or clients to see where they are and where they're not, giving you great insight into where you should focus your sales and marketing efforts. BatchGeo has some advanced features with the paid level, but Google My Maps is free, so....

Send Free Text and Voice Messages

The world is a big place, but technology can make us seem like our far-away friends are right next door. These tools offer free communication across the miles.

Start with...

WhatsApp
Free Text, Phone and Video Messenger
whatsapp.com

WhatsApp's About Us page states that 1 billion people in more than 180 countries use the tool. The premise is pretty basic: WhatsApp gives you free text and voice communications through a secure network via devices and the web. Facebook owns the company, but it's a stand-alone tool for now, even though Facebook Messenger also offers free messaging, as well as audio and video calls. The company claims that its end-to-end encryption equals private communications, though the tool Signal (see below) gets generally higher marks in the privacy category.

Then Try...

GroupMe
Group Text Messenger
groupme.com

Signal Private Messenger
Secure Private Messenger
signal.org

When you're working with colleagues who no longer answer emails or pick up the phone, **GroupMe** may be the answer. You can set up a group for texting and sharing images, videos and even your location.

GroupMe is cool because other members of the group don't have to download the app to make the system work. Oh, and it's free. NerdHerder Celia Fritz-Watson says GroupMe is great for staying connected for a project or team for both work and home. But if you're using it for work, you may agree with one reviewer complaint: "I would give it a 5 star, but I'm in a group with men, and I don't like that the only option to 'like' a comment is a red '♥.'"

The messaging app **Signal** made headlines when White House staffers were accused of using the app to secretly leak news to the press. Signal definitely has the best reputation as a private messaging app, although the tool is less known than WhatsApp and other competitors. You can text and call on this system and rest assured that no one can intercept your communication (at least until someone figures out how to do so).

Also Check Out...

Marco Polo
Video Chat App that Works Like Texting
marcopolo.me

The **Marco Polo** app was made to help family members send little videos back and forth without having to video chat live. NerdHerder Kay Babylon-West says it's great to use for groups and because it's "f.u.n." And Megan Mueller says it helps with long-distance relationships:

> *I started using the app when a best friend moved to Hawaii. Having a 5-hour time difference makes it extremely difficult to connect. With Marco Polo there is no pressure to try and fit a phone call in, and I don't feel like I am neglecting my friend. I love that even though my friends and I may not live in the same city or state, we can see each other's faces and still feel like we are together. You can have fun with doodles and voice filters too!*

A few sales professionals have told me they also use it to communicate with clients. One real estate professional said she had closed several deals going back and forth with Marco Polo instead of just texting or emails. Sounds like a perfect use of its best features.

NerdHerd Thumbs Up: Send and Receive Text Messages on Your Computer

iMessage
Apple-Based Messaging App for Macs and Devices

MightyText
Android-Based Messaging App for Computers and Devices
mightytext.net

The staff at Nerd HQ live all over the country, and we need to communicate all the time. Texting is the fastest way, and Apple's **iMessage** makes texting incredibly easy because we get text messages from other iMessage users on our Macs.

MightyText lets Android do the same thing and more. You can send and receive text messages through your computer, plus make calls, send files and more. As NerdHerder Linda Richards says, "I can copy and paste computer-based content and send in a text message." Bonus! Linda adds, "Also, my phone can be put away, and my boss thinks I'm working and not on my phone! LOL!"

Add Closed Captioning to Your Videos

● ●

This will probably not come as a surprise: 85 percent of the videos on Facebook are watched without sound.

That statistic has been kicking around for years, and I'm not sure where it came from. But I do know that if you're not adding closed captioning to every video and presentation you share, you're losing members of your audience.

Start with...

Rev

On-Demand Transcription and Captioning
rev.com

Temi

Automated On-Demand Transcription and Captioning
temi.com

Rev and **Temi** are related companies somehow, but I use them both even though there's overlap. They're both so easy. Just go to the site, upload audio or video, then choose to have it transcribed by machine or human.

Machine transcriptions (via both Temi and Rev) are great for clear audio, and the service costs just $.10 per minute. Rev lets you choose human transcriptions for $1 a minute, or you can upgrade for different languages and other features. Both will let you tweak the transcriptions before downloading the transcript or a special closed-captioning file that you add to your video during the editing process. They're both super quick . . . usually just a few minutes for machine translations and not longer than 24 hours for human help.

Then Try...

Kapwing
Online Video Editor with Captioning Capability
kapwing.com

I'm really not sure how to classify the multi-talented **Kapwing**, but since I discovered it during a search for ways to add captions to video, I'll put it here.

Kapwing lets you automatically add captions and subtitles to video in its browser tool. But you can also edit images, GIFs, videos, memes and all kinds of things. The site even has templates for collages, montages, slideshows and ... and ... and.... It's just so full of good stuff.

Also Check Out...

AutoCap
Mobile Video Tool with Automatic Captions (Android)
In the Google Play Store

Clipomatic
Mobile Video Tool with Automatic Captions (iOS)
In the App Store

Clips
Apple's Video Editor with Easy Captions
apple.com/clips

When I'm making a video on the go, I like to make sure it is accessible for all. These three apps transcribe your words live on the screen while you speak. Apple's **Clips** is my favorite, but Apple hasn't updated it in a while, so perhaps it's on the way out. Clips records square videos and lets you add fun little "posters" between segments, such as a little drama from "Star Wars." You can also replace your background with fun animated backdrops.

Clipomatic has similar functionality but goes even further. Your captions can be styled as speech bubbles and creative subtitles. **AutoCap** is a similar option for Android devices.

Then Try...

Facebook

Automated Closed-Captioning for Videos on Facebook
facebook.com/help/509746615868430

YouTube

Automated Subtitles and Translations for Videos on YouTube
support.google.com/youtube/topic/9257536

When you upload video to **Facebook** and **YouTube**, you can go into the editors and enable closed captioning. The videos will have been transcribed automatically, and frequently you'll need to clean the text up and republish. But it doesn't take long, and the benefits of having closed captions outweigh the hassle.

Hot Topic:
Add Closed Captioning to Your TV

Tunity
App that Routes Live TV Audio Through Your Device
tunity.com

Tunity is a free app that lets you stream the audio from live TV channels through your mobile device. This gives you the freedom to watch a muted TV and hear the audio on your own.

Connecting Tunity takes seconds…just put the TV in the scan area on your phone, and if the channel is supported, you'll be listening in less than 30 seconds. You'll have to enable location services so the app will find the right feed. It works with about 100 basic cable channels on live TV only; so sorry, no Netflix.

I've found myself using it all over the place, from the waiting area at an airport gate to a hotel room when I didn't want to bother other guests with my blaring TV. And when I told my husband about this tool, he immediately asked me to download it to his phone. In marriage terms, that's a win!

Reference

In This Chapter...

Search Beyond Google

Google dominates the world of search engines with almost 90 percent of the market. Although it's arguably the best tool, other search engines reach other corners of the web and give you different answers to your questions.

Start with...

Wolfram|Alpha

Where All the Knowledge in the World Lives

wolframalpha.com

It's impossible to exaggerate the wealth of knowledge you'll find on **Wolfram|Alpha**, which calls itself a "Computational Knowledge Engine." You can convert measurements, analyze data, look up IP addresses, compare the statistics of The Beatles' White Album to Jay-Z's The Black Album, get step-by-step instructions for a physics calculation... I mean. Wow. From the About page:

> *Our goal is to accept completely free-form input, and to serve as a knowledge engine that generates powerful results and presents them with maximum clarity.*

> *We aim to collect and curate all objective data; implement every known model, method, and algorithm; and make it possible to compute whatever can be computed about anything.*

Then Try...

Dogpile
Search Results of Multiple Search Engines
dogpile.com

Yippy
IBM Watson-Backed Search Engine Compiler
yippy.com

Different search engines will return different results for the same search. Both **Dogpile** and **Yippy** run your inquiry on multiple search engines at once then rank the results for relevance and eliminate duplicates.

Dogpile has the cuter interface, but Yippy has a handy "cluster" results format that groups the types of results you find. And Yippy is another search engine that embraces private and cookie-free searches.

Also Check Out...

Wayback Machine
Search Engine for the Past
archive.org/web

On the web, nothing really disappears. The **Wayback Machine** is the archive of the internet. It has been taking snapshots of publicly available sites since 1996. Just put the site into the search engine, and you can click back in time to see the site on different dates.

NerdHerd Thumbs Up: Search Securely

DuckDuckGo
Search Engine with Privacy Protection
duckduckgo.com

Besides having the most adorable name, **DuckDuckGo** has the reputation of being the most private. When you search using DuckDuckGo, your history isn't tracked or sold to advertisers.

"Google has enough money," Cheryl Smith says. For that reason and the super-duper privacy capabilities, Cheryl uses DuckDuckGo.

Search Beyond Google *with Google*

The regular Google search gets you millions and millions of results in seconds, which is incredible, but that could make it harder to find really specific things you need to look up. Check out these Google specialty searches for more streamlined searches.

Start with...

Google Books

Full-Text Book Search Engine
books.google.com

Google Scholar

Academic Research Search Engine
scholar.google.com

When you search for the word *nerd* in the regular Google search engine, you get the Wikipedia page, the *Revenge of the Nerds* IMDB listing and an invitation to buy Nerds candies.

When you start with **Google Scholar,** you get "Nerd Nation: Images of Nerds in U.S. Popular Culture," an article that appeared in the *International Journal of Cultural Studies*. The search will cover scholarly articles, books and even some newsletters, which is where I found a few references to my sessions in limited-distribution electronic magazines including *College Athletics and the Law*. Who knew?

The bummer thing about this search engine is that the articles are often behind a paywall, but sometimes the abstract is helpful.

REFERENCE

I'm proud to say the first result for "Ziesenis" in the **Google Books** search engine is my first book, *Upgrade to Free."* But then my ancestors take over.

The magical tome *Ene Nederlandsche Tooneelspeelster* takes second place with its fascinating account of Johanna Cornelia Ziesenis-Wattier's career as a Dutch playwright (I think. Google Translate, anyone?).

Like Google Scholar, not every search will give you full-text results, but you'll find entire volumes of some classic works (*Ene Nederlandsche Tooneelspeelster* is available!). And you'll find easy access to where you can get the books.

Then Try...

Google Trends
Search Engine that Shows Trends in Searches
trends.google.com

Which term is more Googled: *geek* or *nerd*? According to **Google Trends,** *geek* is more popular as a general term, but *nerd* takes the lead when it comes to image searches. This search engine offers fascinating insights into world trends in hot topics. You can compare searches or click on trending insights, such as Google searches for political candidates or sports news.

Not only does it show trends, but the platform encourages reporting and research for studies and news outlets. I just got lost in whydocatsanddogs.com, "a visual exploration by cat and dog lover Nadieh Bremer in collaboration with Google Trends." The site investigated the 4400 most asked questions about the world's favorite pets that started with the word *why.* You'll also see serious explorations, like a study of an analysis of mysterious deaths in Mexico.

This site will suck you in with its insane range of topics. I just dug around a little bit and discovered a spike in Google Shopping searches for *milk frother* in the last 90 days, apparently centered around shoppers in Washington D.C. That's 10 minutes of my book-writing time that I'll never get back.

Even if you don't have a need to research specific search trends, check out the Year in Search for insight into popular culture, news, sports and more. For example, because of a rumor in February 2018 that Sylvester Stallone died, he beat out Khloe Kardashian for the most searched people in the world. More head-shaking news from the U.S.: *Unicorn cake* came in just ahead of *Romaine lettuce* for food searches in 2018, followed by *CBD gummies.*

Also Check Out...

Google Dataset Search
Statistic and Dataset Search
toolbox.google.com/datasetsearch

Google Earth
Geography Exploration with 3D Effects
earth.google.com

Where do first-time Millennial homebuyers get their down payments?

How many minutes did Peter Dinklage get as Tyrion Lannister on "Game of Thrones"?

Which dogs on Instagram have the most followers?

For the answers to these and other pressing questions, check out **Google Dataset Search.** The site searches—you'll never guess—datasets...thousands and thousands of them. You can find statistics for almost anything anyone has ever collected statistics on. Some of the dataset sources are paid, but you can find plenty of free ones.

Google Earth isn't a search engine per se, but it is an awesome way to search our world. You can explore in the Chrome browser, use the app on the go or download for more advanced manipulations. Click on the Voyager tool in the menu for geography quizzes, map overlays (such as weather and U.S. congressional districts) and educational articles with geographical significance.

NerdHerd Thumbs Up: Ain't Google Great?

Google—Just... All of It
The Google Empire
google.com

I could write a book this same size on the free and bargain services **Google** offers. There's just so much to love. That's why NerdHerder Debbie Lowenthal mentioned Google as her favorite tech tool. Debbie says, "I like all the things that you can do with Google: docs, maps, teams, sharing. I'm still learning, but the Google tools I have used so far I really like."

REFERENCE

Discover and Manage Podcasts

Although I'm a podcast addict, I'm very boring when it comes to the app I choose. Apple Podcasts is the, well, podcast app for, umm, Apple. It came with the phone. But many of the other podcast options are better.

Start with...

Bullhorn
Data-Free Podcast Tool
bullhorn.fm

Castbox
Free Podcast App for Lots of Platforms
castbox.fm

You have dozens of choices of podcast players, but **Castbox** may be the most popular. You can access it from almost any platform you want, including smartphones, the web, digital assistant platforms and more. And it has a special feature . . . a search engine that lets you search the actual audio, perhaps the only podcast tool with this capability.

Bullhorn also has a unique feature. Most players use data because you need to stream or download, and if you're not on Wi-Fi, you may eat into your limit. Bullhorn lets you call through your phone to hear the podcast, and since you're using minutes, that means zero data.

Then Try...

iHeartRadio
Radio Station Streaming Tool with Podcasts
iheart.com

Spotify
Music Streaming Tool with Podcasts
spotify.com

TuneIn
Another Radio Station Streaming Tool with Podcasts
tunein.com

Of course you've heard of **iHeartRadio, Spotify** and **TuneIn.** They're some of the most popular audio streaming sites. All three will also let you listen to and manage your favorite podcasts.

Bonus! If you have a digital assistant (Page 154–155), just ask it to play the latest episode of your favorite podcast, as in, "Alexa, play the latest episode of 'Reply All.'"

Also Check Out...

Breaker
Social Connections Podcast App
breaker.audio

Bullet
Podcast Snippet Sharing Tool (iOS)
bullet.audio

Dang it all! I'm breaking two of my book rules in this one section! First, I'm mentioning two apps that are right now iOS only. As of this writing, **Breaker** is promising an Android app "very soon." I've heard that before. And **Bullet** doesn't even promise that.

The second rule I'm breaking is that I promised that I'd only include tools that look strong and healthy. I'm not confident that Bullet is going to make it. It has a bare-bones website and only a handful of weak reviews.

But I just can't help myself because I like them both so much for dis-covering and sharing podcasts. Listening to podcasts is a pretty solitary activity, and when I find other people who enjoy them, we excitedly share our favorites and make notes of ones to try. Breaker's podcast app revolves around social circles and recommendations. It goes beyond sharing a podcast's reviews. You connect with other listeners to share and learn. And because they just entered into a relationship with Bullet, I feel obligated to share that cool app as well.

Sometimes you hear a great line in a podcast and want to share it. Bullet is your solution. When you're listening to a podcast (Breaker or another podcast player), you can choose to share it through Bullet. Then you can select a snippet up to 30 seconds. Bullet will then turn the podcast audio into a little video with the transcription. Perfect!

Hot Topic:
My Favorite Tech Podcasts

Freakonomics Radio
Research-Based Socioeconomic Trends
freakonomics.com

Note to Self
Podcast that Examines the Human Side of Technology
wnycstudios.org/podcasts/notetoself

Privacy Paradox
Note to Self's Privacy Project
project.wnyc.org/privacy-paradox

Reply All
Tech Solution Podcast
gimletmedia.com/shows/reply-all

Should This Exist?
New Tech Exploration and Analysis
shouldthisexist.com

Product Hunt (Page 148) is not the only place I keep up with the hottest technology topics. These podcasts also give me great ideas to share. **Note to Self** addresses questions like should we put pictures of our kids on social media and is your phone watching you. The Note to Self team is also behind one of my favorite digital privacy activities, **Privacy Paradox.** I highly recommend it to anyone who wants to understand issues around their own privacy.

Should This Exist? is another podcast that addresses the effect of technology on our world. They interview the creators of new technology such as Woebot, a chatbot that tries to serve as a therapist. Should Woebot exist? That is the question.

Reply All is more humorous, with several nerdy types talking about weird tech mysteries and tracking down the solutions. They had a great episode on tracking down a master robocaller. **Freakonomics Radio** can also be funny…or as funny as socioeconomics can be. The show examines statistics and trends to share hidden insights, with episodes such as "Here's Why All Your Projects Are Always Late—and What to Do About It" and "The Data-Driven Guide to Sane Parenting."

●●

Keep Up with the News

When every moment of our online life is filled with articles, analyses and content, we need a tool that will help us curate the flood of information to find the resources we want to read.

Start with...

Flipboard
Magazine-Style Content Aggregator
flipboard.com

Pocket
Saved Article Library for Online and Offline Reading
getpocket.com

Another book, another cheer for **Flipboard.** Flipboard's 10th anniversary is 2020, and I think I've been a fan since the beginning.

Flipboard is a content curating platform that lets you combine your favorite topics and news sources into a beautiful, easy-to-access custom magazine. NerdHerd member Todd Crow likes it because it's concise, simple, quick and up to date. The sources, topics, political slants and biases are all up to you, so you don't have to worry about an all-seeing content curator that feeds you propaganda. Any fake news in your news feeds is your responsibility.

Once you choose topics to follow, you can save your favorite articles into **Pocket** or a personal channel on Flipboard. I created a board called Nerdy News, where I collect and share my favorite tech content. When I need ideas for the blog or NerdWords newsletter, I go back through my archives to find the ideas I saved.

Pocket allows you to tuck any article or website into a virtual folder to read later from anywhere: Nooks, Android devices, iOS devices, desktops and other devices. You'll find options to save to Pocket on many major sites and readers, allowing you to instantly add articles and pages to your account to read anywhere. A completely useable version of Pocket is free, but the company has a premium level as well.

Then Try...

SmartNews
Trending News App with Super-Fast Loading
smartnews.com

Another news aggregator is **SmartNews.** This app also lets you choose sources and personalize your feed, plus it speeds up the articles so you don't have that annoying zero-point-seven second delay.

Also Check Out...

Good News Network
Your Daily Dose of Good News
goodnewsnetwork.org

Puppies rescued from a burning building? Check.

Rallying community that helps a struggling veteran? Check.

Inspiring teachers surprised by former students? Check.

You get the picture. When you can't stomach another story about strife, murder, corruption or catastrophe, spend a couple of minutes (or a couple of hours) on the **Good News Network** for all the feels. Download the apps for warm fuzzies on the go.

Hot Topic:
Where to Find New Tools

AppSumo
Secret Tech Tool Bargain Marketplace
appsumo.com

NerdWords
Beth Z's Weekly Newsletters
yournerdybestfriend.com

Product Hunt
The Ultimate Source for New Technology
producthunt.com

Speaking of keeping up with the news, here are my secret tech weapons for great app ideas.

Every time CNN talks about a hot new app, you can bet that **Product Hunt** had the scoop first. Based on the Reddit concept where people post ideas and other readers vote up the best ones, Product Hunt members share new app discoveries with the community, and the most popular tools bubble to the top every day.

I use both the app and the site to stay on top of the latest technology, books, podcasts and other products. I use IFTTT (Page 33) to create a recipe: When I upvote a tool on Product Hunt, IFTTT saves it into a Google spreadsheet. When I update presentations, write blog posts and review apps for new books, this spreadsheet is where I start.

I don't subscribe to all the tools that I find, but sometimes I come across ones I just can't live without. That's why **AppSumo** is so cool. The site has super-secret sales on really interesting tech services. That's how I ended up with a lifetime subscription to the video email tool Dubb (Page 112) as well as Lumen5 (Page 103), my favorite app to make Buzzfeed-type videos. And you have to read the story of how AppSumo helped me create my very first Last Will and Testament with Giving Docs (Page 26).

Oh, and I should say that *I* didn't add my newsletter, **NerdWords,** to this list. This recommendation comes from NerdHerder April Tanner, who says…

> *I love the weekly emails from Beth Z and attending her presentations. She reminds me of what I should keep up on and stay alert for in the tech world. She is also funny!*

REFERENCE

Translate Anything

• •

In Star Trek, intergalactic travelers used the Universal Translator gadget to communicate with Klingons and other beings that didn't speak the Federation Standard language (which happened to be English—lucky for us).

Thanks to monumental improvements in artificial intelligence, today's translation technology represents science fiction come to life. It is a good time to be a nerd.

Quick Words or Phrases

Alexa
Amazon's Digital Assistant
amazon.com/meet-alexa

Cortana
Microsoft's Digital Assistant
microsoft.com/cortana

Google Assistant
Google's Digital Assistant
assistant.google.com

Siri
Apple's Digital Assistant
apple.com/siri

Almost any digital voice assistant will do a decent job of helping you with a quick word or phrase. Ask **Google Assistant**, **Siri**, **Cortana**, **Alexa** or anybody else "What's the Spanish word for 'breakfast?'" and all will answer back "desayuno" with an appropriate accent. If

Google has to dig deeper to get the answer, the link to where it got the answer will appear wherever you have the Google Assistant installed. #HelpfulButCreepy

See more about digital assistants on Page 154–155.

One-to-One Conversations

Google Translate (App)
Translation App with Conversation and Augmented Reality Tools
In the Google Play and App Stores

Google Translate may be the only translation app you'll ever need. Check out these features:

- Type to translate more than 100 languages
- Copy text in any app and choose translate inside the app (Android only)
- Download language packs to use offline
- Translate text from a picture or through the viewfinder instantly
- Use the Conversation Mode to carry on a two-way conversation with automatic language recognition.
- Translate words you've written with your finger instead of typing
- Save common phrases and translations in a Phrasebook

Although the camera trick that uses augmented reality to translate words on a screen in your viewfinder is my very favorite feature, the Conversation Mode is really handy. Choose the two languages and activate the microphone. Google Translate will identify each language and automatically translate so you can talk back and forth without touching your phone.

I chased a bilingual painter all around our house trying to get her to try it out with me. I'd give it a B+. Like any voice-recognition tool, the quality of the output depends greatly on the quality of the input. Two people in a conversation might speak quickly in their native languages and use colloquialisms. And you're still going to have to pause every sentence or two to hear the translation.

In 2019 Google added an "Interpreter Mode" to Google Assistant. You can use the Google Home device or Google Assistant for interpreting without having to open Google Translate. Hotels are trying the feature out at concierge desks.

Group Conversations

Microsoft Translator

Translation Tool with Instant Translation for Multiple Languages
translator.microsoft.com

An American, a German and a Russian walk into a bar.

The American says, "Let's all be friends. I'll buy the next round!"

The German and the Russian smile awkwardly and go back to their phones. They don't speak English, so...awkward.

But then the German yells out a happy "Ich habe eine Idee!" and starts pointing to an app on his phone. He gestures for everyone to download **Microsoft Translator**, and within seconds, the three are all using the instant translation feature. The German repeats again, "ich habe eine Idee!" and the American and Russian cheer because his words, "I have an idea!" are now instantly translated on their phones.

Microsoft Translator has been around for a while, but recently they made game-changing improvements that will help all of us immediately. Nerdy tech folks call this technology "deep learning" and "neural networks," but they're just making those terms up. It just means that technology is becoming smarter than we are.

The conversation feature lets someone set up a "room" for chatting. You just put your first name and choose the language you speak. Some languages (such as English, Russian, Spanish, Chinese, Arabic and more) offer instant speech-to-text translations, and many others that will translate text. To interact, you press the microphone and start talking. Up to 100 colleagues can see what you're saying instantly translated on their screens and respond in their own languages, which will be translated on your device.

What's more, Microsoft Translator is now embedded into PowerPoint for instant captioning. See Page 100.

Text and Documents

Google Translate (Online)

Online Translation Tool for Voice and Text

translate.google.com

There's a huge difference between **Google Translate** apps and **translate.google.com.** The online translation site still has the look and feel of 2008's translate tools: Just a blank page with boxes where you can paste or speak one language into the first box and get the written translation in the other.

But if you want to translate a document on your computer, this is the place to do it. Upload files up to 10MB, then choose an output language. You'll get a rich-text translation in a matter of seconds. It'll work with multiple types of documents, including PDFs, PowerPoint slides and even spreadsheets.

But wait! There's more! Both Microsoft and Google have translation tools built into their apps so you can create translations as you go.

REFERENCE

Also Check Out...

iTranslate

Translator App that Really Smart People Adore

itranslate.com

Every time I search around for the best translation apps, **iTranslate** comes up. Since Microsoft Translator and Google Translate do all the things that iTranslate does, I'm not sure why you would pay for it. But seriously, the people who use translation tools a lot adore this tool.

You'll have to upgrade to get all the deluxe features, but again, if you need a superior translation tool at your fingertips, take a look at iTranslate.

Hot Topic:
The Vast Universe of Digital Assistants

I could write an entire book on what digital assistants can do. With the exception of Apple's Siri, you can download whichever one you want no matter your preferred platform. Here's a very short, very limited list of tasks that Siri, Google Assistant, Cortana and Alexa can do.

- Connect and monitor smart home gadgets such as lights, thermostats, locks, appliances and more so you can just ask the assistants to turn on the light, start the laundry, etc.

- Make lists, set reminders and add appointments to calendars.
- Access music, podcasts, news, audio books and more.
- Dictate texts, emails and anything else you need to write.
- Provide sarcasm, amusement and entertainment.
- Translate languages (Page 150).
- Serve as a calculator, dictionary, encyclopedia, thesaurus, atlas, phone book and other reference materials.
- Make phone and video calls.
- Get recipes.
- Access health advice, first aid tips and even pet emergency aid.
- Set timers (Pomodoro, anyone? See Page 28).
- Meditate and find de-stressing tools.
- Make restaurant reservations and more.

Of course, with these conveniences, these digital assistants put both the "helpful" and the "creepy" in #HelpfulButCreepy. These devices hear and record everything you do and ask. Several of these companies have been criticized for having humans review the automated responses, ostensibly to improve the accuracy of the responses. Privacy issues abound, and many people are uncomfortable with the idea that these devices are always listening and recording, and perhaps watching with the video cameras.

Our household has multiple Alexa devices plus a Google Home speaker, and we love the convenience and ignore the creepy factor. You're going to have to make your own decisions about your level of comfort regarding privacy.

Learn a New Language

• •

The best language-learning tool in the world is like the best diet in the world. There are lots of good ones, but the best one is the one that works best for you.

Before you choose one, think for a moment about how you like to learn and what you want to do. Do you like a study buddy, or are you best in a traditional classroom? Are you spending a week in Italy or studying for a job in international finance?

Instead of recommending language-learning apps in hierarchical order, I organized this section so you can choose the best one for your needs and learning style.

Note: To get the best features of most of these tools, you're probably going to have to pay from dozens to hundreds of dollars a year for access.

Traditional Students

Beelinguapp
Language App to Increase Reading Comprehension
beelinguapp.com

Busuu
Language-Learning System with Lessons and Live Practice
busuu.com

Rosetta Stone
Grandfather of Self-Study Language Learning, Now with
Subscription Options
rosettastone.com

Rosetta Stone was the first language-learning tool to create a personal software version, or at least it's the only one that I remember hearing about. They used to charge hundreds per language level, but strong competition in this area has driven down the prices and led the company to join many others with a subscription-based online version with (fairly) reasonable pricing levels. Thus, I'm going to go ahead and add it to the list of tools since the company is consistently on top of reviews in this category.

Oh, and perhaps more significantly, a study by Dr. Roumen Vesselinov from The City University of New York found that clocking 13 study hours of Spanish with Rosetta Stone for two months can help users complete the requirements for the first college semester of Spanish, which is the best result of seven other systems he had tested in the past decade.

In an earlier study, **Busuu** came out on top for conversational fluency. The premium version of Busuu includes very structured lessons coupled with community interaction. The system also includes tests certified by McGraw-Hill Education for English, French, Spanish and German. If you pass, you can share the achievement on social media and print out the certificate to put on the fridge.

If your primary learning goal is to read your first foreign-language novel, **Beelinguapp** will help. You'll see your language and the new one side by side so you can listen and read while following along in your native language.

Game Lovers

Duolingo
Gamified Free Language-Learning System
duolingo.com

Mondly
Language App with Augmented Reality
mondly.com

Duolingo changed the way people learn languages. Instead of listening to language tapes in your car during a commute, Duolingo creates mini-lessons with games and tricks to keep you engaged and encouraged. You get points for completing lessons multiple days in a row and hearts when you get answers correct. Your progress is synced between your app and the web, so you can sneak in a lesson anywhere. It's free for the ad-supported version.

And JOY! In 2018 Duolingo finally released Klingon lessons. (If you have to look up "Klingon," I'm not sure I can be Your Nerdy BFF.) NerdHerder Tracy Taraski says Duolingo is easy and fun.

Yet another language app, **Mondly,** wants to engage you with augmented reality. My Spanish lesson involved an augmented reality teacher who conjured up augmented reality animals for a vocabulary lesson.

Word Nerds and Vocabulary Junkies

Memrise
Gamified Vocabulary Tool for Languages and More
memrise.com

Quizlet
Flashcards for Language Learning and More
quizlet.com

TinyCards
Duolingo Flashcard App
tinycards.duolingo.com

If you're one of those people who still knows your multiplication tables and state capitals by heart, you may enjoy the word-by-word memorization tools for language learning. All three of these tools go beyond language learning, but they shine in this category.

Quizlet is my favorite (and NerdHerder Deborah Hudson agrees with me) because I like the way you can print out language (and other) vocabulary lists to create real flashcards. **Memrise** includes little language lessons with groups of vocabulary words. And **TinyCards** gets bonus points both for its cute interface (cute, tiny cards) and its developers . . . it comes from the makers of Duolingo.

Social Butterflies

HelloTalk
Social Sharing Language Exchange Community
hellotalk.com

Tandem
Language Practice App
tandem.net

Now that you've learned the basics of a new language, you need to find a practice partner. **Tandem** is a community of language learners who help each other practice and learn.

Like Tandem, **HelloTalk** has no lessons or quizzes. Instead the apps bring together millions of members to practice more than 100 languages. You can chat through text, audio recordings, calls (audio and video) and even sketches. In-app translation, pronunciation and correction tools help communication happen even for relative beginners.

A big drawback for both is that the quality of the learning is dependent on the quality of the members. And, as with all chat communities,

REFERENCE

you may encounter con artists, creeps and people you don't want to be stuck talking to at a party.

World Travelers

Drops
Gamified Language App with In-Flight Lessons
languagedrops.com

Drops probably belongs in multiple categories in this section. It's a fun learning tool that lets you play on your screens to connect words and phrases with their translations.

The reason Drops deserves a highlight in the World Travelers heading is because of the Travel Talk feature. Travel Talk focuses on helpful travel phrases, and in 2020, the plan is to partner with an in-flight entertainment provider to offer mini-lessons in the air. That means on your way to Italy you will be able to play games to learn common phrases that will be helpful as soon as you step off the plane.

Bonus: More Flashcard Tools

Anki
Flashcards to Study Wherever You Go
ankisrs.net

Cram
Another Flashcard App
cram.com

Ok, I'm not sure "More Flashcard Tools" can be called a truly hot topic, but I just had to add these resources. One of the winning-est Jeopardy! champions, Arthur Chu (years before Ken Jennings and James Holzhauer), said he used the **Anki** flashcard system to prep for the show. Anki lets you set up decks of flashcards that you can use to study anywhere. You can find a whole host of tools at ankisrs.net or try the apps at ankiapp.com. **Cram.com's** apps also come recommended by attendees from my sessions.

Check the Weather

All the weather apps out there probably rely on the same data sources to provide the forecasts, but the way they present the info is as varied as snowflakes. You have plenty of options when it comes to weather apps, so it may be hard to choose. Here are my recommendations based on your personality.

For the Instant-Gratification Junkies

Dark Sky

Unnervingly Precise Weather App

darksky.net

Dark Sky describes itself as a "hyperlocal" weather app, specializing in micro-forecasts for the two-foot square that surrounds you and your phone. I was walking around on a warm afternoon in Florida when I downloaded it. The forecast predicted a light downpour starting in four minutes and lasting for seven minutes, followed by clear skies. Sure enough, I had just enough time to duck under an overhang before the rain came down. And it lasted almost exactly seven minutes. Not all the predictions have been that accurate, but it's a beautiful, simple, useable resource that has become my favorite weather app.

For the Artistic Types

Yahoo Weather

Weather Forecasts with Beautiful Photos

mobile.yahoo.com/weather

When you open the beautiful **Yahoo Weather** app, you're greeted with an exquisite Flickr photo of the area around you. You have the regular features you need in a weather app...daily forecasts, weekly forecasts and the occasional ad.

For the Dignified Professional
Who Enjoys an Occasional F-Bomb

What The Forecast?!!

Weather Forecasts with Giggles
nightcatproductions.com/whattheforecast

My mama would never let me read forecasts from **What The Forecast?!!** aloud, but the NSFW honest descriptions will make you laugh every time. They have won Webby Awards because everyone loves them. Some of the forecasts are just funny, such as, "It's partly cloudy outside. What's the other part? Shame." and some drop the f-bomb. You can set the profanity filter to keep it clean, but it's funnier when it's naughty.

For the Sarcastic Smart-Aleck

Carrot Weather

Snarky Weather App
meetcarrot.com/weather

I don't know…I've always thought all the Carrot apps (meetcarrot.com) were just too mean to enjoy. The **Carrot Weather** app is more snarky and funny than mean, but their Carrot To-Do app calls you a "lazy human," and don't even get me started on the health app, Carrot Fit, which calls itself "your judgmental fitness overlord." I just don't need that much negativity in my life. Carrot Weather is the only one of their apps that is available on both Apple and Android, so I don't have to cover the meaner ones.

For the Shop-Local Enthusiast

Weather Underground

Best Overall Weather App
wunderground.com

WunderMap

Online Weather Tracker from Weather Underground
wunderground.com/wundermap

If you favor small businesses and farmers markets over big box stores, you'll appreciate the underground community that powers the forecasts at **Weather Underground**. From the About Us page:

> *The beating heart of our brand is the generous and passionate community of weather enthusiasts that share weather data and content across our products. With 250,000+ of our members sending real-time data from their own personal weather stations, they provide us with the extensive data that makes our forecasts and products so unique.*

Weather Underground's resources always show up on "best of" lists for accuracy, clarity and ease of use. Whether you visit the site, play with the interactive **WunderMap** or download the app, you can be assured you're getting the most accurate info from the best sources. (But it won't have an attitude like Carrot or What The Forecast?!!.)

For the Thrill Seekers

MyRadar

Advanced Radar App for Storm Tracking
myradar.com

Storm

Weather Underground's Storm-Tracking App
wunderground.com/storm

If you're a storm tracker, you'll love **MyRadar**. It gives you NOAA alerts, storm tracking and radar views anywhere you need to keep an eye on the skies. Weather Underground's **Storm** (Apple devices only) also gives in-depth info about, err, storms.

REFERENCE

For the Animal Lover

Weather Kitty
Feline-Themed Weather App
weatherkittyapp.com

Weather Puppy
Doggy Weather App with Pound Puppy Pics
weatherpuppy.com

Say it with me . . . aww! **Weather Kitty** and **Weather Puppy** give you your daily forecast with a touch of adorable. Animal non-profits and charities have partnered with these founders to provide an app that features our favorite fluffy friends, and, of course, they change with the weather and time. You can even upload pics of your own dog or cat.

Hot Topic:
"Your Apps Know Where You Were Last Night, and They're Not Keeping It Secret"

In 2018, The New York Times wrote an article titled, "Your Apps Know Where You Were Last Night, and They're Not Keeping It Secret." They found that 17 of the 20 apps they tested shared the exact location of users to about 70 companies that used the info for location-based advertising and marketing research.

When I say "the exact location," I mean these apps know the route you take to work, the soccer fields where your kids play and the restaurant where you celebrated your birthday. They can see these things because we give them permission when they ask to use location services. Some of the apps that the newspaper studied were kids' favorites.

The apps that track locations and the companies they sell the data to claim that although they could individualize the data to know exactly where each person is, they mostly use aggregate data and general locations in their marketing. But the individual data points are there, and we often don't know that they're being collected.

Many of the apps that monetize the location data they collect don't let the users know or bury the information in the smallest of small print. For example, The Weather Channel app asked for location permissions during installation so users can get personalized local weather reports.

In the U.S. as of this writing, there is no federal law governing how location information can be collected and what it can be used for. So what can you do?

Three Quick Steps to Protect Your Location Data

1. Pay very close attention to the pop-up permission screens when you install apps

2. Read the terms and conditions (I know…none of us do.)

3. Google a new app to see if the privacy bloodhounds have uncovered any issues.

● ●

Improve Your Writing

When we're texting with friends or posting on social media, we've become accustomed to abbreviating words, leaving out punctuation and generally ignoring many of the grammar and spelling rules we learned in school in favor of instant communication.

But at work, sloppy writing can leave a negative impression on clients, leads, co-workers and bosses. Use these tools to make sure your writing reflects your professionalism.

Start with...

Grammarly
AI-Powered Editing Tool
grammarly.com

If you miss the days when your English teacher peered over your shoulder as you wrote, you'll like **Grammarly**. Download the Chrome plugin or the software for your Windows computer, and the system will monitor what you write in real time. You can also download a Grammarly keyboard for your mobile devices to avoid those *your/you're* social media conundrums.

Grammarly earned an upgrade in this edition because it has definitely upgraded its services. Using artificial intelligence, the tool promises to elevate your writing even more with four categories of suggestions. One category is grammar, spelling and punctuation; then it goes into clarity and conciseness. A third category aims to make your writing more engaging. And it will also "help you strike the right balance of politeness, formality, (sic) and friendliness."

Check out the screenshot to see what happened when I pasted the last two paragraphs into the tool (Grammarly doesn't have a Mac version of its MS Office software. Bummer!) *Note: I made a few changes to those two paragraphs after I tested Grammarly, but not because it told me to.* :P

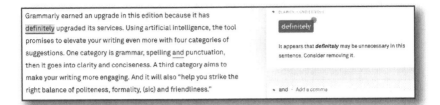

I am a little bit of a writing diva because, you know, five books, a master's degree in journalism, a successful freelance writing career for several years and all that. Right now I'm petrified that you guys have seen typos and problems in this book and are laughing at me, but I will stand my diva writer ground and disagree with both of Grammarly's suggestions.

- Grammarly says the word *definitely* is unnecessary. I disagree because I like to use hyperbole and extra emphasis because I'm emphatically hyperbolic on purpose. So there.

- Grammarly wants me to use the Oxford comma, and I refuse. No comma before a conjunction for me!

And then Grammarly teased me with this...

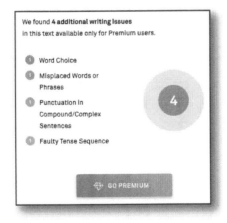

Harrumph again. Four more writing issues? That seems excessive. I'd have to pay $30 for one month or about $140 a year to see what they thought. Now I did see that I needed a semicolon in a compound/complex sentence (fixed it!), but I don't think I'd upgrade, especially since I would have to upload or paste sections of this manuscript into the web tool instead of being able to use the software on my Mac.

Then Try...

Hemingway App

Online Writing Editor
hemingwayapp.com

The online app called **Hemingway** lets you paste or write text on the page, and with one button click, the system analyzes your words and sentence structure to give you tips for clearer, more concise writing.

Hemingway (which is free, of course) gives you a Readability Grade that corresponds to how educated your audience needs to be to get the point. The system recommends you write for Grade 10—not because your readers might not have graduated from high school—but because your message may come out more clearly when you cut down on the verbiage and get to the point.

Hemingway pushes you to eliminate adverbs and passive voice, plus it helps you shrink your sentences and avoid run-on messes. The system color codes your text to show you the problems.

Also Check Out...

PaperRater
Online Writing Editor with Option for Paper Submissions
paperrater.com

Like the Hemingway App, **PaperRater** evaluates text you paste or upload to check for common grammar and spelling mistakes, as well as style. It also gives you an official grade.

One characteristic that stands out with PaperRater is the feature that allows teachers to create a code to collect submissions. Students can check their work then submit their papers to their teachers, and the system will automatically scan the submission for plagiarism—a deluxe feature that PaperRater gives to schools for free.

NerdHerd Thumbs Up: PDF Annotation Tool

GoodReader
Apple PDF Reader and Annotation Tool
goodreader.com

Way back in 2010, Mashable called **GoodReader** "a Swiss army knife of awesome." For its 10th anniversary, GoodReader revamped its interface and functionality. NerdHerder Jeri Hendrie is a big fan of this PDF file manager that gives you the ability to annotate and create PDFs from iOS mobile devices.

Launch a Blog or Website

Small business folks often seek professionals to build major projects like new websites or a blog. If you're a do-it-yourself nerd, give these blog builders a try.

Start with...

Elegant Themes
My Manager's Theme Tools
elegantthemes.com

WooThemes
More Wordpress Themes
woothemes.com

WordPress
Leading Site Builder for Blogs and Websites
wordpress.com

Starting a **WordPress** blog or website is easy, for both personal and business use. For a free hosted site with a URL such as nerdybest-friend.wordpress.com, simply create an account and pick a name at WordPress.com. There, you can also purchase various upgrades, including a custom URL if you want your blog or site to live at nerdybestfriend.com. If you want total control—including a custom URL, a wide variety of plug-ins and the capability to sell your own advertising—you can download the free WordPress software from WordPress.org; but you must arrange and pay for hosting of the site.

The next step in building your site with WordPress is choosing a theme, and here's where the magic begins. You can choose from thousands of free themes, or for less than $100, you can buy an easy-to-install framework for a full site, complete with the embedded blog for dynamic content, or not. I find great templates from Envato (Page 352) and **WooThemes**. My sales manager, Molly, loves **Elegant Themes**. You can further personalize your site with any of the thousands of plug-ins and widgets to do everything from embed video to automatically tweet your posts to Twitter to install a carousel-type photo gallery.

Then Try...

Squarespace
Drag-and-Drop Website Builder
squarespace.com

Weebly
Site Builder with Added Features Like Email Marketing
weebly.com

Wix
Highly Customizable Online Site Builder
wix.com

Confession: I wrote under the WordPress description that starting a blog or website is easy. That's true, but setting up a professional site and making it do everything you want does have a learning curve with WordPress. The system is truly one of the most flexible and powerful, but it can be complicated.

For simple drag-and-drop sites, you can't beat **Squarespace**, **Weebly** and **Wix**. Wix is probably the best of the three because of the ease of set up and hundreds of templates. With all these services, you should expect to pay a monthly fee for hosting and services. I've heard but can't verify that WordPress is better for SEO (search engine optimization), but perhaps that's selective reading on my part because I prefer WordPress.

Also Check Out...

Medium
Modern Blog Site with a Clean Interface
medium.com

There's something calming about the white background and black words of **Medium**, the blogging platform from the founder of Twitter. There are no themes, no blinking boxes, no busy columns. Medium has text and pictures and words and ideas. You write your piece, and the world can respond, even to a very specific area of your post. You can make collections of other content on your pages, and the most popular posts end up on the front page. Medium is simple, stark, beautiful and purposeful; and it seamlessly integrates into your social media world.

> "The problem with quotes on
> the internet is you can never be
> certain they're authentic."
> —Abraham Lincoln

Create Resumes and CVs

Let's face it. I'm pretty much unhireable after all these years as a quirky speaker. But because I'm a writer, I'm often asked to help people with their resumes. Instead, I'm sending them to these resources. Most give you a taste of the capabilities for free, then ask for a reasonable fee to upgrade your results.

Start with...

Resume Worded

Online Resume Reviewer and Writing Service
resumeworded.com

I uploaded my old resume to the AI-powered review feature at **Resume Worded.** I scored a 20/100. Yeah. Unhireable. But I loved this service. Within about 30 seconds, the site had analyzed my resume for all kinds of features that recruiters seek, such as good bullet points, strong verbs and quantified achievements. Many of the recommendations to improve are free, but the specific feedback is behind a paywall that starts at $26 a month.

Then Try...

Zety

Online Resume Creator with Wizard Interface
zety.com

Resume Worded also helps you create a new resume and improve your LinkedIn presence. I'm fond of the wizard-type forms that ask you one question at a time instead of presenting you with a blank screen asking you to get organized. **Zety** helps you gather the information you need for your resume then craft it into something that looks great. If you're feeling lazy, you can upload your existing resume, and they'll pull the info for you.

REFERENCE

Also Check Out...

Canva
Everyone's Favorite Graphic Tool with Resume Templates
canva.com

If you don't want to pay for a resume, **Canva** (Page 94) might be your best bet. The preformatted templates let you fill in the blanks with your info. Just be aware that working with graphic templates rather than flexible documents can be frustrating—like when you add just one more word, and the paragraph adds another line, and the line then covers up the next text box, and when you move the textbox the border moves with it, and then the whole resume is out of whack. I've done this before a thousand times.

> The first written instance
> of the word "nerd" was in
> the Dr. Seuss book
> *If I Ran the Zoo* in 1950.

Discover a Good Book

• •

Since we just talked about how to improve your writing, we should also cover how to discover some great things to read.

Start with...

Hoopla

Public Library Lending App for Videos, Music, Audiobooks, Comics and Ebooks

hoopladigital.com

Libby

Public Library Lending App for Ebooks and Audiobooks

meet.libbyapp.com

Because I'm an author and want to support people who write books, I tend to purchase printed and audiobooks. But my mom was a librarian, and I know she'd love the success of the public library apps that let you enjoy your library's resources without having to actually go to the library itself.

For the more authentic book borrowing experience, see if your local library uses **Libby.** You'll use your library card to "check out" book and audio titles for your phone, tablet or Kindle. Just like a regular library, you'll have a time limit before you have to "return" your items. If your library uses **Hoopla,** you won't have a time limit, and you'll also have access to movies, TV shows, music and comics. And Hoopla lets you stream to several devices and streaming services, including Roku, Chromecast and Apple TV.

Note: Libby is owned by a company called OverDrive, which also has an app. They're phasing it out, so I'm not including it in the official list, but I'm putting it here just in case it survives for a while. Remember what happened with Wunderlist (Page 4).

Then Try...

Goodreads
Online Reading Community with Recommendations
goodreads.com

What Should I Read Next?
Book Discovery Site Based on Title or Author
whatshouldireadnext.com

Whichbook
Book Discovery Site Based on Story Characteristics
whichbook.net

What should you read next? These sites have the answer. All of them help you discover new books. **What Should I Read Next?** asks you to type in an author or title, and you'll get a list of recommendations and other topics to explore. **Whichbook** takes a different approach with a list of characteristics you might look for in a book, such as happy / sad or sex / no sex. You choose four characteristics and slide a marker toward the characteristics you prefer. Then Whichbook does its magic to help you find a new read.

Goodreads is perhaps the best-known reader community online. As soon as you sign up, you can start clicking on rows and rows of books to start teaching the site what kinds of books pique your interest. The more feedback you give, the more accurate your next recommendations will be. Another bonus on Goodreads is that many authors (including yours truly) run giveaways.

Also Check Out...

Audible
Audiobook Provider
audible.com

This is less a revealing of a new app and more of an endorsement of one that's kind of pricy. I was a reluctant **Audible** subscriber, but I am so glad I did it. It's about $15 a month, and you get a credit for an Amazon audiobook every month. Plus they have free titles and some monthly special programs that are produced exclusively for Audible members. I find myself using the credit every month and frequently buying an additional title for a discount. It's worth the investment.

NerdHerder Robin Wedewer agrees with me.

Audible is my constant companion. Routine chores, such as weeding the garden, folding laundry, or dusting my office, are absolutely pleasurable when I can listen to a great book. I use Audible when the books I want aren't available from my local library or OverDrive (Page 175). I would have listed OverDrive as my fave, but a lot of the time books I want aren't available from the library.

NerdHerd Thumbs Up: Bible Study on the Go

Blue Letter Bible
Bible Study Resources
blueletterbible.org

"Better than a whole bookshelf full of books!" is how NerdHerder Kerry Harris describes **Blue Letter Bible**. "I use it almost daily; it has translations (even original Hebrew, Greek and Aramaic) commentaries, side-by-side comparisons and powerful search features."

Utilities

. . . .

In This Chapter...

UTILITIES

Back Up Computer and Files

• •

Although cloud storage services do keep a copy of your files on their servers, experts say you shouldn't rely on them as your backup system. I use a couple of external hard drives as well as duplicate data on both Dropbox (Page 9) and Google Drive (Page 64) to back up everything I own. This system has saved my butt more than once, including the time my computer started smoking right before a presentation, and I had to buy a brand new machine for another engagement the very next day. #justifiablyparanoid

Start with...

IDrive
Backup Service with Extended Archiving
idrive.com

When using online backup services, you generally set up an account; tell them which drives, folders and files to back up; and let them get to work. They can work in the background all the time or back up on a schedule. If your computer blows up, you can restore your files or even every bit and byte of your computer to another machine or recover an earlier version of your files.

IDrive receives a big thumbs up from *PC Magazine* for its reasonable prices, unlimited archiving and other super-extra features.

Then Try...

Acronis True Image
Super-Secure Backup System with Ransomware Protection
acronis.com

Backblaze
Backup Service with Unlimited Storage and No File Size Limits
backblaze.com

SOS Online Backup
Super-Fast Backup Service with Unlimited Version Archiving
sosonlinebackup.com

Each backup service has slightly different characteristics. **Acronis True Image** is super fast (and a little pricier), but the main plus is that it specializes in high-security protections for your computer and data. **Backblaze's** secret weapon is that it's insanely easy to use and it has no limit on storage or file size. **SOS Online Backup** gets great reviews as well and has the added feature of being incredibly fast in comparison to the other services.

Also Check Out...

Syncthing
Open Source Private Data Storage
syncthing.net

I'm often asked about the privacy issues of data we store in someone else's cloud. To be honest, there's always a risk of data leaks, privacy problems and breaches.

If you want to avoid any of the potential risks but still want to make sure your files are backed up, check out **Syncthing.** This free tool lets you synchronize your files among your own devices. You can access them remotely and share them as well.

One More (Iffy) Thing...

Digi.me
Social Media Private Sharing Data Management
digi.me

TFP
Digi.me-Connected App that Finds Questionable Content in Your Social Media Feeds
digi.me/tfp

In 2019 MySpace, one of the social media pioneers, reported that millions of songs, photos and videos were lost in a server migration project. "We apologize for the inconvenience," MySpace offered.

Before Facebook, MySpace had hundreds of millions of users, and in one computer "uh oh," a half-decade of digital memories was lost.

Think about all the special moments you've shared of your kids' lives on Facebook, Instagram and Twitter. What if they disappeared? One of the backup tools I have been searching for is a quick way to store your social media assets without having to visit each site and download the archives over and over.

I'm not sure I've found the perfect tool, but **Digi.me** is worth a look.

The philosophy of the company is that you own your social media data and other cloud-stored facts and transactions.

- You should have access to them.
- You should be able to download them.
- You should be able to control who has access to them.
- You should be able to monetize them.

After reading Digi.me's fine print and other explanations, I'm still not sure how all that happens. I do know that the app is very thorough about asking permission and explaining privacy policies at every level. I don't know if the company will make it, but it has some features that seem smart and handy.

Digi.me has several tools and apps that connect with the data you want to share. Several of them analyze your social media posts for insights, such as the most popular time to post and your mood. The handiest of these apps is the one that searches your posts for potentially offensive language content like curse words and drunk pics. This is a good check for people who work with the public or someone applying for a job, but I find the name crass: **TFP,** which stands for "That [Bleep-ing] Post."

Other apps connect to your health and financial data. Again, I'm going to keep an eye on these tools to see where they go.

UTILITIES

> 2020 marks Pac-Man's 40th birthday. Ms. Pac-Man came out two years later and became even more popular.

Make Screencaptures and Videos

I find myself needing to grab screenshots from my computer all. the. time . . . from grabbing a shot of an error I'm having to troubleshoot to stealing a funny meme from a page that has disabled right-click downloads.

I also need to capture video of the things I'm doing on my laptop quite a bit. I demo tools that I share with you guys, show new team members a process and, again, capture errors to troubleshoot (I get a lot of errors when I try out all this stuff).

Start with...

Grab/Screenshot
Mac Screenshot Tool
On your Mac

Snipping Tool and Snip & Sketch
Windows Screenshot Tools
On your PC

To paraphrase Glinda the Good Witch when she tells Dorothy to click her heels three times to go back to Kansas . . . you don't need to be helped with screenshots on your computers. You've always had the power to do them.

Both Mac and Windows have built-in, easy-peasy tools to quickly capture images of your screen.

Macs snap screenshots best with quick shortcuts, or you can launch **Grab/Screenshot** (it's called both when you search) for more options.

Mac Screenshot Shortcuts:

Capture entire screen	Command-Shift-3
Capture an area	Command-Shift-4 to make a crosshair icon, then click and drag to capture the area
Capture a single window or screen	Command-Shift-4 plus Spacebar to change the crosshairs to a camera, then click camera icon on the window or screen you want
Open the Screenshot tool for more options	Command-Shift-5

Windows has lots of options for capturing screenshots through the **Snipping Tool** and **Snip & Sketch.** You can also hit the famous **PrtScn** button on your keyboard to capture the whole screen and copy it to the clipboard. Bonus! Use the settings under Ease of Access > Keyboard to turn your PrtScn button into a launch key for the Snipping Tool.

As for shortcuts, **Windows logo key-Shift-S** will "open the new modern snipping experience," Microsoft says.

Snip & Sketch adds the ability to annotate and edit your screenshots with another built-in Windows tool.

UTILITIES

Then Try...

Jing
Old Favorite Screencapture Tool
techsmith.com/jing-tool.html

Monosnap
Free Screencapture Tool for Screenshots and Video
monosnap.com

Snagit
The Best Screencapture Tool
techsmith.com

Although the built-in tools in your device are handy, they just don't do much. For better features, I go to my absolute very favorite screen-capture tool, **Snagit.**

Snagit is the big sister of a tool that *used to be* my absolute very favorite screencapture tool: **Jing.** Jing was a pretty little sun icon that sat on my desktop and made me happy every time I used its screen- and video-capture services.

Sadly, Jing's technology is slipping into obscurity, so I had to upgrade to Snagit for $50. It's a one-time price, but they keep upgrading it and asking for more money for the newer, shinier version. And I keep paying.

Just because Jing is a little old doesn't mean people have stopped using it. NerdHerder Carol Campbell says, "Jing is sitting discretely on the top of my computer screen, letting me capture images that can't be copied and pasted." Sniff. I miss using Jing.

The beauty of Snagit is that it can take just seconds to grab a screen-shot, draw some arrows, write a note then click a button to copy or share the image...ditto with the video capture after you demo some-thing on the screen, with a narration, if you like.

You can choose to edit your capture with Snagit's advanced editing tools such as borders and stamps and a blur tool to obscure private information. You can also capture scrolling screens with Snagit. I particularly like the ability to make a GIF (Page 326) from a video clip. It's great for a little preview of a video in my newsletters.

Monosnap is a free download for Mac and PC, and it works like a lightweight Snagit. You capture a screenshot or video then mark it up. In the free version, you can save to your computer and upload it into your Monosnap cloud account to share with a link. My favorite feature . . . you can drag any file onto the Monosnap icon to upload it to the cloud with a link as well. I'm not sure why I would use that instead of Dropbox (Page 9), but it sure is fun!

Also Check Out...

Screencast-O-Matic
Browser-Based Screen Recorder
screencastomatic.com

Screencastify
Another Browser-Based Screen Recorder
screencastify.com

Recording your screen with either of these tools could hardly be easier. For **Screencast-O-Matic**, just go to the site and launch the recorder—no registration needed, although it may look like you should. When I upgraded these tools for this book, I got snookered into creating an account when I didn't have to.

Screencastify has a browser plugin that you can click from any tab. Both let you record and narrate what's happening on your screen, with or without a webcam. They both have very modestly priced pro versions and robust free versions. The biggest difference is that Screencastify records video in a web-specific format that you'll have to convert if you want to use it in a video editor. Screencast-O-Matic offers more traditional video formats. And it has the coolest name.

Just One More...

Reflector

Screen Mirroring Tool for Your Mobile Devices

airsquirrels.com/reflector

If you need to capture a video demo from something on your mobile device, some smartphones have the capability built in now. But the phone tool is not as professional as the **Reflector** app. Reflector enables you to mirror your mobile screen on your computer, where you can record your movements and capture a voiceover as well.

Convert Almost Anything

Let's say you're working with an incredible graphic designer. He sends you the first draft of the incredibly important graphic you've commissioned—a graphic you have to unveil at a meeting you're having in three minutes. You click on this file, knowing you're about to see a masterpiece; and then a frustrating pop-up announces, "Windows cannot open this file. What do you want to do?"

Don't waste a moment of your precious time trying to fight with a file that won't open. Here are a few tools to help you identify random files and convert on the go.

Start with...

Zamzar
File Converter Extraordinaire
zamzar.com

This is my fifth technology book, and **Zamzar** has been in every one. I searched high and low for a better conversion tool, but I'm still in love. Why mess with the best?

Zamzar has saved my hide multiple times. Simply visit the site, upload a file, choose what you want to turn it into and press a button. In a matter of minutes, your file is transformed into the format you need.

Wait, there's more! You can convert files via email as well, just by writing to [format]@zamzar.com. For example, you can send your Microsoft Word file to pdf@zamzar.com. In a few minutes, you'll receive a link to your new pdf. Or you can send your PDF to doc@zamzar.com, and the opposite happens. It's magic either way.

UTILITIES

Then Try...

CloudConvert
Online File Converter with Zapier Automations
cloudconvert.com

If I had to replace Zamzar, I'd use **CloudConvert**. Just like Zamzar, you can upload a file and choose a conversion format without registering. You can also create an archive of the files you're uploading. CloudConvert also integrates with Zapier (Page 33) for automating some extra tasks, such as automatically saving a converted document into a Google Drive folder.

Both services have file size and number limits in the free versions.

Also Check Out...

FileInfo
Reference Site to Identify File Extensions
fileinfo.com

Just like I am stuck on Zamzar, I'm going to stick with **FileInfo** because it's still so good. When extensions look suspicious, I head over to FileInfo to check them out before clicking. The site is kept up to date with every possible file extension. You can search by file type (audio, game, executables, etc.) or simply enter the extension into the search engine. After you know what you're dealing with, the site gives you a list of applications that will open it.

Measure Areas and Objects

• •

When Apple and Android devices integrated augmented reality tech-nology into their operating systems, the days of running around a room with a tape measure faded into memory.

Kind of.

These measuring apps are great to get an idea of the size of the living room, but they can't be counted on for precise measurements. But they're really fun to play with.

Start with...

Moasure
Motion-Based Measuring App
moasure.com

The other apps in this section use augmented reality to measure, and I've yet to get a consistent measurement with any of them. **Moasure** uses your phone's accelerometer and gyroscope capabilities to meas-ure the distance your phone goes across a room, a table or up a wall.

It's like a 1000-foot tape measure, and it even makes a little sound like you're spooling out the tape. Once I figured out how to use it, I found Moasure accurate and, well, fun. For more precise measure-ments, you can get the Moasure One gadget for $250. But the app by itself works pretty well for casual users.

UTILITIES

Then Try...

AR Ruler
Augmented Reality Measuring App
grymala.by

Measure (Apple)
Apple's Augmented Reality Measuring App
In the App Store

Measure (Google)
Google's Augmented Reality Measuring App
In the Google Play Store

Why both Apple and Google decided to name their in-house augmented reality measuring apps **Measure,** I have no idea. They both do about the same thing, as does **AR Ruler.** Augmented reality apps first ask you to scan the floor so the sensors can get the perspective and understand where your phone is in a 3D world. You can point the viewfinder around the room to place virtual markers on surfaces, walls or floors. As you pan to the end of your measuring area, a virtual line follows you, measuring out the distance.

As I mentioned before, I have never found these things to be very accurate. I always have trouble anchoring the points where they need to be, and I never trust the findings and end up going to find the tape measure anyway. But any of the three will give you a pretty good estimate, and both Apple and Google provide their apps for free. AR Ruler adds a few features, such as the ability to measure angles or compute volume.

Also Check Out...

MagicPlan

Measuring App for Floor Plans

magicplan.app

My real estate friends love this app. Instead of having to spend an hour walking from room to room with a tape measure, they scan each area to mark the corners and room features. Use **MagicPlan** to estimate your square footage or how much paint and trim you need to renovate.

The past, present, and future walked into a bar. It was tense.

UTILITIES

Scan Documents

Gone are the days when scanning a hard-copy document required a scanner. You have many choices of tools to snap a picture of documents and transform them instantly into PDFs and more.

Start with...

iScanner

NerdHerd Favorite Scanning App

iscannerapp.net

In the scanning department, you have lots and lots of choices. NerdHerder Julie Larson shared a great case study of how **iScanner** saves her paper, time and sanity . . . and what she does with it can work for any of these tools.

> *If I am away from my office and need to scan a document or receipt into a pdf to email or save, I can do so with this app. The best part is after I scan in the item, I also have the option from within the app to send the pdf to my Dropbox account, to whichever file folder I would like.*

> *Here is how I most use this app: every year when we get our taxes done, I hated having to gather all of our medical bills and copay receipts for our accountant. After I got this app, I created a folder in Dropbox called (year)Tax Documents. Then every time I take my kids to the doctor or pay a medical bill, I scan my payment or receipt using iScanner, label it with the date and doctor appointment and send it to that Dropbox file.*

> *At the end of the year when I go to the accountant, I can easily access the entire year's worth of medical bills/payments to add up and print a copy for our tax file!*

Then Try...

Adobe Scan

Adobe's Free Document and Business Card Scanner
acrobat.adobe.com/us/en/mobile/scanner-app.html

Office Lens

Microsoft's Free Document Scanner
In the Google Play and App Stores

Office Lens is a free, simple scanning tool with a hidden game changer. Like many scanners, you can snap a picture of hard-copy documents to turn them into PDFs or images. The secret sauce comes in with your subscription to Microsoft Office 365, which starts at about $69 a year. When you have the subscription, Office Lens lets you snap a picture of a document and immediately edit in Microsoft Word. No hassle. No fuss. Just snap, process, upload and edit.

Office Lens is a NerdHerd favorite. Jeanette Alston-Watkins says using the app on the go "makes my life so easy when I need to make changes to a PowerPoint or PDF." David Crain says he also uses the app to convert documents when traveling, adding that it's helpful in the office.

> *Office Lens does a great job of capturing whiteboard notes and making them into a PDF. We frequently brainstorm on a large whiteboard, and Office Lens makes it so easy to email the notes to everyone after the meeting.*

Both **Adobe Scan** and Office Lens have business card scanning functionality. Adobe Scan will recognize business cards, and it'll even autocapture when it finds them. The biggest drawback is that it takes a couple-three minutes for a saved scan to analyze the text, but then you have a one-click option to save as a contact.

Office Lens has a specific image capture option for business cards. It does a great job of capturing, but then you reach a dead end. Your most useful save option is into the default contacts folder in OneNote (Page 13). And that's where it will sit with its recognized text. There's no way to export the contacts into any other system.

UTILITIES

Also Check Out...

CamScanner
Popular Scanning App that Got in Trouble
camscanner.com

Genius Scan
Robust Smart Scanning Tool
thegrizzlylabs.com/genius-scan

Scanbot
Great Free Scanner
scanbot.io

From the category of #ThisCouldHappenToYou, tech watchdogs discovered a malware ad service in the popular scanning app **CamScanner** in the summer of 2019. Google Play removed it from the store, and there was quite a kerfuffle. The company, which also owns the even more popular CamCard app (Page 199), swore it didn't know that the app was showing ads that exploited users' data, and after a couple of patches and a few more apologies, Google Play let it back into the store. This story is a cautionary tale that even the tools we love the most might be doing things we hate.

 Maybe it's just the cuteness of the name, but I just love **Scanbot**. This little app is fast, easy and effective for making PDFs and image files of your hard-copy documents. You can upgrade for OCR. But it sucks. So don't.

Genius Scan is equally as popular, just as easy to use and exactly the same amount of free.

Scan Business Cards

I'm just going to say it straight out: I don't like business card scanners in the slightest. To me they're much more work than they're worth. I get piles of cards at the same time after a presentation, and it's a waste of my time to scan each one and check the transcription and then put my cursor in those tiny little fields and retyping and just all of it.

So I don't use them. When I get the cards, I snap pictures of them and send them off to Fancy Hands (Page 41). These virtual assistants access the online photo album I've created with all the pics. Then they retype them into a spreadsheet. It's worth noting here that Contacts+ (Page 118) also has human transcription at their paid levels. Dang it, people. It just works better!

But that's just me. Other professionals love the tools below, and you're welcome to give them a try. I'm gonna pass.

Note: Several of these scanning apps are going to show up in different areas of the book. Check out scanning apps on Page 194 and contact management tools on Page 118.

Start with...

Google Lens
Google's Image Analyzer Feature
lens.google.com

Notes
iPad and iPhone Native Camera Scanner
apple.com

The first level of business card scanning apps includes the free tools that are either built into the device you already own or are easy to download.

The only reason I'm including **Notes** app on Apple devices is to mention that it's pretty much worthless for business card scanning. Yes, the app will immediately recognize a document as a business card if you take or import a picture (it'll also recognize other documents). Yes, it'll scan the card and label it as a business card. But then all you can do is keep it in Notes or turn it into a PDF. You can't save the info into contacts or export into another system.

Google Lens, on the other hand, is amazing for recognizing business cards. On Android devices, Lens is generally integrated into the native camera. Just snap a picture and hit the little icon that uses artificial intelligence to recognize the contents. A business card scan will instantly pull up the option to save as a contact. It'll also give you the immediate option to push one button to Google information on the card, which is handy if you want to check out the company of your new contact.

On Apple devices, take a picture with the regular phone camera so it ends up in your Album. Then open Google Photos, which you need to have synced with the phone so all Album photos are available. Just click on the business card picture and the little AI icon. Google Lens will do the same magic.

Note: Google Lens is phenomenal in so many ways. The AI feature will identify all kinds of elements of your images, such as cats, wine glasses, friends and family. . . . Then it'll show options for Googling or similar images or all kinds of glorious stuff. It's hours of fun.

Then Try...

ABBYY Business Card Reader

Card Scanner from a Company that Scans Well
abbyybcr.com

CamCard

Card Scanning App
camcard.com

ScanBizCards

Card Scanner with Human Transcription
circleback.com/scanbizcards

Me at my sessions: "What's your favorite business card scanner?"

Everyone: "**CamCard!**"

I'm exaggerating here, but CamCard is definitely a universal favorite. You just snap a picture of the card, verify the info, then add to your contacts. Batch scanning helps speed up the process. You can also exchange electronic cards with people and export/integrate with other systems. The free version is robust but does limit the number of scans. The paid versions start at about $50 a year. If you use Salesforce, CamCard also has a separate app for seamless integration. You can also use CamCard's brother app, CamScanner (Page 196).

ScanBizCards runs a very close second in the number of mentions by audience members, but it's the one I'm most drawn to because of the human transcription options. The pricing is a little confusing to me. There's a really good free app, and a premium app for about $3. And then there's a free ongoing subscription and a paid level starting at $100 a year. Plus you can buy human transcription credits starting at about a quarter each. But I can't figure out if you can buy transcription credits when you use the free version or if the premium app includes some extra subscription features or.... And by the time you read this, the company will have changed it again.

At any rate, ScanBizCards offers many of the same features as CamCard: card scanning, batch scanning, contacts export and integration with other apps. A bonus feature: you can use ScanBizCards to capture leads at events with name badge scanning.

Even though the pricing of this app seems hefty, I have to say good things about **ABBYY**. For years this company been at the top of the scanning heap. Each of their scanning apps is incredibly accurate, and they stand out in many top scanner lists.

Their scanning is all digital with no human help, and I had a tough time figuring out their pricing. The app itself is $60, and then you'll have to pay nickels and dimes here and there to increase the functionality. But it really is one of the best scanners out there.

Also Check Out...

BizConnect
NerdHerd Favorite Business Card Scanner
bizconnectus.com

"I have too many business cards that sit in a box. With this app I now have them easily put into my contacts in my phone (and synced with my email)," says longtime NerdHerder Lisa Farquharson. Lisa compared **BizConnect** to the only business card scanner I ever loved, CardMunch, which went the way of a digital dodo bird.

Security

● ●

In This Chapter...

Protect Your Computer and Mobile Device

Moments ago as I was researching this section, I paid for a premium subscription for antivirus protection and more from Bitdefender. I locked in $40 a year for five devices, and I feel good about it. I just have too much to lose if my computer gets a serious infection or threat.

But that doesn't mean the free tools aren't enough. As I update this section from *The Big Book of Apps,* the same free tools are still at the top.

Note: Another contender, Kaspersky Free Antivirus, has also been rated very highly. But the U.S. government banned the Moscow-based cybersecurity company because of allegations of ties to the Russian government. Kaspersky says it's not a threat, but I don't want to get involved. I'm not good with conflict.

Another note: The tools in this list overlap quite a bit with other categories in this book since so many antivirus tools contain other tools to protect your privacy and increase your security. For more, check out adware blockers (Page 222), VPNs (Page 206) and password tools (Page 212).

Start with...

Bitdefender Antivirus Free Edition
Antivirus Tool with Great Malware Removal Tools
bitdefender.com

Bitdefender has moved to the top of this list because it just keeps coming out on top in all the lists. This is the tool I chose for my Mac just now. The tool has proven itself effective in finding and eliminating viruses and malware and for generally keeping your devices safe.

Then Try...

Avast Free Antivirus
Feature-Rich Antivirus Tool with Password Management
avast.com

AVG AntiVirus FREE
Essential Antivirus Protection
avg.com

Although **Avast** and **AVG** are still separate entities, Avast bought the other company in 2016. Both have been around for a long time and are some of the best tools out there for antivirus. The two guard against malware, viruses and other bad-people techniques for stealing your data or messing up your life. Both offer software/apps for PCs, Macs and Android devices, and Avast adds an app for iOS.

Also Check Out...

Malwarebytes
Malware Finder with Anti-Ransomware Updates
malwarebytes.com

Malware is software such as viruses, worms, Trojan horses and spyware. Isn't it disgusting that we have that many words for the horrible things that bad guys dream up to muck up our computers? Jeeze. **Malwarebytes** has been the best free tool in this category for years. It's the one I use. I like that you can upgrade to get robust protection from ransomware, the programs that literally hold your files hostage and make you pay to get them back.

Hot Topic:
Ransomware Protection

No More Ransom
Site to Identify and Remove Ransomware
nomoreransom.org

When I wrote *The Big Book of Apps* in 2017, bad guys holding computer files hostage and asking for a ransom to unlock sounded like a problem that only big companies would have. But two years later, I have met real people and small businesses who have had this happen. And it can happen to you.

McAfee and governmental cybercrime officials from the Netherlands got together to help the victims of ransomware without having to pay the bad guys. The site has tools to identify ransomware and some of the keys that will unlock the encrypted data.

But, **No More Ransom** says, it's a lot easier to prevent ransomware attacks than it is to recover from them. Here are the tips the site recommends.

1. **Backup Your Files**
   I use Dropbox, Google Drive and a couple of external hard drives to duplicate the files on my computer. And because I use a Mac, the built-in Time Machine tool is always making copies. If something happens to my computer, I can wind back the clock on my computer and files to a time before the attack or catastrophe happened. I've had to do this more than once.

You should be able to do the same. Make sure you have a cloud service or external device that keeps older versions of your files and even your entire operating system.

2. **Use Computer Security Tools**

As I mentioned, many of the tools that offer antivirus protection also have features to protect against ransomware.

3. **Keep Your Software Up to Date**

Updates to your operating systems and programs often contain security patches. If you don't update, you increase your risk.

4. **"Trust no one. Literally."**

You've heard this before: Don't click on any links you're not absolutely positive are safe. Don't open unknown attachments. Don't visit sites if you see a warning from your browser.

5. **Change Your Settings to Show File Extensions**

Keep an eye out for malicious files that end in *.exe, .vbs* and *.scr.* The bad guys may disguise these with double extensions that you may not be able to see, such as naming a file *invoice431.doc.exe.*

6. **Act Quickly to Limit an Attack**

If you are the victim of a cyberattack, disconnect immediately from all network connections to keep it from spreading.

SECURITY

Use a VPN

· ·

I have a confession to make.

Although I fuss at you guys to avoid public Wi-Fi (Page 209), I'm guilty of resorting to it every once in a while, when my hotspot is spotty or if I'm just being lazy. It's just so easy to connect to the free network and start surfing, right? And besides, I'm kind of intimidated by VPNs. They sound complicated, like something only IT folks would use.

As the warnings about public Wi-Fi continued to grow, my unease did, too. So I finally broke down and researched VPNs so I can use public Wi-Fi without worrying about the bad guys.

1.1.1.1
Free Mobile VPN
1.1.1.1

ExpressVPN
VPN Consistently Rated the Best
expressvpn.com

NordVPN
VPN that Includes Multiple Installations
nordvpn.com

TunnelBear
Easy-to-Use VPN
tunnelbear.com

Windscribe
VPN with a Free Version
windscribe.com

Here's what you need to know before you get your own VPN:

1. **Don't Argue with Me: You Need a VPN**

   A VPN is a virtual private network. It hides where and who you are from hackers and encrypts the data you're sending and receiving so bad guys on public Wi-Fi can't intercept what you're typing or reading or sending. This means much greater security when you have to check your bank balance in a Starbucks or compose an email with critical business information to your boss while you're at a conference.

   The first VPN I tried out was **Windscribe** because it has good reviews as a free option.

   The free version was very limited with data, and after the first couple of weeks, I stopped even bothering to turn it on because I exceed the free limit almost immediately. I suppose I could have saved the data for when I had to do something private, but I just forgot about using it. Finally I decided to go ahead and pay the money.

2. **You're Going to Have to Pay for One**

   If the product is free, you are the product.

   Nowhere is that truer than in the VPN world. Think about it: You're installing a tool that manages your data and where it goes. Imagine if you're a bad guy who wants to see that data. It's all right there!

   Many free VPNs can be bad actors that are trying to steal and sell your data or worse. And speaking of worse, you'll find a lot of misleading information about VPNs.

   When you Google "best VPN," you'll see a host of sites like bestvpnreviews and vpnforever, toptenVPNcheerleaders and whatever. They're probably like the "best website hosting" sites that are run by the tools that they "review," thus are complete scams.

One exception to the free VPN conundrum: Cloudflare's **1.1.1.1** thingy. It's a mobile app that speeds up your connection and protects your data. It's free. Nerds love it.

3. **The Top VPN Lists Are Similar**

    When you look at the lists of top VPNs, many include the same names. **ExpressVPN** came out on top in almost every list. I ended up going with another highly recommended one: **NordVPN**. The main reason was because it was a little more affordable (I paid $108 for three years of coverage), and I can install it on up to 6 devices.

4. **You Don't Have to Know Anything About VPNs to Use a VPN**

    Like I said, I was intimidated to use a VPN because I thought it was complicated. It's anything but. You install it on your device, and when you connect to the internet, it just works. **TunnelBear** gets great reviews for the easy interface, but none of them are very complicated. Your VPN chooses a different server somewhere in the world so that the hackers don't know where you are, and it scrambles your data. But all that is automatic, so you don't have to do anything special.

5. **You Can Get Around Some Blocked Sites**

    I speak in Canada several times a year, and sometimes my streaming video sites are blocked because I'm not in the right country. No problem! I just choose a server on my VPN that is based in the accepted country, and I can stream away.

6. **It's Going to Slow Down Your Connection**

    Even though I'm excited to feel protected, I'm frustrated by some issues that having a VPN creates. One of the worst ones is that you may (or may not) notice a significant slowdown in your internet connection rate. As I write this, there's a rumor going around about new technology that is supposed to solve this problem.

7. Some Sites Won't Work Properly

It's a mystery to me why some sites mess up when I have the VPN on. I'll go to a run-of-the-mill website and find an error and a blank screen. I turn off the VPN, and poof: the website reappears. I also use Adblock Plus (Page 222) to block popups, ads and malicious web content, and sometimes weird things happen when I have that enabled on a site as well. I don't know what the plugin is blocking, but it's annoying. Sometimes I can play around with the VPN options to get the page to come up, but it's easier just to disable it for a few minutes.

Hot Topic:
Why You Shouldn't Use Public Wi-Fi

Let's start with the opening sentences from a column in USA Today:

"I don't really need to worry about online privacy," I used to think. "I've got nothing to hide. And who would want to know what I'm up to, anyway?"

So begins the tale of a technology journalist who wrote an article on a plane then was approached by a stranger when he got off. The stranger knew what the journalist had been writing because he had hacked into the plane's Wi-Fi and could see everything that the other connected passengers were typing.

Many of you have heard the warnings about using public Wi-Fi, but you're still using it without taking precautions. I totally understand. I do it sometimes, too [I'm wearing a face of shame]. It's easy. It's fast. It looks official. Where's the danger?

Why Is Public Wi-Fi Dangerous?

When you connect to Wi-Fi, you're sending data to and from the router. The organization that set up the router may have taken extra steps to increase safety, but many don't. And even if they do, hackers know ways around it. Because you're opening up your data and connections, hackers can do a number of things to mess up your world.

Another reason public Wi-Fi is dangerous is that hackers create spoof Wi-Fi names that look like the official connection. So you may see "Grinds Coffee" and "Grinds Coffee Wi-Fi" in the available networks list. It's hard to know which is safe.

What Are Wi-Fi Hackers Trying to Do?

Hackers' biggest motivation for getting access to your machine is to steal your identity and your money. And if that happens to you, it's a total nightmare to get everything straightened out.

What Can Hackers Do When They Get Access?

See what you're typing

Hackers may be able to see any plain text you're typing, including logins, emails, images, private documents, etc. They can use this kind of info to steal your identity, expose private information, hack your accounts, steal your credit card and bank info and all kinds of nasty stuff. "But I don't have anything worth taking, really," you might say. But they don't care. They're digging around to see what they can get, hacking as many people as they can until they find useful stuff to help them be bad people.

Install malware, viruses and ransomware

Hackers want to put programs on your devices for all kinds of reasons. They install keyloggers to capture passwords and private information. They infect your machine with tools that let them use your computer as a host for attacks on websites and networks in what they call a Denial of Service (DoS) or Distributed Denial of Service (DDoS) attack. That's where a hacker will send a kazillion inquiries or hits to a system at once, causing complete overload and meltdown. And you probably won't know that your device is part of the mayhem.

Hackers can also use this vulnerability to install ransomware, which locks down all your files until you pay a ransom. This has taken down small businesses, hospitals, governments and lots of normal people.

What Won't Protect You from Hackers

Some people say, "I'm careful because I never logon to banking sites or whatever when I'm on public Wi-Fi." Sorry, folks. This is not good enough. You're still probably logging into social media sites, email and more, and hackers can get those passwords. And many (many) of us reuse the same username/password combos....yeah. You know. Plus, it's a mess if a hacker gets control of your social media.

What Will Protect You from Hackers

Using your own data
Data plans are expensive. I know that. But it's worth it if you need to use Wi-Fi outside of your own network regularly. I have an unlimited plan on multiple devices, so most of the time I can use my hotspot in hotels, airports and restaurants.

Using a VPN
A Virtual Private Network (VPN) routes your data through a safe tunnel rather than the open channels. Although there are a few reputable free VPNs, you have to be very careful because bad guys create free VPNs to have full access. See Page 206 for a few of the top options vetted by reputable tech sites.

Manage Your Passwords

••

One of the most common online security mistakes we make, besides picking passwords that are too easy, is using the same password for multiple sites.

The bad guys know this, and when they hack into a site, they get our username/password combos and try them on other sites and eventually get to some pretty valuable information. It's time to truly take charge of your password and Internet security issues.

Start with...

LastPass

Everyone's Favorite Password Manager

lastpass.com

To understand why **LastPass** is consistently rated as one of the best password managers around, just ask the NerdHerd.

From Amanda Glass...

> *Like my beloved Trapper Keeper from childhood, LastPass is a password keeper that keeps everything in one secure spot. In addition, as a password generator it creates for me and allows me to use the craziest, longest, most secure passwords without worry of forgetting. It keeps important codes, numbers, etc. in one location, accessible from the app or the website.*

From Brooke Dilworth...

> *I only have to remember ONE password for the rest of my life! LastPass integrates with the security on my phone and lets me into my apps by facial recognition. It also stores my form fills, such as addresses and credit card information, so I never have to fill that in!*

From Carol Hamilton...

> *I don't have to worry about passwords anymore! I know they are available whether I am using my phone, my iPad, my laptop or my*

work computer. There is a free version and a paid version. The paid version is worth every penny!

From Leslie Davidson...

LastPass is a safe way to store passwords, credit card numbers and anything else you just can't remember. We all know we should have a different password for each site/app we use, and LastPass makes that much easier! Works great with Chrome and iPhone apps.
Additionally, you can set it up to share in case of an accident or your death, so your loved one has all your passwords.

[Editor's note: I said the same thing about using it to get your affairs in order on Page 24.]

And wait . . . there's more! Joyce Pleva loves that you only have to remember one password. Kathleen Fitzpatrick says it's helpful for keeping track of household email accounts. Laura Troyer likes that the mobile version is protected with fingerprint technology. And Christine Guise says simply, "LastPass is trusted because Beth approved."

In case you haven't picked up on the praise for LastPass' features, LastPass is a password manager that lets you generate unique, very complicated passwords for every site you visit then makes them accessible so you never have to remember them.

After an unnervingly quick search, LastPass discovers all the usernames and passwords you've ever used on your computer and stores them in a vault. You access your entries via one giant password—the last password you'll ever need. (LastPass—get it?) When you visit a page while you're logged into LastPass via browser plug-ins, the tool will fill in your username/password automatically.

I use LastPass over the other top password managers for a few reasons. The biggest factor is probably that I tried LastPass first, and once everything was set up, I was too lazy to change. Also, I've been pleased with their responsiveness to major security challenges, including their solid response after a fierce hack attack in 2015.

More reasons I love this tool . . . LastPass makes it very easy to share passwords with people. And the premium version is insanely cheap ($3 a month). Plus the regular improvements have made it increasingly easy to use.

Then Try...

You can't really go wrong with any of the top password managers. Here's a quick list of the best and their unique features.

1Password
Top Password Manager with Offline Storage and Manual Sync
1password.com

Dashlane
Top Password Manager with Online/Offline Storage Options
dashlane.com

Keeper
Top Password Manager with Extra Secure Security
keepersecurity.com

Unlike the other password managers on this list, **1Password** doesn't have a free version. You pay per device, per user and per version. The service keeps an eye on the newest breaches and alerts you if one of your sites or services shows up on a hacked list. Check out the Travel Mode, which removes your password vault from your device when you're traveling, so if an official searches your device, your private info won't show up (and won't even look like it was ever there).

If I hadn't started off with LastPass, I would probably embrace **Dashlane** for my password management, though the premium pricing is quite a bit higher. They both have attractive interfaces, seamless synchronization and easy ways to change multiple passwords at once. Dashlane gets bonus points for letting you choose whether you store your passwords locally or in the cloud. The free version is limited to 50 logins, but its Premium and Premium Plus levels include bonus features such as dark-web monitoring and even credit moni-toring and identity-theft insurance. You also get a VPN, which I paid for separately (Page 206).

Keeper is a new recommendation for me, but it has earned its place in the list of best password tools, especially with a reputation for even better security. The free version limits you to one device, but the per-sonal and family levels are priced about the same as others in this category. Keeper also has a secure chat tool for private messages.

Also Check Out...

DataVault Password Manager

NerdHerd Favorite Password Manager
ascendo.co

NerdHerder Jeffrey Horn likes **DataVault Password Manager** for his password security.

I use it in the Apple environment. My passwords on all my devices and computers are always in sync. Change a password on one device, and all the devices are up to date. They're always accessible and highly encrypted!

Bonus: How Do You Know If Your Password Has Been Hacked?

Have I Been Pwned?

Search Engine for Hacked Emails and Usernames
haveibeenpwned.com

If you're worried about your passwords, visiting **Have I Been Pwned?** can help you rest easier (or get really nervous). Enter your emails and usernames into the search engine, and the site scans mil-lions of records that have been released after data breaches. A couple of my emails and one of my usernames have shown up on the lists, along with the data breach information with the sites and the dates.

Hot Topic:
Three Bad Password Habits
You Didn't Even Know Were Bad

It's incredibly hard to do everything you need to do to keep your passwords safe. Here are some common mistakes that are easily fixed with a password manager.

1. Reusing Passwords

The biggest mistake that the biggest number of people make is reusing passwords. "But Beth," you say, "I only reuse passwords on sites that don't matter!" If you're reusing passwords, it's going to bite you in the butt someday. You may think it's ok because you have different passwords for important sites like your bank or Amazon, but you really, really need to have a unique, unguessable password for every site you visit. Every single one. That way when (not if) there's a breach, you don't have to worry about where you used the same password. You can just change that one password and move on.

2. Saving Passwords in Your Browser

Chrome, Firefox and other browsers will offer to save your usernames and passwords to make it easier to login. Chrome has been improving its password management options, now offering to generate passwords for you and then save them. That's safer than reusing passwords, but it's not as safe as a dedicated password manager.

3. Keeping Your Passwords in Your Contacts

You didn't think I knew about that trick, did you? Many people store their passwords in their contact lists, thinking that no one would think to look there. The bad guys know this. And they look there.

Take Your Password Management to the Next Level with Two-Factor Authentication

When your bank, email platform or company login page ask to send a code to your account, that's two-factor authentication. You should enable this wherever it is offered. The secure factor goes through the roof when you use it. According to a study on two-factor authentication from Google:

> *Our research shows that simply adding a recovery phone number to your Google Account can block up to 100% of automated bots, 99% of bulk phishing attacks, and 66% of targeted attacks that occurred during our investigation.*

And if a service does not offer two-factor authentication, you may be able to safeguard your account with a third-party authenticator.

Google, Microsoft, LastPass (Page 212) and other companies have created authenticators to help with password security. They generate one-time-use codes that you need to input in addition to your username and password every time you log in to applications that allow the extra service. The authenticator is on your phone. When you want to log in to a site that uses two-factor authentication, you provide your username and password then run the authenticator app. The app displays a code and transmits to the site, which then asks you to input it to proceed.

Protect Your Email Address

● ●

In Spammer 101 Class, the bad guys learn that having your email address is the first step for all kinds of frauds and inbox-filling spammy mailing lists. Here are several ways to guard your email privacy.

Start with...

Burner Mail
Fake Email Addresses
burnermail.io

I can't tell you how much I have come to love **Burner Mail.** The extension hangs out in my Chrome browser, and every time I'm confronted with a form that asks for my email, Burner Mail adds a one-click button to generate a fake one.

The fake email is connected to my main email address, so whatever I sign up for will go to my regular inbox. I can click on whatever verification link the company sends or interact any way I would normally, but the organization never gets my primary info.

I have used Burner almost daily in researching tools for this book, which means I have avoided sharing my business email address with hundreds of companies I've tested. When I have learned what I need to know about a service, I simply switch off the email, and nothing ever comes to my inbox again. The free version of Burner gives you five simultaneous burner emails and a 7-day mailbox history, but I use it so much that I upgraded to Premium for $30 a year. So worth it.

Then Try...

EmailOnDeck
Free Temporary Email Addresses
emailondeck.com

Mailinator
Instant @mailinator.com Email Inboxes
mailinator.com

Both **EmailOnDeck** and **Mailinator** work to stop spammers from collecting your contact info in the first place. EmailOnDeck's home page generates a one-time-use email address that you can plug into a registration site to download a great whitepaper or what-have-you. If the site requires you verify your email address or sends the download to your inbox, your EmailOnDeck address is good for a small period of time so you can retrieve your mail.

Mailinator lets you create an email address on the fly with this formula: [anything]@mailinator.com. The inbox for your made-up address is already up and running at malinator.com. Just put in your [anything], and all the mail for that address shows up. Note: Unlike EmailOnDeck, every email on Mailinator (in the free version at least) is public.

Also Check Out...

Newslettrs
Site and Email Address for Your Newsletters
newslettrs.app

Another way to keep spam out of your inbox is to never let it into your inbox in the first place. Use **Newslettrs** to sign up for email subscriptions. You can choose from curated newsletters through their site or sign up for your own with your own Newslettrs email address.

Hot Topic: Tracking Packages (and Being Tracked)

Rakuten Slice
Passive-Aggressive Package Tracker
slice.com

By the end of 2018, the U.S. had more than 100 million consumers willing to shell out $120 a year to get packages delivered by the dozens through Amazon Prime. And about half of the Prime members make purchases at least once a week.

I'm one of them, of course, which means that I'm almost always expecting a package.

Rakuten Slice is single-minded in focus. It sweeps through your cloud-based email (Gmail, AOL, Yahoo, etc.) to find all the receipts and shipping notifications. Then when you're trying to find a particular delivery, you can just open the app or go to the website to track every purchase and package.

A huge benefit of Slice is that it monitors the prices of your recent purchases and alerts you of price drops. I've saved hundreds of dollars from drops at Overstock.com and Nordstrom with zero effort on my part. Slice will also let you know if a product you've purchased has been recalled.

The Bigger Question Is... Are Email-Monitoring Apps Tracking You?

Two of the tools that I love and recommend are Unroll.Me (Page 224) and Slice. The two services, owned by a company called Rakuten (which also took over the coupon company Ebates), provide convenient, handy information for absolutely no money. They don't even have upgrades you can buy. So how do they make money?

Newsflash: if the product is free, you are the product.

Unroll.Me and Slice came under fire in 2017 when The New York Times revealed that the rideshare company Uber was buying data about other rideshare companies from Slice, which was getting the info from receipts Unroll.Me was finding in users' inboxes. That means that when you received your Lyft receipt, Unroll.Me was pulling that data and selling it. Privacy experts accused Unroll.Me of dishonesty. Now when you go to the site, there's a big link that says, "Why we don't charge you for this amazing service" with an explanation of how the company uses the data.

Facebook collects mountains of data that it lets advertisers use to target you. Google reads your emails and tracks where you go on the web. The aggregation and sale of browsing history and interests are massive. If you're taking advantage of the good things the connected world has to offer, someone is taking advantage of you.

What can you do to protect your privacy?

I highly, highly, highly recommend you sign up for the free (and non-intrusive) email series called The Privacy Paradox (Page 144). The five emails give you simple steps to understand and examine your privacy options in today's tech world. When I listened to the series, I came to the conclusion that I'm comfortable with trading my data for the convenience that tech tools and services offer me. But you may not be. The first step is to listen to the series to become aware of what's happening. Then you can decide what, if anything, you want to do about it.

Improve Your Browsing Efficiency

Every time a browser updates the software, you'll see faster loading, more security features and increased privacy. But you can also take more proactive steps to make your browsing more efficient and safer.

Start with...

Adblock Plus
Browser Ad Blocker that Prevents Pop-Ups, Tracking, Malware and More
adblockplus.org

Just by installing a quick plugin for your browser, you can speed up web pages and stop annoying ads from cluttering up your screen. I'm amazed at how fast pages load without the ads. You can find plenty of ad-blocking options, but **Adblock Plus** is a favorite as an open-source product that works on a whole bunch of different browsers, including mobile ones.

Then Try...

Print Friendly
Multi-Platform Print Management Tool
printfriendly.com

Printliminator
Simple Bookmark for Print-Friendly Sites
nerdybff.com/printliminatorbookmark

Have you ever tried to print a simple 500-word article from the web only to end up with 14 pages of ads, promos and other webpage crapola? Both **Print Friendly** and **Printliminator** (NerdHerder Lisa Priepot's favorite) analyze websites and pages before you print, allowing you to eliminate graphics, ads, footers and other extraneous material that eats up ink and paper.

Also Check Out...

Down for Everyone or Just Me?

Utility to Discover Whether a Site is, Umm, Down for Everyone or Just You

downforeveryoneorjustme.com

Fast.com

Netflix Internet Speed Checker

fast.com

SpeedTest

Another Internet Speed Checker

speedtest.net

Most of us depend on a strong internet connection to make sure we can upload, download and access what we need from the web and the cloud. **Fast.com** and **SpeedTest** both run tests on your connection to make sure you're fast enough to do what you need to do. I've used them to prove to my provider that my connection wasn't as fast as it should be. And when I travel, I check a connection before choosing between my personal hotspot or the hotel's.

Have you ever been surfing the web and come across a down page? Maybe I'm a little paranoid, but my first thought is always, "I wonder if this is down for everyone or just me?"

Guess what? There's a site for that. Just type the URL in question into the perfectly named site **downforeveryoneorjustme.com**. The service checks the offending site to see if it's an isolated problem.

SECURITY

Manage Spam: Email Edition

Any email you don't want is spam, from sincere offers from Nigerian princes to the newsletter you signed up for three years ago with gluten-free recipes. Thanks to these tech tools, you don't have to put up with spam in your inbox anymore.

Start with...

Unroll.me
Email Subscription Manager and Unsubscribe Tool
unroll.me

If your Gmail (Page 106) inbox (or Yahoo! or AOL or more) overflows with subscriptions, promotions and just plain old junk, **Unroll.me** can help (but first check out an important conversation we need to have about privacy issues, Page 220). It analyzes and categorizes your email, making it easy to unsubscribe from what you don't want and organize the rest into a daily or weekly digest.

Note: Unroll.me works wonderfully for things like newsletter subscriptions and social media notifications, but it can go all kinds of wrong with forum notifications. Experiment a little with the different types of subscriptions in your inbox to make it work for you.

Then Try...

Gmail

The Most Versatile Cloud-Based Email Service
gmail.com

Go to Page 106 for the full description of **Gmail**, but the tool belongs in this list because it's hands down the very best filter for removing spam from your inbox. Seriously.

Also Check Out...

To avoid getting on spammers' lists in the first place, use temporary email address tools like those on Page 218.

> Rich Skrenta was 15 when he wrote a "dumb little practical joke" computer program that we now recognize as the first computer virus. Thanks, Rich.

SECURITY

Manage Spam: Phone Edition

Although it seems like we're losing the battle against robocallers, you don't have to sit idly by while they take over your phone lines. Use these tools to block, identify and control unwanted calls.

They can help you by . . .

- Comparing incoming calls with a database of known spammers and suspicious callers.
- Using technology to determine if the incoming call is coming from the real number or a spoofed one.
- Putting an interactive barrier between you and the caller.
- Digging deeper for the real caller ID.

Start with...

Your Carrier's Tools

Your Phone Settings

Different carriers and some phones take steps to stop calls from ever reaching your line. In 2019, the U.S. government called upon call service providers to implement a technology called STIR/SHAKEN, which verifies that the calls are real and not spoofed (coming from a faked number to make it look familiar or legit).

As of this writing, major carriers including Verizon, Sprint, AT&T and T-Mobile are rolling out STIR/SHAKEN technology. Many carriers and some phones are also offering free basic spam-filtering tools. In most cases, for a few bucks a month you can upgrade the call information to include reverse-call lookup, additional info on callers and more.

Because of the regulatory changes in this arena, I was hopeful that I could leave this section out of this book, thinking that these steps would make robocalls disappear! But the major changes just address one area of the problem . . . robocallers that make it look like the call is coming from a different number so it looks more familiar to you. And no one thinks this will solve the problem. Even if it catches some calls, the bad guys will probably find another way around it.

Then Try...

Hiya
Spam-Blocking App
hiya.com

Nomorobo
VoIP Number Spam Protection with Mobile App Option
nomorobo.com

RoboKiller
Spam-Blocking App with a Sense of Humor
robokiller.com

These three tools all seek to identify, filter and block spammers and scammers. Register your phone numbers with **Nomorobo** to remove your VoIP landline from robocall lists, or pay a small monthly fee to register your mobile device number. **Hiya** and **RoboKiller** have free services to identify spam, but for a small fee, they both do much more to keep your phone spam free. RoboKiller has a bonus feature that makes it a top choice for NerdHerder Ed Weaver. The service recognizes a scammer's call and will let you enable an Answer Bot that will waste the scammer's time with hilarious fake conversations. While the scammers spend time with the Answer Bot's grumpy old man, drunken waste-oid or clueless Southern Belle, RoboKiller says it's detecting voice patterns and then searches for numbers with the same "audio fingerprint."

Also Check Out...

YouMail (Page 115)

Check out the section on managing calls (Page 115) to read more about **YouMail,** a voicemail/call-management system that also helps manage robocalls.

Celebrate Nerdiness all year long!

- January 9: Word Nerd Day

- May 25: Geek Pride Day

- June 20: National Hike with a Geek Day

- July 13: Embrace Your Geekness Day

- July 15: Be a Dork Day

- July 18: Insurance Nerd Day

Manage Spam: Junk Mail Edition

· ·

You can call it kitchen table spam, birdcage liner or plain old junk mail. But whatever you name the piles of catalogs and mailers that fill up your mailbox, you probably don't want it in your house.

These tools help you dump the junk snail mail and find your kitchen table again.

Start with...

PaperKarma

Junk Mail Eliminator

paperkarma.com

After some ups and downs and a temporary demise, I'm thrilled to say that one of my favorite apps is healthy and happy.

PaperKarma makes being green easy. Just snap a picture of the junk mail you receive, and the app will contact the company to remove you from the mailing list. Not only does it cut down on the junk mail that hides your kitchen table . . . it also helps companies save money on catalogs that you'll never open. Get a year's worth of junk mail zapping for $20, or just gather all the extra mailings in your house and blast through them in a month for $2.

Then Try...

DMAchoice
Direct Mailing Filter
dmachoice.org

Catalog Choice
Catalog Unsubscriber
catalogchoice.org

The people who mail you catalogs are members of ~~The Direct Mailing Association~~, I mean the ~~Data & Marketing Association~~, oops, now it's the Association of National Advertisers (ANA). Heck, I don't know what the organization is called anymore, but it still runs a site called **DMAchoice.** For two bucks, you can register your name and address for 10 years, giving you control over what types of junk mail actually reach your mailbox, no matter if you're on the official mailing list or not. DMAchoice is also handy for email opt-outs and canceling mail after a person passes away.

You can also go to the nonprofit site **Catalog Choice** to remove your name from mailings.

Also Check Out...

OptOutPrescreen.com
Service to Opt Out of Credit Offers
optoutprescreen.com

Under the Fair Credit Reporting Act, we can block credit and insurance companies from sending us solicitations. In other words, no more "You're PREAPPROVED!" letters with the little transparent windows.

Travel

∙∙

In This Chapter...

TRAVEL

Organize Travel Plans

Traveling in the age of the smartphone is more complicated than ever. Because we're tethered to both home and office via email, text and social media, we're expected to be able to respond in an airport just as quickly as if we were sitting on our couch.

Luckily technology can help us keep our travel plans organized so we can multitask on the go, no matter how far we're going.

Start with...

TripIt
Effortless Travel Organizer
tripit.com

The first time you use **TripIt**, you'll wonder how you ever lived without it. The concept is simple—just forward all your travel confirmations to plans@tripit.com, which is connected to the email address you use to forward. TripIt absorbs your confirmation and makes all the plans available on your mobile device. Besides the effortless transfer of travel details, TripIt links parts of your trip together, combining your flight, car rental and hotel under one trip.

> A photon checks into a hotel and is asked if he needs any help with his luggage. He says, "No, I'm traveling light."

The modestly priced Pro version adds features such as real-time flight alerts plus fare watches. I've received more in fare refunds than I've spent on the yearly membership. I mean, come on. There's just nothing better. The NerdHerd agrees:

Kim Mydland	TripIt is not a new app, but it continues to be one of the most used apps on my phone…and totally worth the paid upgrade to Pro.
Marti Wangen	TripIt notifies me of gate changes before the airport does. Best travel assistant ever!
Jeanne McAuliffe	You can set up your inbox so it automatically syncs plans from your email to the app, putting all the details in one location. No need to look up each reservation separately.
Michael Brown	Easy to use and so handy while on the road!
Rita Tayenaka	Can't travel without it. TripIt reminds me to check in, shares my plans with family, offers me refunds if my ticket price adjusts and gives me updates on my travels even before the airlines does.
Fran Rickenbach	When I am trying to manage three or more trips at a time, having TripIt means I no longer have to rely on my memory or bunches of slips of paper. It even picked up my niece's itinerary that she sent to me and reminded me when to get to the airport to pick her up!

TRAVEL

Then Try...

App in the Air
Travel Planning Organizer with an Emphasis on Flights
appintheair.mobi

CheckMyTrip
Free Trip Planning App
checkmytrip.com

If you don't want to spring for TripIt Pro, **CheckMyTrip** is free with many of the same characteristics. Reviewers are often pleased by how quickly they get flight updates, which makes sense because CheckMyTrip's parent company is involved in the airline booking and status business.

App in the Air has some of the TripIt functionality as well, but the focus is on the flight travel itself. It works independently as a planner app, or you can double the travel planning by importing TripIt.

Also Check Out...

Planapple
Free Site for Simple Trip Planning
planapple.com

Skyscanner
Travel Tool for People with Wanderlust
skyscanner.com

Part of me is worried about including **Planapple** in this book because the site looks a little weary. But it seems so handy if you are planning a trip with friends and want a place to put everything together. You just visit the site and start planning. No cost, no hassle. The site is designed for mobile, so no need to download an app. It'll integrate with TripIt (Page 232) as well as export your plans for another calendar. And if you are worried about offline access (or want to go old school), you can click a button to print your plans out.

And if you and your friends have no idea where to go, **Skyscanner** lets you explore anywhere and everywhere. NerdHerder Stephanie Shapiro loves this tool.

> *If you're like me and you like to explore everything with no preference on location but more on convenience/price, you can easily search the app or site to take you anywhere, see the cost over entire months, view high/low trends, etc. It makes finding a flight to anywhere you want to go so easy and fun!*

NerdHerd Thumbs Up: Track Your Loyalty Points

AwardWallet
Travel and Credit Card Points Tracker
awardwallet.com

Road Warrior and NerdHerd member Tim Buckley uses **AwardWallet** to track all the points and miles ("826k and counting!"). It'll show the rewards you have for credit cards, frequent flyer programs, hotels and rental cars, along with their expiration dates. Tim adds that AwardWallet will also track trips, but he prefers TripIt Pro.

TRAVEL

Navigate Smartly

• •

Not much has changed in the lineup of the best navigation apps since the last edition of this book. You hear fewer horror stories about navigation tools leading you into the middle of nowhere as GPS and technology improves.

Start with...

Google Maps

Worldwide Navigation System with Real-Time Updates
google.com/maps

Let's get straight to the point: **Google Maps** are the very best. There's just so much to love. . . .

- Let Google tell you which lane to be in to prepare for the next turn.
- Use the Explore Nearby feature to find restaurant reviews, gas prices, local events and more.
- Add your work address for real-time commute updates and advice.
- Download maps to save your data.
- Tap into Google's #CreepyButHelpful features with personalized recommendations in the For You section.
- Walk with step-by-step directions to your destination using the augmented reality direction prompts that appear on your screen.
- View the beautiful world around you with the satellite view instead of the standard map.
- Let Google remember where you parked.

Not only does Google have the most to offer, but it's continuing to invest in improvements with navigation and innovative technology.

Of course, some of these innovations may sacrifice our privacy. For a double dose of creepy, open your timeline to see how Google has tracked you every step you've taken. I clicked through a few of the days on the calendar, and Google had aggregated every single place I had been, gathered all the pictures I had taken in each place and even guessed at the places I had eaten and slept.

Here's one day:

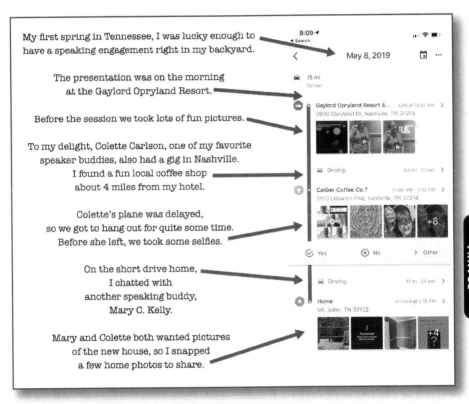

My first spring in Tennessee, I was lucky enough to have a speaking engagement right in my backyard.

The presentation was on the morning at the Gaylord Opryland Resort.

Before the session we took lots of fun pictures.

To my delight, Colette Carlson, one of my favorite speaker buddies, also had a gig in Nashville. I found a fun local coffee shop about 4 miles from my hotel.

Colette's plane was delayed, so we got to hang out for quite some time. Before she left, we took some selfies.

On the short drive home, I chatted with another speaking buddy, Mary C. Kelly.

Mary and Colette both wanted pictures of the new house, so I snapped a few home photos to share.

Then Try...

INRIX Traffic
Traffic-Focused Navigation App
inrix.com

Waze
Crowdsourced Navigation App with Real-Time Updates
waze.com

Waze is the personality-rich social navigation app that helps people avoid traffic and hazards by encouraging users to share things they see. You can connect with fellow drivers and send neighborly honks to your friends. You can also change the navigation voice in Waze to guest celebrities like Arnold Schwarzenegger and Cookie Monster, who will help you nerd out on your commute with messages about the next turn. Plus, and perhaps most importantly, you can send your route and ETA to people waiting on you to avoid those "Where are you now?" calls.

Waze used to be my favorite, but I couldn't handle the crazy routes that it kept choosing when I was driving more than 50 miles. One time in the Northeast, Waze suggested a 6-hour route for a 100-mile trip! In my experience it just doesn't do well for longer navigation.

Just because I don't trust Waze for all my travels doesn't mean the NerdHerd has abandoned it. Jamie Rice uses it to avoid D.C. traffic. Laura Featherston swears she can't live without it, "and trying to beat the estimated arrival time makes life interesting." Misty Seidel adds, "As someone who is directionally challenged and gets very nervous driving somewhere I don't know where I'm going, Waze is amazing! I don't have to refuse to go places now, because Waze will help me get there!"

Like Waze, **INRIX Traffic** aggregates crowdsourced data to help understand traffic. Its goal is to learn a driver's habits to recommend trips and departure times, keeping you updated about the latest weather and changing road conditions. It's a favorite of many attendees in my sessions.

Then Try...

CityMaps2Go
International City Map App with Travel Insight
ulmon.com

HERE WeGo
International Map App with Transit Options
wego.here.com

Rome2rio
Transportation Option Resource for Travel Anywhere
rome2rio.com

HERE WeGo shares many of the characteristics of Google Maps, including the capability to download maps and use them offline to avoid big data bills when you're traveling overseas. It has maps for hundreds of major cities around the world, plus 3D maps of thousands of malls, airports and other facilities.

CityMaps2Go is a great app for your backpacking trip through Europe. It's a favorite for its colorful, easy-to-read city guides and bonus cultural facts and articles.

NerdHerder Susan Motley also recommends **Rome2rio** for transportation options around the world. Susan says Rome2rio is excellent for logistical trip planning. Just put in any two points and get options for getting there including trains, planes and automobiles…plus feet and ferries.

TRAVEL

Also Check Out...

Weather Route/Highway Weather

Weather Forecast App for Travel

weatherroute.io

You're leaving home for a 6-hour road trip to your dream vacation. Will you have sunny skies all the way? This app is called **Weather Route** on iOS and **Highway Weather** on Android. Plan your route up to three days before you leave to see weather forecasts along the way.

NerdHerd Thumbs Up:
Download Topo Maps to Navigate the
Great Outdoors Offline

BackCountry Navigator TOPO GPS

Offline Topo Maps

backcountrynavigator.com

NerdHerder Joe Lattimore recommends **BackCountry Navigator** for, well, backcountry navigating. "It's a great GPS app for adventures in the woods."

Stay Safe on the Go

Have you ever seen Creepy Stalker Guy hanging out near your car in a dark parking lot? Or felt uncomfortable answering a knock at the door in a hotel? Or walked home after dark alone? These apps link you to technology that links you to a support system that can help you feel safer.

Start with...

Noonlight

Safety Button that Reaches Authorities in a Flash

noonlight.com

Noonlight (formerly SafeTrek) was developed by college students for college students. If you're worried about your safety, you open the app with one tap then hold your thumb on the big button and just keep walking. When you take your thumb off the button, you have 10 seconds to put in a code. If the code is not entered, the system is notified, and Noonlight sends your location, name and number to the nearest police station.

Bonus feature: As of this writing, you can't say, "Alexa, call 911" to summon police to your home, but you can say, "Alexa, tell Noonlight I need help." We set this up for my mother-in-law so if she falls or has an emergency, help is just a request away.

I guess we'll have to trust that it works because I'm scared to do a test run and end up with a hotel room full of policemen. I am happy just paying my $30 a year for peace of mind.

TRAVEL

Then Try...

FOREWARN
Background Checker for Real Estate Professionals
forewarn.com

FOREWARN was created for real estate professionals to help them run a background check before they meet a stranger. With as little as a prospect's phone number, an agent can see real names, addresses, criminal records and even some financial facts such as past bankruptcies or liens. Individual agents pay $20 a month, and associations and brokerages can buy multiple licenses for a discount.

Also Check Out...

Nextdoor
Social Network for Neighborhoods
nextdoor.com

As Sesame Street folks used to ask, "Who are the people in your neighborhood?" **Nextdoor** is a social network that keeps you abreast of what's happening where you live. You can find local recommendations for plumbers, reliable babysitters, garage sale hotspots—and, more importantly—news about suspicious characters and neighborhood crime.

Travel with Specific Needs

If you have a food allergy or are roadtripping with someone in a wheelchair, travel can be challenging. Here are a few apps for specific needs.

Accessible Travel

brettapproved
Site that Helps People with Disabilities Travel Easier
brettapproved.com

Wheelmap
Nonprofit that Shows Accessible Places for Wheelchairs
wheelmap.org

If you're wondering whether a "wheelchair accessible" hotel has a truly navigable ramp, there are a few apps for that. The challenge with all the ones that I found is that they're mostly based on crowdsourced reviews and updates, which can lead to a whole lot of unreviewed places. I searched several sites for rated locations in the Nashville area and came up with very little. But they're a good place to start.

Unsurprisingly founded by a guy named Brett, **brettapproved** lets disabled travelers discover and rate places to eat, stay and play. I like the thorough reviews, especially those by Brett. He wrote about several businesses in Nashville with comments such as, "When you drive up to the restaurant, you'll no doubt think to yourself, 'Wow, this is small and probably a challenge.' And you'd be right! It is extremely small and presented numerous challenges during the crowded lunch hour." Although this business only received two out of five checks, Brett ended with, "The staff, owner and patrons, along with the food obviously, make Arnold's worth visiting. The pecan pie is the best I have ever had, and I can't wait to go back."

A plus for both brettapproved and **Wheelmap** is that both have online searchable sites so you don't have to download apps. Wheelmap makes rating easy, so I was able to find a few local resources.

TRAVEL

Food Restrictions and Preferences Finders

AllergyEats
Food Allergy Restaurant Finder
allergyeats.com

Find Me Gluten Free
Gluten Free Restaurant Finder
findmeglutenfree.com

HappyCow
Vegetarian and Vegan Restaurant Finder
happycow.net

When my hubby was training for his second Ironman (yeah, one of those fun events where participants swim, bike and run for a total of 140.6 miles), he went hard-core vegetarian for a while. We used **HappyCow** to discover highly rated local restaurants that would cater to his athletic goals. Perhaps it's unfortunate that I am able to eat ANYTHING because I don't have any food allergies or sensitives, but if I did, I'd use **AllergyEats** and **Find Me Gluten Free.** All three of these tools let you search online or download an app.

Traveling with a Pet

BringFido
Site to Discover Pet-Friendly Businesses
bringfido.com

Petswelcome
Pet-Friendly Hotel Finder
petswelcome.com

If you just can't leave your pet pig at home, search **BringFido** or **Petswelcome** for pet-friendly restaurants, hotels, parks and more.

But make sure you tell the hotels you find on Petswelcome where you got their name. Petswelcome takes referrals pretty seriously. Here's their warning:

IMPORTANT: If you find a lodging through our site, please tell them that petswelcome.com sent you....Otherwise we'll automatically download a screensaver to your computer with dozens--nay, hundreds--of images of former New York Mayor Rudolph Giuliani in drag.

NerdHerd Thumbs Up: Speaking of Pets...

My Talking Pet
Animal-Animating App
mytalkingpet.app

At first glance, you may question the purpose of an app that animates a picture of your dog so you can make a video of him saying, "May the Force be with you." But when you post on a lot of dog sites like NerdHerder Nanci Saucier does, the **My Talking Pet** app is a huge hit. Nanci adds, "It's fun to imagine what my dogs would say if they could talk."

Also Check Out...

GasBuddy
Tool that Tracks Gas Prices to Find the Lowest Near You
gasbuddy.com

This really works! **GasBuddy** searches prices of all the gas stations within driving distance to help you find the best rates.

NerdHerd Thumbs Up:
Finding More Time to Travel

Countdown!!
Countdown Clock to Retirement (and More) (iOS Version)
In the App Store

Countdown Widget
Countdown Clock to Retirement (and More) (Android Version)
In the Google Play Store

When I asked NerdHerder Mark Figg for his favorite app, he said "Retirement Countdown." When I asked him why, he said, "Guess...." If you're looking forward to having more time to travel like Mark is, try Sevenlogics' **Countdown** apps. They have different names on iOS and Android, but they both let you create countdowns for all kinds of things and see them at a glance in the widget area on your mobile devices.

Pack with a Purpose

∙ ∙

I have made every packing mistake there is, from forgetting my suit pants on a business trip to not being able to find a toaster after a move until six months later when I already replaced it. Now I have these apps and won't make these mistakes again (I'm sure I'll find others to make).

Start with...

Sortly
Packing Organization Tool
sortly.com

The hubby and I moved from San Diego to Nashville in December 2018. My friend Aaron had told me about **Sortly,** an app that helps you organize boxes and inventory. Our move from San Diego to Nashville in 2018 was the perfect time to give it a try.

Snap pictures of your belongings as you put them in the boxes, then organize them in the app. Then use the app to generate color-coded labels with QR codes for each box. It's easy to find the right box when you need to retrieve an item. So when my husband asked, "Where did you hide the toaster?" I'd open Sortly and respond, "It's in the box labeled Kitchen 14."

TRAVEL

Then Try...

PackPoint

Travel Packing App
packpnt.com

Let's say last week you won the lottery, so in a couple of days you're leaving for a round-the-world trip. You're too busy with media requests and calls from long-lost relatives to look up the weather for your destinations. How in the world are you going to pack the right clothes and sundries for your trip?

Ok, you're probably not going to have that particular problem, but you'll probably be faced with a "what should I bring?" travel challenge. Just download **PackPoint** and put in your travel dates, duration and destination. The app will calculate how much you need to bring then looks at the weather forecast to further advise you. You can also tell it whether you're going to a fancy dinner or the beach to make sure you don't forget the specialty clothing items.

Your packing list gets its own website, so you can share it with your travel companions. With the paid version, you can even hook it up with TripIt (Page 232) so your packing lists are automatically generated.

Eliminate Airport Hassles

Note: You're never really going to speed through an airport, but these apps can help.

I go through airports more than 150 times a year (I'm afraid to count). These days *everything* is a hassle. But you can use these apps to make things a little easier and avoid some headaches.

Mobile Passport
U.S./Canadian Border Crossing App
mobilepassport.us

TSA Pre✓
TSA's Security Shortcut Program
tsa.gov/precheck

When I started traveling a lot, I invested in **TSA Pre✓** on the recommendation of my speaking colleagues. Then my hubby and I were planning a trip together, and I issued this warning: "If you don't get TSA Pre✓ before our trip, I will leave you in a heartbeat and be at Starbucks while you take an extra half hour to get through the line."

TSA Pre✓ makes a traveler's life soooo much easier. No more long lines (most of the time). No more pulling everything out of your bag (most of the time). And, most importantly, no more hopping on one foot trying to shove your foot back into your shoe as you try to rush to the gate (most of the time).

Yes, it's $85, but that's for five years, and renewing is a snap. I haven't upgraded to other services such as Global Entry or NEXUS because 90 percent of my trips are domestic.

But when I travel to Canada, **Mobile Passport** comes in handy. This app digitizes your passport for expedited processing between the two countries. It is not a pre-screened program. Anyone can use it. It simply eliminates the hassle of filling out the entry forms and makes moving through the process a little bit easier.

TRAVEL

Track Mileage (and Expenses)

• •

With the explosion of the gig economy, mileage-tracking apps have gotten better and more comprehensive. If you're still logging miles into a little notebook in your dashboard, these apps are for you.

Start with...

Everlance
Mileage Tracking App with Expense Tracking
everlance.com

Even if you're not a Lyft driver, the little errands you run all day add up: Office supply runs for the office, volunteer carpool to the community fundraiser, back-and-forth trips to the doctor's office. And all those errands could be deductible, if only you would track them.

Everlance takes the work out of tracking mileage. It logs your trips passively without you having to remember to open the app or start a tracker. At your convenience you can quickly classify your trips and get reports on your deductible miles, along with the current IRS rates. The info is ready to plop into your taxes for your well-earned credit. You get only 30 tracked trips a month with the free version, so you're probably going to have to upgrade to the $60/year Premium level. It'll easily pay for itself in time and tax savings.

In addition, Everlance is one of those tools that serves double duty for small businesses and entrepreneurs. You can track other expenses on the go for a real-time snapshot of your business costs in one place.

Then Try...

Stride Tax
Free Mileage Tracking App with Expense Tracking
stridehealth.com/tax

Did you notice **Stride Tax's** URL? The company is Stride *Health*. The company makes money helping small businesses find healthcare and dental insurance, which makes it kind of crazy that it has a mileage tracker and expense manager tool. But it bills itself a resource for small businesses and entrepreneurs, so perhaps it makes sense.

Anyway, I'm including them because it's big in the rideshare driver community, and those guys know mileage tracking. Like Everlance, Stride Tax tracks mileage and expenses, giving you an official report for your taxes.

Also Check Out...

Hurdlr
Business Expense and Mileage Tracker
hurdlr.com

Praised for its mileage accuracy and low battery use, **Hurdlr** is a great choice for automatic mileage tracking. And it does much, much more for solopreneurs with multiple income streams (aka side hustle pros). It also lets you track income and expenses and gives you real-time calculations for taxes. Another great feature is the ability to set rules for tagging transactions from imported bank statements as business or personal.

TRAVEL

Find a Parking Spot

In the last edition of *The Big Book of Apps,* I covered one parking app as an afterthought. But so many parking tools have cropped up in the last few years that it deserves its own section.

Start with...

ParkMobile
Pre-Purchase Parking Service
parkmobile.io

ParkWhiz
Another Pre-Purchase Parking Service
parkwhiz.com

SpotHero
Pre-Purchase Parking Service
spothero.com

Nothing can spoil a day at the beach more than having to drive around forever looking for parking. These three apps all let you find and reserve parking so you'll have the perfect spot without having to rely on luck. You can use the apps to find spots on the go or plan ahead online. You can even find the occasional discount coupon.

I'm listing **ParkMobile, ParkWhiz** and **SpotHero** in the same conversation rather than picking one over the other because they all have similar ratings in app stores. In fact, the reviews are so similar that many of them look fake. I may be wrong here, but when you see a dozen 5-star (or 1-star) reviews in a row all with the same review pattern, such as "best app ever" and "worst app ever," you get suspicious.

Another reason all these belong together is because you may need to download several to cover more areas. For example, I searched for parking at the Nashville airport, and each app had a different vendor.

Then Try...

SpotAngels
Parking Community App for Free Parking and More
spotangels.com

This app only works in some major cities, such as San Francisco, Seattle, New York City and, umm, Jacksonville? But if you're in or visiting one of the cities, **SpotAngels** will be very helpful.

SpotAngels helps you find free street parking, helps you remember where you parked and updates you about street cleaning schedules and the like. But the coolest thing is that when you use the app to find a spot, SpotAngels will update people around you when you're leaving. It's a lot easier than circling block after block trying to find someone pulling out (sometimes I feel like a stalker when I follow people to their cars and wait).

Also Check Out...

Local Parking Apps
Parking Apps from Your Area or Vendor
In the Google Play and App Stores

Check to see if your city or favorite parking lot vendor has an app. For example, Austin has its own app, as does Boston, White Plains, NY, and the City of Corpus Christi. You can also get a parking app if you use The Parking Spot airport parking locations.

TRAVEL

Hot Topic:
Help Stop Accessible Parking Abuse

Parking Mobility
App for Citizen Volunteers to Report
Accessible Parking Violations
parkingmobility.com

One of my best friends suffered a life-threatening spinal cord injury, and she was in a wheelchair for quite some time.

If you've never had to maneuver a wheelchair in a parking lot, let me tell you…it's incredibly difficult. The first time we went on an errand together, I didn't have a disabled parking pass, so we parked in the far corner of the parking lot because that was the only place we'd have enough room to park the wheelchair by the side of the car. I swear it took 15 minutes for us to untangle the foldable wheelchair from the trunk, get Ingrid in the right position to get out of the car, swing her body into the chair and then stabilize everything, shut everything and lock everything…and that was just getting us into the store.

Contrast that with the thoughtless able-bodied people who park in accessible spots, so they'll save 11 seconds during their errand. Every time I see someone parked in one of those spots without a permit, it burns me up.

That's why I'm thrilled to share **Parking Mobility**. This app lets users quietly report vehicles parked illegally in accessible parking spots.

You'll see several very grumpy reviews on the app—mostly because of their strict rules. According to Parking Mobility, you have to take 2-3 pictures of the vehicle from the app's camera, then retreat to a safe distance nearby to report. You cannot snap a couple of pics with your phone's camera then upload later from home.

When you submit your report, the staff reviews the violation then forwards it on to local law enforcement. Some communities partner with Parking Mobility for violators, who then can avoid harsher legal penalties by taking the nonprofit's 4-hour online course about accessibility. As of the summer of 2018, Parking Mobility says more than 12,000 offenders have taken the class. If your community doesn't participate, Parking Mobility uses the opportunity to encourage law enforcement to focus on education solutions rather than punitive.

Another big no-no for Parking Mobility volunteers: When you're reporting a violation, you must avoid a confrontation at all costs. They will reject a report where confrontations were involved.

TRAVEL

Search for Travel Bargains

On your next flight, you could sit next to someone who is paying hundreds of dollars less than you to go to the same place. These tools even the playing field when it comes to finding the best prices for travel.

Start with...

Hopper
Travel Shopping App to Find the Best Time to Fly
hopper.com

Skiplagged
Flight Search Engine for a Sneaky Discount
skiplagged.com

This travel app caused me all kinds of hassle . . . not because it's not helpful but because it is TOO helpful! **Hopper** lets you plug in details for a trip you want to take, and it will make predictions about the price and tell you when it's best to buy. You'll find yourself shopping for flights for January, and all of a sudden you'll be putting in alerts for the best prices to visit all your Facebook friends.

Let's say I need to fly from Nashville to Newark in two weeks. United's non-stop flight at 6 am will get me there for $172. But if I book a flight to Syracuse that just happens to go through Newark, I can get on the same non-stop flight and get off in Newark and pay just $105.

Skiplagged helps you find these "hidden-city" loopholes where you book a longer trip but get off during a layover. You can save hundreds on flights if you're willing to travel without checked luggage and with a little bit of chutzpah. The workaround is not illegal, but it is controversial.

Airline companies *hate* this practice. On very rare occasions they have punished or sued skiplagging passengers for the money they should have spent on the shorter flights. That's why Skiplagged has several do's and don'ts before you book a hidden-city flight through the site:

- Do bring just a backpack just in case they want to check your carry-on.
- Don't add your frequent flyer account because airlines may punish you if they find out.
- Don't rule out the chance bad weather will cause re-routing.
- Don't do this often because airlines may catch on.
- If the airline requires you to have proof of a return ticket, buy a return ticket and then cancel it within 24 hours (or buy a refundable ticket).

By the way, I will probably never try this. Because I have so many giveaways and materials for every speaking engagement, I almost always travel with about 100 pounds of luggage.

Then Try...

Google Flights

Google's Travel Tool with Price Alerts

google.com/flights

This is yet another step in Google's plan to take over our lives. **Google Flights** lets you search for flights on most major airlines to compare fares, schedules, stops and more. Search results show you cost-saving tips like "Save $32 if you leave the day before and depart the day after." Google also gives you the option to track the trip to receive price alerts.

In 2019 Google experimented with a price guarantee. For a couple of months, if you booked through their site and the price decreased on a ticket that Google was very confident about, Google would give you the difference back.

Also Check Out...

AirHelp
Service that Pursues Your Compensation for Flight Delays
airhelp.com

In 2005 a European Union regulation established compensation allowances for flight delays, cancellations and denied boarding for flights in and out of the European Union countries. A delay of 3 or more hours to your dream vacation in Paris could entitle you to up to 600 euros. But getting the airlines to pay up can be a daunting task. **AirHelp** and a few competitors will review your trip to see if you qualify. If you do, they'll file your claim for free and even move to litigation if they're sure you're entitled to the money. If the airline pays up, AirHelp takes a fee and gives you the rest.

If your airline troubles don't fall under AirHelp's services, you can still learn a lot from the resources on their site. They explain in clear language what you can do about lost luggage, overbooking, airline strikes and more.

NerdHerd Thumbs Up:
Super-Duper Flight Search Engine

Matrix Airfare Search
Google's Super-Duper Airfare Search Engine
matrix.itasoftware.com

You can't buy tickets through the **Matrix Airfare Search,** but you can dig deep, deep into options, preferences and more complicated routes. NerdHerder Steve Snyder says he always checks Matrix before booking any flight because it gives you all the real-time airfare costs for all airlines (except Southwest, of course. They don't play with anybody).

Discover New Sights and Sites

In 1996 my sister and I spent 6 months working our way around the country. Armed with a Rand McNally Road Atlas and a *Let's Go USA* travel guide, we visited 26 states without strangling each other.

We mapped our route with a highlighter and just crossed our fingers that we'd run across cool things to see. Now it's soooo much easier to plan the road trip of a lifetime (or even a Sunday drive).

Start with...

Roadtrippers
Road Trip Planner
roadtrippers.com

Roadtrippers lets you make your plan to get from A to B, whether you want the most direct route to save money or the drive that brings you past the best taco stands in Southern California. You can use the app or the site to plot start and end points, then have fun with all the possibilities in between. Share your trips with friends to make sure everyone sees what she wants to see.

A side note about Roadtrippers...it's addictive. When I wrote the original *The Big Book of Apps* in 2017, I played around with the site. Before I knew it, I was planning a vacation and a drive from San Diego to Portland. Poof! Two hours disappeared. I'm afraid to go there again.

Then Try...

iExit
Interstate Exit Guide
iexitapp.com

It's so hard to find the nearest Cracker Barrel off the highway (just kidding...they're everywhere). Download **iExit** or check your route on the app. You'll discover restaurants, gas stations, grocery stores and other resources you may need on the go, organized by each exit off your interstate.

Also Check Out...

World Around Me

Augmented Reality App to Find Local Sites and Resources
worldaroundmeapp.com

World Around Me (WAM) is an award-winning app that deserves the accolades. Look through the viewfinder of your phone to see information about your surroundings via augmented-reality overlays that show you where to go. The app shows restaurants, shopping, churches, ATMs, transportation options and emergency services. And it is so cool to use.

Super Tool Spotlight: RunPee

RunPee

Database App that Shares the Best Time for a Bathroom Run During a Movie
runpee.com

When you're drinking super-triple sodas while watching the summer's best blockbusters in a movie theater, you might need to take a break. **RunPee** tells you the best time to run to the restroom so you don't miss anything critical. Each movie costs a "PeeCoin," which can be earned by watching ads or buying them (10 for a buck!).

When the movie starts, set the timer on the app to get a little vibration when you can step away. You'll also find the important plot points, for, ummm, reading material during your potty break. The app also includes bonus tips like a summary of the first couple of minutes so you know what's going on if you're running late. And you'll also find out whether there's a surprise you should stay for after the credits.

Finance

· ·

In This Chapter...

FINANCE

Track Receipts and Expenses

• •

OK, 'fess up. Do you have a pile of wrinkled, stained, faded receipts sitting around your office that you're supposed to do something with? It's time to take control with these receipt management tools.

Note: Even though these apps are affordable and handy, you don't need a specific receipt-scanning app to scan your receipts. Check out these three other sections for similar functionality plus other features:

- Scanning apps frequently recognize receipts as a separate document type (Page 263).

- Several apps that track mileage will also help you keep track of expenses (Page 250).

- Systems that help you manage budgets and spending also have receipt integration and tracking (Page 269).

Start with...

Expensify
Expense Manager with SmartScan
expensify.com

"**Expensify** changed my life when it comes to getting expense reports done quickly and on time," says NerdHerd member Wade Koehler. Wade's opinion is one of the reasons Expensify moved up the charts from the last book. It has been so solid for so long and just keeps improving. My favorite feature is a chatbot-type "Concierge," that walks you through features and functionality one at a time so you're not faced with a setup page with a bunch of blank fields.

A skill they call SmartScan helps Expensify technology automatically read your receipts and input the merchant and totals. You can submit receipts for SmartScan via app, email (just forward to receipts@expensify.com), direct upload or a Chrome extension. Expense reports are super easy, and you can choose to forward receipts immediately to the people waiting breathlessly to reimburse you.

When you enable location tracking on the app, Expensify will use your travels to better identify where you obtained your receipts, plus it will keep track of your mileage (see other mileage tracking tools on Page 250).

The free version gets you 5 SmartScans a month plus unlimited manual submissions. But it makes good business sense to spring for the $4.99 a month for unlimited scans.

Then Try...

Receipts by Wave
Free Receipt Scanner for a Free Accounting System
waveapps.com

Wave
Free Accounting System
waveapps.com

Two things to know about **Receipts by Wave** and **Wave** itself.

1. Out of almost every single free tool I've used, Wave is my fave.

2. I can't believe no one knows about it.

If you have a small business, you will love Wave. It's a super easy online accounting system with invoicing, budgeting, expense tracking and more. It even works for personal budgeting, although the tools on Page 269 are more tailored for that purpose. H&R Block bought Wave in 2019, but I talked to someone at the company who assured me that the free version and its wonderful functionality will not go away.

Small business or employed professional, you'll love the ease (and free-ness) of Wave's receipt scanner, cleverly called Receipts by Wave. Snap a picture with the app or forward an email receipt to your account. Receipts by Wave will digest the receipt details so you can submit them to your account.

FINANCE

Receipts by Wave doesn't have the bonus features that Expensify does. In fact, it pretty much does the one task of scanning receipts on the go. But gosh. It's free. We love free.

Also Check Out...

Smart Receipts
Affordable Receipt-Tracking App
smartreceipts.co

Smart Receipts is built on open-source resources, so the price point for the premium version is just ten bucks a year. NerdHerder Nancy Silva says it's great for quick and easy receipt uploads. The app will "automatically categorize receipts by vendor, total spent, date and payment type, and the data is fully searchable and editable," Nancy says. She also likes the expense report generator.

NerdHerd Thumbs Up:
Financial Reporting Linked to Excel

F9
Financial Reports from Microsoft
Excel Connections
F9.com

Like many of us, NerdHerder Robert Newman relies on Microsoft Excel for critical business data. Robert shared how a tool called **F9** helps him link Excel files to general ledger data. F9 uses financial cell-based formulas, wizards and analysis tools to create spreadsheet reports that can be calculated, filtered and drilled down. "F9 is simple and user friendly," Robert says, "and it saves time by eliminating the need for double entry."

Pay Someone (or Get Paid)

My baby sister's favorite phrases at a restaurant when the bill comes:

- "Oops. I forgot my wallet."
- "I don't have any cash."
- "Can I write you a check later?"

My father and I laugh, and we pay, knowing that the money will never come. (Sarah would TOTALLY pay us back, but we never ask because having others take care of her is the benefit of being the baby sister.)

But watch out, baby sister. Your excuses for not being able to chip in have disappeared with these (mostly) fee-free tools to transfer money via your phone.

Start with...

Venmo

Fee-Free Payment Tool

venmo.com

When **Venmo** co-founder Iqram Magdon-Ismail forgot his wallet on a trip to see the other co-founder, the two guys were convinced that there had to be an easier way to reimburse a friend than scrambling for cash or sending a check. They created an easy money transfer tool that would let people connect their debit and credit cards to send and receive money from friends and family without a fee.

More than 10 years later, the company name is a verb. "Just Venmo me," the cool kids say. To use the tool, find the username of the person you want to pay or request money from. Then you can use a cute emoji as a description of the transaction and even share the activity in a social feed so others can see.

FINANCE

Venmo has a couple of security challenges, one big one being that it's pretty easy to pay the wrong username. I did it once, and the nice person returned the money, but that's not always the case. Some scammers ask for Venmo payments, and since (as of this writing), the transactions are not protected like bank or credit card purchases, if you send money you're not supposed to and the person doesn't give it back, you're hosed.

Now that PayPal owns Venmo, users are able to pay businesses and online stores, with the businesses picking up the fees. And as a consumer you'll face fees if you want the money in Venmo transferred immediately into your bank account vs. waiting a couple of days for the free slow-boat transfer. The money can also remain a spendable balance in Venmo until you request the transfer.

Then Try...

PayPal
Vintage Payment Tool
paypal.com

Square Cash
Another Payment Tool
cash.app

Venmo is the O.G. in this category, but it has a lot of competitors now because its functionality is so popular. Even though **PayPal** owns Venmo, it has another payment app. And **Square Cash** comes from Square, the groundbreaking company that brought low-cost mobile credit card processing to millions of small businesses (including mine).

PayPal lets you send a paypal.me link to people who owe you money, and it has a much higher transaction limit. Square Cash lets you buy and spend Bitcoin, which is pretty cool. You can also request payment via email by copying request@square.com. Plus Square Cash offers promotions from time to time and has a super cool website.

Also Check Out...

Apple Pay
Apple's Payment Tool
apple.com/apple-pay

Google Pay
Google's Payment Tool
pay.google.com

The **Apple** and **Google** payment tools are different but the same. But mostly the same.

Similarities

- They're both integrated completely into their own system so you can text or email payments to people with a click on the native devices.
- They both let you save other items, like a digital wallet for your loyalty and gift cards, boarding passes and more.
- You can use both of them at a bunch of retail stores just by holding them up to a card reader and confirming your ID.
- They both have the higher transfer limits.

Differences

- You can use your Google Home digital assistant to pay a friend.
- Google only charges a fee if you use your credit card. Like Venmo, Apple charges fees for both credit card use and for expedited bank transfers.
- Apple released the Apple (Credit and More) Card in the summer of 2019. It has no annual fees, international fees or penalty fees. It also gives you cash back immediately rather than yearly. You can use it like a regular credit card even if the place won't take Apple Pay.

Zelle

Bank-Linked Payment Tool
zellepay.com

You guys, I just don't know about **Zelle.** I tried out all these services for a newsletter a while ago, and Zelle was the only one that I just gave up on. With Zelle, you can transfer money from your bank account to someone else's by putting in someone's email or phone.

BUT ... the email or phone has to be attached to a bank account, and that bank has to be a member of the Zelle community. And ... get this ... if a scammer talks you into sending money through Zelle, it's not protected like a check or debit card transaction would be. You would think that a transfer directly to a bank would be secure. Pass.

> I just got fired from
> my job at the keyboard factory.
> They told me I wasn't
> putting in enough shifts.

Manage Budgets and Spending

I probably shouldn't be the one to tell you about budgeting tools because I'm absolutely the worst at keeping track of my spending. But if I did aim to balance my checkbook every month, boy howdy, I'd use these tools.

Start with...

Mint
Award-Winning Budget Management Tool
mint.com

You Need a Budget
Four-Rule Budget Management Tool
youneedabudget.com

Fifth book—fifth recommendation for **Mint**. This personal finance budget and money manager is always at the top of any list of best money tools. If you're new to money management tools, start here. Just ask everybody.

You guys know how much I love free stuff, so it's painful to recommend something that's ~~$50~~ now $84! a year. People adore **YNAB** (that's what the cool kids call it).

One thing I admire about YNAB (see how cool I am?) is its four-rule approach to budgeting. Rather than just seeing all your money come in and out and defining what it's doing, YNAB asks you to take proactive steps because, well, You Need a Budget. Another thing I like...they share their process and tips on their site for free.

FINANCE

YNAB Rules:

- **Rule One: Give Every Dollar A Job**
  Let's say you make $100 a month. Your rent is $70. That money has a job. Now YNAB wants you to give each dollar of the remaining $30 a job.

- **Rule Two: Embrace Your True Expenses**
  In the above scenario, you have $30 for other expenses. But every six months you have to pay $18 for insurance, which is obviously a big chunk of your monthly budget. YNAB wants you to put $3 a month aside, so when your insurance is due, the money is in the bank.

- **Rule Three: Roll with The Punches**
  Every month you budget $5 for cupcakes. But you're really spending $10 on cupcakes every month and feeling like a budgeting failure. Just change the allocation for cupcakes to $10 and move around other expense categories.

- **Rule Four: Age Your Money**
  YNAB wants you to slowly stash a little every month so eventually you have at least one paycheck in the bank. That means you're spending money that is at least a month old, so you're not living month to month.

That all sounds so reasonable. No wonder they're so popular. They're aiming for people at the beginning of their careers because they give all students a free year then a small discount to renew.

Then Try...

Digit
Delightful Text-Based Savings Chatbot
digit.co

Honeydue
Finance Manager for Couples
honeydue.com

My husband's a bankruptcy and student loan attorney. He says one of the saddest things about his business is when a couple is in his office to file bankruptcy, and for the first time in their married lives, they have to reveal how much they're spending. D.J. has seen arguments and tears and all kinds of drama from partners who haven't ever looked at finances together.

The **Honeydue** tool seeks to eliminate that problem with its "argue less, save more" functionality. It's designed to track bills, balances and budgets together. You don't have to worry about who is paying which bill and whether you're meeting your savings goals. You can set monthly household spending limits and get alerts when the limits are near. If you and your partner keep some finances separate, you can choose what information you share.

Digit is a chatbot that works through text messaging. I used it for about 6 months, loving the adorable GIFs and comments it would send as the system snuck small amounts out of checking and into savings based on my spending patterns. I was able to squirrel away several hundred dollars without feeling a strain. I also like the "Goalmoji" feature, which lets you choose an emoji as a goal, such as 👞 for that new pair of Converse hi-tops. Digit costs $2.99 a month, not much to pay to manage your money, in my humble opinion.

Also Check Out...

Credit Karma
Credit-Checking Tool
creditkarma.com

We all should be incredibly paranoid about credit monitoring sites. Many of them require a credit card for "free monitoring," and then the site charges your card every month even though you stopped monitoring your numbers, like a gym membership you never use. It took me a while to believe that **Credit Karma** was really not going to start draining my credit card with monthly charges once I signed up. But it kept its word, and I now keep track of my actual credit score with no strings attached. Yay for Credit Karma, and it is incredibly convenient and easy for me.

BONUS: Credit Karma helped me get real money! Read "Two Weeks, $260 in Savings with Apps" starting Page 278.

Do More with Spreadsheets

• •

I'm hardly the best person to give tips for using spreadsheets . . . I have managed to live my entire life without ever doing a pivot table. That's why these tools help me manage my data in a spreadsheet-happy world.

Start with...

Google Sheets

Google's Spreadsheet Tool with Magic Analysis Buttons
google.com/drive

Google Sheets is awesome for people like me with no formula skills. The somewhat-boring spreadsheet app from Google has a secret strength that will make you forget that you never took an Excel class.

Google Sheets has a little button in the bottom right corner of the sheet: Explore. When you click on the button, a pop-up window analyzes the data in your sheet and guesses what kinds of information you might be looking for. Ask it a question in natural language, and the Explore feature will answer. If you're interested (which I'm not), it'll reveal the formula that it used to pull the info. You can also highlight certain columns or rows to get specific data points. Super helpful. Also, the charts and data you're offered depend on the type of data you're using. Again, I say . . . #omg!

FINANCE

Then Try...

Airtable
Spreadsheet Tool with Database Capabilities
airtable.com

If you're using a spreadsheet to manage inventory, layers of data or larger projects, it might be time to upgrade to **Airtable**. This tool adds layers of organizational tools to spreadsheets to help you do what Excel wizards can do: group, sort, pivot, link, reference, filter . . . the advanced capabilities go on and on.

What's more, Airtable can be finagled to do all kinds of things, from keeping track of sales to managing contacts. Anything that involves lists and data can be managed in Airtable. You don't have to start from scratch . . . Airtable has tons of templates to help you set up your databases.

Airtable has plenty of raving fans, including NerdHerder Toni Fanelli. "Online forms that drop into tables make life easy!" Toni says.

Also Check Out...

PivotTableGuy
Guy Who Talks about Pivot Tables (and More)
youtube.com/pivottableguy

If you're really, really into spreadsheets and get all excited about pivot tables, NerdHerder Denise Merlino loves Nate Moore, aka **PivotTableGuy**. Believe it or not, PivotTableGuy shares video tips on pivot tables . . . plus a bunch of other Excel tips. "He has saved me so much time in working in Excel," Denise says.

Save Money

The TV show *Extreme Couponing* is no longer on air, so we have to look different places to learn how to save money. Luckily tech nerds have put the answers at our fingertips. Check out these easy ways to save money and find discounts.

Start with...

Honey
Browser Extension for Coupon Codes and Savings
joinhoney.com

Rakuten (formerly Ebates)
Cash-Back Browser Plugin
rakuten.com

Money-saving browser extensions are the bomb! Just now I took a break from writing to buy some new orange Chuck Taylor High Tops (because I only have seven pair). When I got to the checkout page, both **Honey** and **Rakuten** popped up with ways to save and earn money.

It's the passive-aggressive way to save money while you shop online. The tools are integrated into your browser and alerts you when the site has a promotion code. If you're an Amazon addict like I am, Honey works extra hard to find you the best prices from Amazon sellers that Amazon may not show you. Rakuten offers hard, cold cash back for many purchases instantly, which is why NerdHerder Dianne Richards loves it. With Honey you earn "Honey Gold" that you can trade in for gift cards. I use both to get better coupons through Honey and better cash back from Rakuten.

FINANCE

Then Try...

RetailMeNot
Coupon Site with Mobile App for Bargains
retailmenot.com

I mostly use Honey now because I am lazy and don't like to have to go hunting for coupons, but **RetailMeNot** is still a great resource. If Honey can't find a discount, I pop on over and check with this site. Some retailers do not allow posting of codes by users; in this case, check the comments to see if there is anything useful. Also check the maximum number of codes you can use per order because some sites let you use more than one.

And one big benefit of RetailMeNot is its mobile app. With Bonus! The RetailMeNot app uses geolocation capabilities to let you know when the store you're near has coupons and sales.

NerdHerd Thumbs Up:
Store Apps to Save Time and Money

Target
Shopping and Savings App for Target Stores
In the Google Play and App Stores

Walmart
Shopping and Savings App for Walmart Stores
In the Google Play and App Stores

Busy professionals have no time to mess around with shopping, says NerdHerd member Blair Brown. That's why she listed the apps for two stores as her favorites: **Target** and **Walmart.**

> *I have children and dragging them to stores quite frankly sucks...trying to figure out time to get to the store in between work, nap schedules, sports, bedtimes, etc....#Not Fun!!*

I love that I can order groceries in the middle of the night if I want and then swing by on my way home from work the next day to pick them up. I love that when the sitter texts me during the day that she is low on diapers and wipes, I can immediately go online and order pick up or drive up and just swing in and grab my items on my way to pick the kids up.

Need a last-minute gift? No problem. Go to one of the sites order it and pick it up on your way to the party.

These types of apps have saved me so much time and money (sanity, too). I'm not walking through stores for hours and coming out stressed with tons of stuff I didn't need. And you don't have to listen to kids beg you for everything cool they see.

Now my family actually gets to eat a normal dinner since I'm not waiting a month to go to the grocery store!! HAHA Well usually....

Also Check Out...

Key Ring
Loyalty Card Organizer
keyringapp.com

Stocard
Another Loyalty Card Organizer
stocardapp.com

If you're like me, chances are you have a pile of grocery, pharmacy and other loyalty cards in your wallet, and a couple of peeling, pathetic ones on your key ring. These are the cards you need to scan to receive store discounts and garner loyalty points.

Key Ring and **Stocard** are NerdHerd-approved smartphone apps that allow you to enter all your loyalty programs into your phone so you don't have to carry the physical cards. To enter your cards, just snap a picture of the card's barcode, and your card is permanently and instantly cataloged in your app.

In addition, the loyalty programs frequently offer other discounts and specials through the app and make it easier for you to sign up for new cards as well. NerdHerder Julie Kellman says Stocard reduces the stuff she needs to carry around. And W. Craig Henry calls Key Ring "a quick and easy way to keep all loyalty cards (and their barcodes) in one convenient place on your phone. No individual apps, just a virtual key ring in your pocket."

Tools in Action:
Two Weeks, $260 in Savings with Apps

It's one thing to write about apps that are supposed to save money. It's another thing to put my money where my apps are (or something like that) and quantify exactly how these tools can mean money in the pocket.

In two weeks in the spring of 2019, I saved/found $260 using apps. Here's the math.

GoodRx: $130 in Prescription Savings

Allergies, allergies, ALLERGIES! I needed several prescriptions when I moved to Tennessee to combat all the wonderful new pollens and allergens in my new home state.

The pharmacist asked for more than $200 for two prescriptions, but I pulled out the **GoodRX** app (Page 303) and for instant savings.

With GoodRX, you just look up the name of the medication on the app. I did it while I was standing at the checkout counter. You don't even have to have an account with GoodRx, and you can also search for the pharmacies with the best prices.

GoodRx led me to a brand name drug's manufacturer website for a $80 coupon on one prescription. And the app provided a list of pharmacies with coupons for a second drug, leading me to another $50 in savings.

Slice: $40 in Sale Refunds

We had finally finished all the renovations in our new Tennessee home, and the new purple walls in my bathroom clashed with my old burgundy towels.

I ordered new towels on the Target website. Before they even arrived, my **Rakuten Slice** app (Page 220) sent me an email. Target's towels had just gone on sale!

Don't you hate it when that happens? But Slice had my back. Not only did they notify me of the sale, they also provided a link to the Target site where I could ask for a credit back. Within about five minutes, I had a $40 Target gift card.

Note: some retailers (I'm looking at you, Amazon) don't refund the difference if the price goes down. But I've gotten back hundreds over the years from Overstock, Nordstrom and more.

Credit Karma: $90 in Unclaimed Money

I love **Credit Karma** (Page 272), a site that tracks your credit for free. They make money by suggesting credit cards and the like that would fit your budget and credit score, but I've just used the free features.

When I checked the site that spring, I saw a notification. "You have unclaimed money!" Credit Karma told me.

The alert included a link to the California Unclaimed Funds site, and with a few clicks I had applied to get the check that I had forgotten about. I was also able to dig around in other states where I had worked and found another $25. I would have never known to check if Credit Karma hadn't been keeping an eye on these claims.

Runner Up Money Savers:

TripIt: Hundreds in Savings Over the Years

I didn't get any money back from **TripIt** (Page 232) over these two weeks, but over the years the Pro version ($49/year) has more than paid for itself. TripIt Pro watches the prices of the flights you are tracking in its travel organizer. If there's a fare difference, you'll get a notification. They take into account change fees, but really the only airline I've ever had success with is Southwest because they don't have change fees and they have lots of sales.

Honey: Hundreds Over the Years

Well, my savings with **Honey** (Page 275) might not add up to hundreds of dollars, but I save several bucks here and there all the time. Honey is a plugin for Chrome that watches for the best prices and for coupons whenever I buy something online.

It's especially helpful in Amazon. You know how you see pricing on the first page of a product, then see "other sellers" in fine print? Honey does the math for you for all the different sellers and calculates the best prices based on shipping, etc. Frequently I'll see that I can save several bucks from another seller, even though it may take a few more days to get to me.

On other sites like Walgreens Photo, etc., Honey will try a whole bunch of discount codes that it has collected. I regularly end up with 10 percent off or free shipping or whatever. Hey, every dollar helps!

• •

Reuse and Recycle Your Old Devices

• •

Newer devices have more protections against phone spam, and many of us upgrade our phones every couple of years. This can lead to the dead-eye stare of an old smart device as it sits lonely in the junk drawer.

Here are a dozen ways you can repurpose your old device even after you move on to the shiny new gadget.

1. Contribute to the Greater Good

BOINC
Research Center that Uses the Power in Your Gadgets to Fight for Academic Research
boinc.berkeley.edu

Folding@Home
Research Center that Focuses on Understanding Diseases
folding.stanford.edu

I'm starting off with my favorite idea first. Researchers have found a way to put the unused processing power of your devices to work on important research projects. The Berkeley Open Infrastructure for Network Computing, affectionately known as **BOINC** (giggle), links researchers with the power of a computing grid that taps into individual devices. You can hook up your old computer or Android device to work on climate studies, humanitarian research, astronomy projects and much more. Another service, **Folding@Home**, gives your computing power to researchers working on understanding diseases such as AIDS, Huntington's, Parkinson's and even cancer.

2. Keep Your Home Safe (Or Watch the Kitties from Work)

Alfred

Security Camera System that Works with Old Devices
alfred.camera

Old devices are wonderful as security cameras. Install **Alfred** on your old device as well as your new one. Then login to both, and you'll be able to monitor the viewing area of your older device. You can also monitor the video feed on a computer and share with others.

3. Be Prepared for Emergencies

When you upgrade, wipe your old phone and insert a pre-paid SIM card. Then throw it into a junk drawer until you have a phone emergency. Bonus prep idea: buy a solar-powered device charger to bring the emergency phone to life if the power goes out.

4. Install a Dashcam

Nexar

Dashboard Camera App for Your Device
getnexar.com

Nexar combines your device's own sensory-gathering info (like speed, etc.) with traditional dashcam video monitoring to create a record of sudden stops, traffic events and more driving hazards. You can use the service and the cloud video storage for free or buy their dashcam and get more features for about $90.

5. Create a Media Center

Purchase a video cable to connect your device to a monitor or TV, then load up your device with all your streaming media apps: Hulu, Netflix, Amazon Prime and more.

6. Keep an Eye on the Baby

Baby Monitor 3G

Baby Monitoring App that Uses Your Old Devices

babymonitor3g.com

Apps such as **Baby Monitor 3G** let you set up your old devices to listen for baby cries and general kid-watching activities.

7. Wake Up with Style

The charging station for my phone is in the living room, and when I need an alarm to get up for an early-morning flight, I stress about running out of juice. Set your old device up as an alarm (with the cool tools on Page 286) or even a sleep monitor to end the back-and-forth swapping of your primary device.

8. Create a Digital Photo Album

Share your online photo albums with friends and family (read: Grandparents!) to keep the most updated family photos playing on everyone's old devices. (P.S.—Want to send the grandparents real photo albums? Check out Page 338.)

9. Use Your Device as a Remote Control

SURE Universal Remote for TV

TV and Smart Device Remote for Android

tekoia.com/sure-universal

A quick search of the Google Play Store reveals dozens of apps like **SURE Universal Remote for TV** that enable you to turn your Android phone or tablet into a remote control for your TV and other Wi-Fi–connected devices. Apple limits using your device as a remote for, unsurprisingly, Apple products.

FINANCE

10. Donate to a Charity

Cell Phones for Soldiers
Donation Site for Old Devices that Go to Soldiers
cellphonesforsoldiers.com

Gazelle
Company that Buys Old Computers and Gadgets
gazelle.com

Secure the Call
Donation Site for Old Devices that Are Transformed to 911-Only Phones
securethecall.org

Cell Phones for Soldiers is a site with many resources for the military community. They refurbish old devices to give to soldiers. **Secure the Call** uses your old device to create 911-only phones that the community can use to summon emergency services for events such as domestic violence.

I've sold a couple of older computers to **Gazelle**. They make it easy to send in old devices to receive cash or Amazon gift cards. Using Gazelle you can also set up your own electronics drive for a charity group and get a 15 percent commission.

Health

. . . .

In This Chapter...

HEALTH

Sleep Better and Wake Up Refreshed

The Centers for Disease Control and Prevention says adults need 7+ hours of sleep a night, and a whole host of new devices and tech tools are trying to help us get them.

Start with...

Sleep Cycle
Motion-Activated Sleep Monitor and Alarm
sleepcycle.com

The **Sleep Cycle** alarm is my new choice for sleep tracking and smart alarms. The app monitors your sleep motion patterns in two ways: either through sound from your nightstand or motion directly from your mattress. The alarm has a 30-minute wake-up phase that ends at your real alarm time. As the time to wake up approaches, Sleep Cycle uses its motion sensors to figure out when your body is in a lighter sleep stage.

Their home page is full of fascinating statistics including the number of app users asleep right now and the average sleep time for everyone. I also like the stats on the countries that snore the most or wake up the earliest.

Then Try...

Alarmy
Annoying Alarm Clock
alar.my

Alarmy calls itself the world's most annoying alarm clock, and I think it qualifies. Set alarms in three modes. One makes you get out of bed and take a picture of an object you've chosen. Another makes you shake the dang phone until you're wide awake. The third alarm option asks you to solve a math puzzle before the alarm stops sounding.

See? Annoying.

Also Check Out...

Alarm Clock for Me (iOS)

My Alarm Clock (Android)
Beautiful Nightstand Alarm Clock
apalon.com

Apalon makes customizable, beautiful alarm clocks for both Apple and Android devices. I have no idea why they named one **Alarm Clock for Me** and one **My Alarm Clock**, but they're the same app. Both have attractive interfaces, versatile alarms and weather updates. There's even a flashlight built in. The Android version is also available on Amazon devices, which is wonderful since their Fire Tablets are so inexpensive. Get one for less than $50 for bedtime reading and a handsome nightstand alarm. Bonus: Amazon frequently offers really, really good discounts on these things.

HEALTH

NerdHerd Thumbs Up:
Wearables for Sleep Monitoring

Fitbit Devices
Smartwatches that Track Activity,
Exercise, Sleep and More
fitbit.com

AutoSleep Tracker for Watch
Sleep Tracking Apple Watch App
autosleep.tantsissa.com

Sleep Tracker: by Sleepmatic
Sleep Tracking Apple Watch App
In the App Store

Many smart watches go beyond measuring your 10k
daily steps. **Fitbit's** sleep-monitoring technology helps
NerdHerder John Gann with insight into his sleep
patterns, including statistics on REM, deep sleep, awake
time and more.

As of this writing, Apple Watch doesn't yet have sleep-
tracking functionality. That's why Kimberly Lilley uses
the **Sleepmatic** app.

> I wore a Fitbit for years, and I really liked the sleep
> tracking. When I upgraded to my Apple Watch, I
> missed having that data. Sleepmatic was the solution.
> It has a similar dashboard showing periods of wake,
> restlessness and sleep.

AutoSleep Tracker is similar, but it also adds the ability
to start and stop your watch on the nightstand if you
don't like to wear your watch to bed.

Get Active

Are you wearing a fitness tracker right now? The fitness wearables market is going strong. Researchers have debated whether having these things helps us increase our activity levels and lose weight. But even if they don't, we're still buying them and using tech tools that go with them.

Start with...

StepBet
Activity App that Earns You Money (Or Not)
waybetter.com

Zombies, Run!
Running App with Zombies
zombiesrungame.com

I'm always partial to tools that begin with a Z, but I truly do love **Zombies, Run!** This activity app is still my favorite, and it has sparked a whole store's worth of zombie merchandise. Way to find a way to monetize! The game motivates you to lace up your running shoes with adventures and storylines around blood-thirsty zombies.

The WayBetter company structures its apps on financial motivation. Commit to an activity goal with real money. If you make your goal, you split the winnings with the other people in the community who met theirs. And if you don't meet your goal, well, your loss funds everyone else's gains. WayBetter has **StepBet,** DietBet, RunBet and SweatBet.

HEALTH

Then Try...

MapMyFitness
Comprehensive Fitness Tracker
mapmyfitness.com

MapMyHike
GPS Tool for Tracking Hikes
mapmyhike.com

MapMyRide
Bicycle Fitness Tracker
mapmyride.com

MapMyRun
Fitness Tracker for Runners
mapmyrun.com

MapMyWalk
Fitness Tracker for Walkers
mapmywalk.com

Sworkit
Workout Videos for a Custom Fitness Program
sworkit.com

One of my biggest excuses for not working out is that I'm always on the road. **Sworkit** takes away that roadblock (get it? On the road with roadblocks? Ha!) by offering exercise plans that can be done anywhere for any length of time without any equipment. Easy-to-follow videos walk you through a workout. The paid version provides access for you to create unlimited custom workouts and offers more fine tuning.

Both of these companies have several activity apps for your favorite way to sweat. **MapMyFitness** is kind of an umbrella app for Under Armour's collection of fitness apps. You can use it to track any workout with any fitness app. If you're into more specialized workouts, such as cycling and hiking, you can try other apps in the series: **MapMyRide**, **MapMyRun**, **MapMyWalk** and **MapMyHike**. These tools have online resources as well as apps, and all of them integrate into health-tracking tools. Under Armour also integrates its nutrition app, MyFitnessPal (Page 296).

Also Check Out...

Strava
Fitness App for Runners and Cyclists
with a Rabid Fan Base
strava.com

If you don't need to chase zombies or win money to get motivated to go for a run or ride, you may be a candidate for the **Strava** community. Strava members track their stats then compare them with everyone else's stats to find out who has the very best stats and therefore wins a competition that no one else knows about. And they love it. The Strava community are fierce competitors who enjoy challenging themselves and others.

Strava has had some bad PR because of privacy concerns. Public Strava data revealed the location of U.S. military bases in Afghanistan and Syria. Not good. In addition, one of the phrases that will come up when you Google *Strava* is *Strava stalking*, referring to the ability members have to see where their connections are working out. Not good. But members are still sharing more than a million activities a day, so the concerns about privacy are not a deterrent. Them people be crazy. By "them people," I don't necessarily mean NerdHerder Darcy Burnett. She says Strava is "a great way to track, share and see everyone's accomplishments!"

HEALTH

NerdHerd Thumbs Up: Apps to Keep Up with Your Favorite Competitions

The Open
Official App of The British Open
Golf Championship
In the Google Play and **App Stores**

Race Monitor
Race Results for Motorsports
race-monitor.com

NerdHerder Tim Zielenbach takes his golf obsession very seriously, like all good nerds do. He loves **The Open,** the official app for the British Open, the golf championship that began in 1860.

> *Golf was my first love, having picked up a club when I was 6 and set my sights on wiping Jack Nicklaus' records off the books. A back injury in my teens and a distinct absence of exceptional skills prevented me from ever seriously competing beyond then.*

> *These days, golf remains a passion for me, and The Open is a joy to watch each year. If I cannot be in front of a TV or laptop, firing up the app fuels my continued addiction to the befuddling and joyous game...and shows all of us just how far the difference is between casual players and the world's best.*

Although Tim didn't achieve a career as a golf professional, another member of the NerdHerd is on the right track to make a name for himself in car racing. Andrew Rucker uses **Race Monitor** to see real-time race scoring from events around the world. Andrew says he and his race team can see detailed results and statistics that help his team improve.

Venture Outside

• •

Nerds like me don't get out much (really not kidding about this one), but when I do enjoy the great outdoors, I take my tech with me. Here are some super-techy tools for outdoor activities.

Start with...

Merlin Bird ID
Wizard-Style Bird Identification App
merlin.allaboutbirds.org

PlantSnap
AI Plant Identification App
plantsnap.com

Our home in Tennessee has about 2 acres, and when we first moved in, we had no idea what kinds of plants we had. Thank goodness for **PlantSnap,** an app that uses artificial intelligence to recognize leaves and blooms of hundreds of thousands of growing things.

The hubby and I walked every inch of our huge yard identifying dozens and dozens of local plants we had never seen in San Diego. But apparently we didn't identify ALL the plants because I failed to recognize all the new foliage. Boy was I embarrassed when I went to the dermatologist with a mystery rash, and she pronounced it poison ivy. I learned "leaves of three, let it be" in grade school, but I guess I forgot. [Scratch, scratch.]

Merlin Bird ID asks a series of questions about a bird you want to identify. As you answer, the app narrows the database of options and customizes your list to the species you're more likely to see in your area. Once you ID your bird, you can read all about it and listen to the audio.

HEALTH

Then Try...

SkyView

Augmented Reality Stargazing App
terminaleleven.com

Gazing at the sky on a clear night is a pleasure you should share with people you love. And the app you should share while doing it is **SkyView**. Load the app then stare through the viewfinder at the sky. SkyView's augmented reality feature will superimpose constellations, stars, planets and other heavenly bodies onto the dark sky so you can finally find Orion's Belt. The app also keeps up with sightings and events such as meteor showers and satellite flybys.

Note: The app is available for iOS and Android, but the site only mentions iOS. Just search the Google Play store.

Also Check Out...

Komoot

Mapping Tool for Outdoor Adventures
komoot.com

Relive

3D Video Maker for Outdoor Activities
relive.cc

Going for a hike? First, head over to HikerAlert (Page 313) to make sure people know where you are, then download **Komoot** and figure out where you want to go. Komoot helps you route a hike, road bike race, mountain biking adventure or other cross-country event. Once you plan your route, you can use the turn-by-turn voice navigation to stick to the plan . . . this is much better than having to ride your bike and figure out the map on your phone at the same time. Plus, your map works offline, so you can go into the woods without losing your way.

When you take your three-day bike tour through Italy, you'll want to use **Relive** to, umm, relive the adventure. Relive hooks up with your fitness app of choice (except Strava (Page 291) as of the summer of 2019, which made everyone mad). Then it turns your trip into a trippy 3D video to which you can add pictures and exhausted emojis to show the pain you went through. You can link your Relive trip to your teammates' accounts to show how each of your little icons moved around together.

NerdHerd Thumbs Up: Explore Tennessee Parks

Healthy Parks Healthy Person TN
Tennessee Parks Guide with Rewards
for Enjoying the State
healthyparkstn.com

I am so biased about this web app! Yes, I know that **Healthy Parks Healthy Person TN** is only for Tennessee (my new home state), but it's a brilliant idea that should spread.

Not surprisingly, it was Candi Rawlins from the Tennessee Recreation and Parks Association who submitted Healthy Parks Healthy Person TN as her favorite. The web app helps you discover Tennessee parks, gives you ideas for activities and rewards you for getting out there and enjoying them. You earn points by checking in to different parks while you're hiking, riding bikes, etc. Then you can redeem points for free food, rounds of golf, guided hikes and more.

HEALTH

Watch What You Eat

I just ate two frozen yogurt pops in a row while writing this section, so I'm not sure I'm the right person to give you advice on great dieting tools. But I'm ok with a do-as-I-say-not-as-I-do approach to this category if you are.

Start with...

MyFitnessPal
Calorie and Activity Tracker
myfitnesspal.com

Lose It!
Calorie and Activity Tracker with Food Image Recognition
loseit.com

Of these two apps, **MyFitnessPal** is the most well known and perhaps the most beloved. Under Armour bought it in 2017, expanding its extensive reach even further. The app integrates into the very popular fitness series named MapMy . . . Ride, Fitness, Run, Walk, etc. (Page 290), as well as many other fitness trackers and other wellness tools.

Lose It! also has many fans, but it's the Snap It! feature that makes it stand out, at least in theory. You snap a picture of your meal, and the app uses image recognition to determine what you're eating and how much.

Then Try...

SparkPeople

Weight-Loss Tool with Supportive Community

sparkpeople.com

If it makes you feel better that Brittany in New Hampshire is trying not to eat her second frozen yogurt pop tonight, too, you should try **SparkPeople**. It has thousands and thousands of food items in the database, but its best feature is the connected community of supporters.

Also Check Out...

Calorie Mama

Food-Recognition App to Calculate Calories on Your Plate

caloriemama.ai

For those of us who still believe that a quart of Ben & Jerry's is one serving, there's **Calorie Mama**. Snap a picture of your meal, and Calorie Mama recognizes the food and calculates the calories. #NerdyWorkaround! Throw a leaf of kale over your cupcake, and the app will never know.

Eat, Drink, and Be Merry

● ●

Ok, so this is actually a section on great apps for adult beverages, but I couldn't come up with a great headline. These tools help you find and mix interesting beverages beyond Bud Light and Fuzzy Navel wine coolers.

NOTE: Please drink responsibly. If you find yourself enjoying these tools too much, use your app to summon a rideshare driver. Around the best drinking holidays, many offer free rides or discounts.

Wine

Vivino
Wine Identification Tool and Tracker
vivino.com

Wine Picker
Restaurant Guide for Best Wine Pairings
winepicker.co.uk

My husband is a wine (and beer and other alcohol) snob. When we first started dating, I'd open the **Vivino** app in the wine store to try to find the best bottle to bring over for dinner. Instead of just picking the wine because I liked the label, I snapped a picture of the label with the app to learn all about it.

I'm looking forward to trying **Wine Picker** the next time I go out to dinner. This app lists the wines available at local restaurants—a quick search in my Nashville area showed six connected restaurants. Then you put in what you're having for dinner, and the app finds wines from the restaurant list that pair the best. You can also put in a wine from the wine list to read about it and get recommendations for dinner.

Beer

Untappd
Microbrewery Beer Rater
untappd.com

When it comes to beer apps, you have some beer pong tools and a few "fake drinking a beer" apps. **Untappd** stands pretty much alone in its field. This app solves the problem we all face when we go to a fun little microbrewery and see a beer menu with Robohop Imperial IPA next to Geriatric Hipster Club and Space Station Middle Finger American Pale Ale. How can you possibly choose?

Untappd lets people rate and track craft beers at bars around the world. You can check in at different places and keep track of your favorites plus see the ratings of new brews.

Mixed Drinks

7UP Digital Bartender
Web App to Measure Your Favorite 7UP Drinks
7up.com/digital-bartender

Even though I haven't had a 7UP in years, I just love the **7UP Digital Bartender.** Visit the site from your phone and choose a recipe. Then set your phone on the counter next to your glass. The app shows you the levels to pour your ingredients to in order to make the drink, like this recipe for a Summer Pisco.

What a clever use of a web app!

Hot Topic:
Augmented Reality in Products

Living Wine Labels
Augmented Reality App to Bring Wine Labels to Life
livingwinelabels.com

One day I was having a drink with some fellow speakers in Houston. A delivery van pulled up in front of the bar, and I started to squeal. "OMG! That's the 19 Crimes truck! Get out there and scan with this app!"

My colleagues were quite startled, but within minutes we were all looking through my phone with **Living Wine Labels** at the labels on the Australian wine brand 19 Crimes. Each bottle is named for a real convict who was banished to Australia by Queen Victoria after the Revolution of 1776. When you point the app at the label, the featured figure comes to life to tell his or her story.

Besides seeing 19 Crimes criminal stories, you can watch zombies break through the bottles on The Walking Dead wine or listen to a winemaker highlight the best features of Chateau St. Jean wines.

Stay Healthy

Technology has given us many options for monitoring, improving and reporting on our health. As always, check with your personal healthcare provider and insurance folks to make sure these are the best resources for your needs.

Start with...

Apple Watch
Smart Watch with Advanced Health Monitoring
apple.com

A mother of three had a seizure. Her **Apple Watch** detected her fall and notified her husband. A 13-year-old boy's Apple Watch alerted him to a sharp spike in his heart rate. His father got him to the hospital before it was too late.

Ok, here I go again breaking my rule about Apple-only products. But in my defense, I think the market will soon see multiple wearables with health-monitoring features that the Apple Watch Series 4 and up include. The watch can pick up on sudden impacts and falls, and EKG technology can alert wearers to arrythmias and unusual changes in heartrate.

Yes, these devices are expensive. But they are saving lives, which puts them into the category of #WorthThePrice for many of us.

Then Try...

Ada
AI-Powered Medical Advisor App
ada.com

AskMD
Medical Care and Follow Up
sharecare.com/static/askmd

You Google what could be causing your hacking cough. Wouldn't it be nice if someone followed up in a few days to see if you're doing better? **AskMD** from Sharecare does just that.

Googling health symptoms is never a good idea. You get a sore on your little finger, and after an hour on Google, you're convinced you have necrotizing fasciitis. (By the way, I just Googled *necrotizing fasciitis* to make sure I was spelling it correctly, and DON'T DO IT!)

Both AskMD and **Ada** guide you through a series of questions to narrow down the choices. Then they both lead to guidance toward treatment, whether it is something you can do yourself or you need to seek treatment.

Ada is powered by artificial intelligence, the result of many, many data points about your symptoms and the possible outcomes. I like that both will encourage you to check back in so the system can keep monitoring your improvement.

Also Check Out...

CareZone

Record Keeper for Your Family's Health

carezone.com

GoodRx

Pill Identifier and Prescription Price Comparisons

goodrx.com

CareZone is an app that organizes your medical information—it's as easy as scanning your prescriptions into the app. CareZone then alerts you about refills and helps remind you to take your pills. What's more, you can keep track of other people's prescriptions and health info—a wonderful feature for those of us who are keeping tabs on elderly parents or kids.

GoodRx helps you identify pills and understand their effects, but the best feature is the comparison tool that searches the prices of your prescription at area pharmacies and lets you know where it'll be cheapest.

HEALTH

Hot Topic:
Apps for the Greater Good

Child Protector
Child Injury Assessment Tool
childrensmercy.org/childprotector

TraffickCam
Web App to Fight Sex Trafficking
traffickcam.com

My brilliant college roommate, Dr. Raquel Vargas-Whale, is a child abuse expert. She recommended the **Child Protector** app for both child care professionals and lay people. The app assesses the risk that a finding or situation represents maltreatment and gives a plan of action. "It's a good teaching tool with helpful animations," she says.

Another easy-to-use app that may help victims of sex trafficking is the **TraffickCam** site, which lets ordinary travelers like you and me upload photos of your hotel rooms. The photos are added to a searchable database to help sex trafficker investigators identify locations of trafficking activity.

Family

● ●

In This Chapter...

FAMILY

Keep Your Sanity as a New Parent

Nerd HQ's own Molly Veydovec and her husband welcomed Baby Jack into their lives in June of 2018. I asked her to share some of the tech tools that help them all keep their sanity.

New Mama Molly's Five Awesome Apps for New Parents

Tinybeans
Private Family Photo Album
tinybeans.com

I'm not a huge social media sharer. But I still want to share pictures of Jack with my immediate family and friends. I also don't want to drive said family and friends nuts with a bunch of pictures of our drooly newborn.

Enter **Tinybeans**. This app allows you to save and share pictures and videos on a timeline of your family's life. The fam gets a daily email, and they can choose how many pictures they want to see. Our aunties and grandmas live for this, and it's a great way to semi-privately share your little one.

Bonus: You can keep track of special milestones and print photo books.

The Wonder Weeks
Baby Development Resource
thewonderweeks.com

Did you know that babies are KA-RAY-ZEE? They are. And, as first-time parents, we didn't know that part. Fortunately, we came across **The Wonder Weeks** app, which breaks a baby's early development down into "leaps." The Wonder Weeks gives you a helpful summary of what your baby is going through and ways you can help them during each stage.

Kinedu
Age-Appropriate Activity Ideas for Babies and Toddlers
kinedu.com

Kinedu is a cool app that gives you a daily activity you can do with your wee one from the time they are born to the toddler years. Think simple things like sharing facial expressions and blowing bubbles… things that seem silly to us but are mind altering to a little baby.

White Noise Baby
Hair Dryer Sounds and More for Cranky Babies
tmsoft.com/white-noise-baby

Yes, babies are crazy, and you never know what will work to appease the tiny human. We discovered that the sound of the hair dryer helped Jack to sleep.

White noise is super helpful because babies are used to sleeping to loud sounds of the womb. Some kind stranger actually created a Hair Dryer app (downloaded thousands and thousands of times). Note: your kid might prefer the lawn mower app or the thunderstorm app, etc.

Note from Beth: There really is such a thing as the hair dryer app. Molly's favorite hair dryer app was iOS only, so I replaced it with **White Noise Baby***.*

Libby (Page 175)
Libby is just the best app ever, kids or no kids. It just happened to save me in the first months of mommyhood. There is a lot of quiet sitting with baby in your arms napping and nursing. I could only watch so much TV (although Beth can tell you I watched pretty much every baking show plus two seasons of *Riverdale*). My brain fried, and I turned to my love of reading.

One cannot turn pages while holding a fat baby, so my tablet was my life saver. Libby allowed me to borrow any book from my local library! Magazines and audiobooks are available, too. From my favorite best-selling authors to new classics, like *Oh, Crap! Potty Training*, Libby is a must-have for new moms and dads.

Bonus: Apps for Parents with Older Kids

GameChanger
Sports Tracker for Parents and Grandparents
gc.com

Photomath
App that Solves Math Problems with a Click
photomath.net

Can't make your nephew's 75th softball game this year? See if the team has **GameChanger**. The app lets parents, grandparents and far-away aunts follow kids' baseball and basketball games. The coach sets up the app for the team, and family members follow the plays no matter how far away they are from the action.

You paid attention in math class, but when your kid comes to you for help with homework, your old math skills seem to have disappeared. **Photomath** uses your mobile camera to solve math problems in real time, and will even take you step by step through the solution. Parents tell me it's easy to snap a picture of a math problem when your kid steps away from his homework for a bathroom break. Then when your little student returns, you're suddenly empowered with the answer, just like you knew what you were doing all along.

Guide Your Kids in This Crazy Digital World

Parents have always worried about their kids, but in today's high-tech world, they REALLY worry about their kids. They wonder where they are, who they're texting, what they're looking at on their computers and how much time they're spending staring at screens.

Technology has tools to help us monitor our kids' time with technology. Even if you don't have school-age kids, you probably know someone who does, so please share this with worried parents in your circles.

Start with...

Bark
AI-Powered Social Media Monitoring
bark.us

I've heard from many parents that they're flummoxed when it comes to keeping up with their kids' social media, texting and other online interactions.

How do we monitor the conversations to protect our kids from bullies, predators and other creeps?

How can we better see the signs when our kids express troublesome thoughts?

How are we supposed to decipher this???

One answer to everything but the emoji text is **Bark**. Bark uses artificial intelligence to monitor 24+ social media sites to watch for bullying, release of personal information, predators, suicidal ideation and more. A year's subscription is $99 and covers all the kids. Right now the system focuses on mobile devices — not regular browsers. The alerts also cover the installation of new apps — especially suspicious ones. Plus it covers text messages and even analyzes images to look for nudity and other imagery that kids shouldn't be sharing.

What I really like about Bark is that YOU don't have to do the monitoring. Your kids are free to talk to their friends and communicate like kids do without fearing that you're sneaking peeks at their phone (or outright monitoring everything). You simply let the kids be kids and feel confident that Bark will watch out for warning signs.

The success of Bark with your family will probably depend on your existing relationship with your kids. Yes, you can install the apps without your kids' permission, but it's best to talk to them directly about why you worry and what you worry about.

Then Try...

Qustodio
Screen Monitoring and Content Blocking Tool
qustodio.com

Qustodio shows up regularly on the top screen-monitoring tools for families on all kinds of devices. It'll track time spent on social media networks so you can limit the number of hours your kids can watch toy unboxing videos. It doesn't keep an eye on what they're posting like Bark does. Use Qustodio to watch how much they're using their devices and where they're spending time.

Also Check Out...

OpenDNS FamilyShield
Free Router-Level Parental Control Tool
opendns.com/home-internet-security

This tool is a little different. **OpenDNS FamilyShield** is software that works at the router level to block adult content and suspicious content. But I'm a nerd, and even my head was swimming as I read the instructions.

What you're going to have to do is change the DNS server settings to the OpenDNS server addresses. And then there's some cache flushing. The site gives you step-by-step instructions for lots of different types of routers, but that didn't help me any. I was still confused.

It turns out our router already has parental controls, and the DNS server settings are hard to get to on purpose. With our router settings, I can even cut off data to my husband's devices at dinner. I didn't complete my test of the software, but other users love it. You can also install it on individual devices, such as gaming systems and Apple TV.

Keep Track of Your Loved Ones

My wonderful husband is a crazy Ironman triathlete-turned avid camper, and he's frequently on all-day bike rides or multi-hour hikes. When I haven't heard from him in a while, my worry gene kicks in. So, I use the Find iPhone app to track him down.

If you have more people to keep track of, start your stalking career here.

Start with...

Life360
Family Location and Communication System
life360.com

We don't like to call **Life360** a stalking tool, but that's what it is since it helps you keep track of your family 24/7. Life360 eliminates the text messages that ask, "Are you there yet?" Once you set up your "circles," you can view family members on a map, send messages and receive alerts when they arrive at home, school or work. NerdHerder Greg Hummel is like many of the parents who mention Life360 in my sessions. "It's the best way to know where your kids are and what they are doing," Greg says.

Other features (some premium) include crash alerts, stolen phone protection and round-the-clock access to a live person for emergency help as well as roadside assistance (like a family-oriented OnStar with a side of AAA).

Then Try...

Glympse
Simple Location Sharer
glympse.com

If you're a worrywart and want to ~~stalk~~ track your loved ones, **Glympse** is a fast, free app that shares your location. You can share your location for a set amount of time, alert people of your travel plans and set up a group to track everyone. People can ~~stalk~~ track each other through the apps or online.

Also Check Out...

HikerAlert
Safety Service for Hiking and Outdoor Activities
hikeralert.com

Kitestring
Text-Based Emergency Service
kitestring.io

Glympse and Life360 use GPS for passive tracking, but sometimes you want to let your loved ones know where you're going because weird things happen in this world. **HikerAlert** calls itself "A modern approach to the age-old rule: Always tell someone where you're going and when you expect to return." Register with the site ($5.99/year) and share the details about your hike, camping trip, long run or whatever you're going to be doing that puts you out of reach. When you finish your adventure, check back in on the web app (no download needed). The system will text you if you don't check back in, and if you don't text back, your trip details are sent to the emergency contacts you provided. What's more, if you have hiking buddies, you can link accounts for group trips so everyone's emergency info and details are linked.

Kitestring is similar, but it's more designed for a blind date-type situation, and it's mainly text based. When you're headed out, text a duration to Kitestring. Then text "ok" to end a trip. It's free if you only use it three times a month and only choose one contact. If you don't text, your contacts will get a notification.

FAMILY

Use Alexa for Family Management

On a trip to see my husband's family, my nerd neurons started to tingle when I realized how some simple technology might solve some of the challenges his brothers and sisters have with taking care of Nana, the family matriarch.

Brother Paul and his wife, Becca, are the most involved in Nana's life because she lives in a literal mother-in-law apartment on the first floor of their house. I interviewed Paul to hear about his processes and concerns, and then I came up with techy solutions that would help.

Essential Solution Gadgets and Tools

Before I set up the new systems, we needed to buy a few pieces of equipment and sign up for some services:

- Amazon Alexa Devices (See digital assistants, Page 150)
    - A big-screened Echo Show for Nana
    - A smaller Echo Spot for Paul and Becca so they could see the calendar and reminders but didn't have to pay the higher price for the Show
    - Several Echo Dots so the two households had connectivity and connections in various places around the two living areas.
- Google Calendar (Page 6)
- Noonlight (Page 241)
- IFTTT (Page 33)

Solution One: Google Calendar for the Helpers

Nana's schedule was written on a big calendar and kept in the kitchen drawer. Paul used to send pictures of the calendar to his siblings to keep them all up to date. So the easiest solution was to set up a calendar in Google Calendar (Page 6) that everyone can see and update. All the siblings can add the group calendar to their regular one (keeping their work and other appointments separate). They can get reminders for different events. I used Paul's Google account as the base calendar, then went into settings to invite his family members. If they didn't have a Google account themselves, they could receive the invite via their regular email address then sign up for an account later.

Solution One-A: Keeping the Hard Copy Calendar

Nana was concerned when she heard that the calendar was going to be electronic, but we decided to keep the handwritten one in the drawer as well. The siblings can just write a note on the printed version and add the appointment to the digital version via Alexa.

Solution One-B: Keeping Calendar on the Alexa Screen

We wanted to be able to see the calendar on Alexa at any time, and after goofing around with the settings a while, I found that Alexa will only display the calendar if an event is scheduled during the next few days. So our workaround was to add a recurring event daily so it'll always show up. Paul's recurring event was, "Good Morning, Nana! We love you." So cute.

Solution Two: Alexa for Communication

The other challenge Paul talked about had to do with communication. Nana's apartment is on the bottom floor of Paul's house. What if Nana has a problem and needs help? Paul has video monitors, but the family doesn't monitor them 24/7. And what if Nana just needed to ask someone upstairs a question? We wanted to find a way to make communication easier and safer.

It's Alexa to the rescue! We put Alexa devices in both living areas. Nana's big screen Echo Show and Paul and Becca's Echo Spot show reminders and calendars on the screen, as well as extra features such as song lyrics (this thrilled the granddaughter).

We also added several inexpensive Echo Dots in other rooms.

After I set the devices up, I worked with Nana to introduce her to all the things it can do.

Since Nana sometimes has problems with her short-term memory, I suggested that they write out specific phrases for common tasks that she might want to do:

- How to play music
- How to get the news
- How to add things to shopping lists
- How to set reminders
- How to add appointments
- How to increase/decrease volume
- How to drop-in (intercom) to different devices around the house
- How to cancel an activity, such as "Alexa, STOP" or "Alexa, CANCEL"
- How to call for help
- How to call people's phones (Alexa can call regular phone lines)

Solution Three: Alexa for Safety

One of the family's biggest worries is that Nana is pretty independent and refuses to wear one of those "I've fallen, and I can't get up!" buttons. I don't blame her. Who wants to be tethered like that all the time? [Beth looks down at her Apple Watch and sighs.]

So we set up the emergency service Noonlight (Page 241), which has a special feature for Alexa. Noonlight started out as a big button on your phone. If you're walking along and feel uncomfortable, you just open the app and put your thumb on that big button. When you release your button, you have ten seconds to put in a code. If you don't put in that code, emergency services will be called

Noonlight expanded to Alexa and other platforms as well, so after it's set up, Nana can say, "Alexa, tell Noonlight to send help."

Next Phase: Expanding the Technology

Amazon Skill Blueprints
Amazon's Custom Alexa Skills for Business and Home
blueprints.amazon.com

IFTTT (Page 33)

Zapier (Page 33)
I cannot tell you how over-the-moon happy I was to be able to give the family a hand. I wish I could go back every couple of months to keep tweaking the system and adding capabilities. But alas, I had to do that "making a living" thing. So I left them with two ideas for expansion.

- **Amazon Skill Blueprints** lets you create your own Q&A for caregivers for questions like "where are the spare hearing aid batteries?" and "What time does Nana like lunch?" They can make up a list of FAQs that caregivers need to know and just program them into Amazon's template.
- IFTTT and Zapier (Page 33) are tools that help connect one cloud service to another. When I lose my phone, I just say, "Alexa, trigger find my phone," and IFTTT sends a little signal to make it ring. As they fine-tune the caregiving system, they can use these tools to be even more efficient.

FAMILY

Manage Family Schedules and Projects

• •

As a working adult, you need to track tasks, keep in touch with team-mates, manage inventory and schedule meetings and events. What about your duties at home? Running a household isn't all that different from running a business.

Start with...

Cozi Family Organizer
Family-Friendly Calendar Manager
cozi.com

Year after year, parents in my audiences tell me the best calendar tool for families is **Cozi Family Organizer**. Cozi lets you set up calendars for each family member and combines them on your master calendar. You can also import other calendars, such as soccer and school sched-ules. The system also includes family-oriented lists to help with shop-ping, chores and more. The free version works for many families, but advanced users can get a subscription to Cozi Gold for less than $30 a year.

Then Try...

TimeTree
100 Percent Free Family Calendar
timetreeapp.com

TimeTree is a family calendar that welcomes even non-TimeTree users, allowing you to share the schedules with people who don't want to bother adding the app. The tool is ad supported, so you get the full version without a subscription.

Also Check Out...

AnyList
Grocery List and Recipe Manager Tool
anylist.com

Out of Milk
Home-Centered To-Do List Tool
outofmilk.com

Gone are the days when we have to call around from the grocery store to see what we need to bring home for dinner. Tools like **AnyList** and **Out of Milk** both manage family grocery lists in real time, giving all household members the ability to add and check off list items whenever they need to. AnyList gets bonus points for its ability to import and keep recipes and add ingredients to the shopping lists.

What did E.T.'s mother say to him when he got home? "...Where on Earth have you been?!?"

Help Others

• •

Much of today's technology is created to help make our own lives better, but some tools let you help others. These apps and sites make it easy to give back, and it's easy to get the whole family involved.

Start with...

AtlasGO
Fitness Tracking App that Raises Donations and Motivates Teams
atlasgo.org

Charity Miles
Fitness Tracking App that Raises Donations

charitymiles.org

WoofTrax Walk for a Dog
Activity Tracker that Benefits Animal Shelters
wooftrax.com

If your family is going to go for a hike anyway, you can reap benefits beyond burning of the day's cupcake. Both **AtlasGO** and **Charity Miles** track your workouts to raise money for charities. Every mile you log running, walking or biking earns donations. The organization finds corporations to sponsor your activities. If your friends, family and co-workers get jealous of your generosity and fitness level, AtlasGO lets you put together challenges with groups and companies.

Dogs need walks. Animal shelters need donations. Doesn't it make sense to link these two needs? **WoofTrax** thinks so. This app lets you turn your afternoon puppy outings into fundraising opportunities for your favorite shelters.

Then Try...

Olio
Food and Sundries Sharing Community
olioex.com

I wasn't really sure how to describe **Olio** in one line (above). It's a service that connects people who have surplus food and sundries with people who need food and sundries. The goal is to share with those who have less and reduce food waste.

The site is free, while the app cost me a buck. I was really excited to see the Olio community around Nashville, but it found no one but me in the area. So I searched Dallas. And New Orleans. And Denver. Nothing.

And then I saw on the activity feed that someone was giving away five croissants and six assorted baps! Bingo! I checked out how close they were and it was...4176 miles away.

I should have known. I've never heard of a *bap* before.

The company is in London, and that's where most of the action is. I saw a few items in San Francisco and Seattle, but it doesn't have much of a following here. Yet. Y'all...you and your family can get something going in your neighborhood!

Also Check Out...

Be My Eyes
App that Lets Sighted People See for the Visually Impaired
bemyeyes.com

Give the visually impaired a little help through **Be My Eyes**. Sighted volunteers receive notifications when someone needs their help to identify objects, read labels or discover colors. As of this book's printing, the Android app is still in the works.

FAMILY

Photo and Video

· ·

In This Chapter...

PHOTO / VIDEO

323

Try Special Graphic Effects

You have plenty of reasons to try out these special effects for multimedia, but the biggest motivation may be to elevate your social media and marketing.

Note: For more (many, many more!) graphic and video tools, check out my companion book, *The Little Book of Video Tools.*

Specialty Filters

Huji Cam
Take a Picture Like It's 1998
In the Google Play and App Stores

LENS FX
Epic Special Effects for Images (iOS Only)
brainfevermedia.com/lensfx.html

Remember the questionable quality of those disposable cameras in the '90s? NerdHerder Ashley Simon uses **Huji Cam** to relive those retro photos. When you open the app, it actually looks like a disposable camera, and you can add the light-leak effects that ~~ruined~~ enhanced your photos back in the day.

From his description below, how do you think NerdHerder Victor Goodpasture feels about **LENS FX**?

Is your vacation photo just a tad bland? Well, how about adding dinosaurs, spaceships and giant robots? Not enough, you say? Well, how about adding explosions, fire-breathing effects, lasers, lightning and jet fighters? Still not enough?? Did I mention dinosaurs? Like, lots of different dinosaurs??

The variety of 150 effects, attention to detail and multiple levels of editing capabilities make this app a must-have for anyone's photo editing library.

By the way, I did mention dinosaurs, didn't I?

This is an inexpensive app that will give you hours of enjoyment turning the throw-away photo into a sci-fi masterpiece. You will NOT be disappointed.

Frame Effects

If you need your face on the cover of a magazine or hanging in an art gallery, head over to these sites. I love these for quick graphics for my blog and newsletter.

Pho.to
Image Editing for Fun Frames, Filters and Editing
pho.to

Photofacefun
My Favorite Photo Frame Site
photofacefun.com

Collages and Mosaics

EasyMoza
Photo Mosaic Site
easymoza.com

PicPlayPost
Video Postcards to Jazz Up Marketing
mixcord.co/partners/picplaypost.html

Picture Mosaics
Photo Mosaic Site with App
picturemosaics.com

These three tools all do basically the same thing: create an image out of a whole bunch of other little images. **EasyMoza** and **Picture Mosaics** are both web-based (Picture Mosaics has an app). Pick a main photo then a whole bunch of other photos to fill it. You can connect to Facebook, Instagram and other photo repositories for your images. Both sites allow you to download and share low-res versions. EasyMoza sells the high-res files for up to $10. Picture Mosaics sells prints for a whole lot more.

Putting **PicPlayPost** in the category of collages is doing it a disservice. Sure, you can make great photo collages with just a few clicks. But its secret sauce is the capability to make some of the images in your collage out of videos and GIFs. The end result is what I would consider a video postcard that makes a great social media post. NerdHerder Maddie Williams likes PicPlayPost because you can make a quick video with your own photos right from your phone.

Hot Topic:
Schedule and Optimize
Social Media Posts

Buffer
Social Media Scheduler
buffer.com

Hashtagify
Twitter and Instagram Hashtag Helper
hashtagify.me

Now that you have learned how to create all these wonderful graphics for social media, when do you have time to post them everywhere? **Buffer** will schedule, track and report on social media posts across a whole host of platforms. The app has lots of flexibility, even with the free version, and provides great stats.

My brilliant speaker friend and NerdHerd member Lois Creamer preloads all her social media posts into Buffer. "Besides being an excellent program, their responsiveness if a problem arises is amazing."

Another NerdHerder, Judith Briles, boosts her social media posts with the help of **Hashtagify**.

Hashtagify is a terrific tool to expand your hashtag horizon. Add the one you think is right, it gives you a percentage of usage, top users, what parts of the world most used in AND variables of other complimentary hashtags to use as well.

PHOTO / VIDEO

Touch Up Your Photos

• •

Do you remember buying the retouching addon package for your senior pictures? Or sighing when you snapped the most adorable picture of your family…only to see a telephone line running through everyone's heads?

The retouching tools you have at your fingertips will help you post the pics you want without the pimples and background clutter you don't.

Start with...

Remove.bg
Site for Instant Background Removal
remove.bg

This site was the most clicked link in my NerdWords newsletter in 2019, maybe because I loved it so much I included it like four times.

It's just so amazingly simple! Upload a picture to **Remove.bg**, and within five seconds, the background disappears, leaving you with a transparent picture with just the person showing in the foreground. When I shared it, I received at least five emails from people saying, "Where has this been all my life??"

The site was an overnight success, leading them to create a downloadable program and a Photoshop extension. You buy credits for the number of images you need to transform. It's fun to drag a whole folder into the program and watch all the backgrounds disappear.

Then Try...

TouchRetouch
App that Gets Rid of Unwanted Objects and Flaws in Images
In the Google Play and App Stores

Although I adore Remove.bg, it's kind of all-or-nothing in that it wipes out whatever is in the background to make a transparent PNG. Sometimes you just need to wipe out a telephone line or remove a for sale sign. **TouchRetouch** does that for you with just a touch (thus the name). Use the tutorials to learn how to very quickly and (more or less) expertly clean up images.

```
            And the smiley was born...

19-Sep-82 11:44 Scott E Fahlman              :-)

   From: Scott E Fahlman <Fahlman at Cmu-20c>

    I propose that the following character
            sequence for joke markers:

                     :-)

       Read it sideways. Actually, it is
        probably more economical to mark

  things that are NOT jokes, given current trends.
                For this, use

                     :-(
```

Edit Images on Your Phone

• •

From adding filters to cropping on the go, having an image editor on your device is essential at work and home.

Start with...

Afterlight
All-In-One Editing App
afterlight.co

Snapseed
Google's All-In-One Editing App
snapseed.com

Several apps are Swiss Army knives of image editing. They have filters, art effects, background-removing options, cropping capabilities, text and stickers and much, much more.

NerdHerder Addison Simon likes **Afterlight** for on-the-go editing. Afterlight has apps for Android and iOS, but the Android one is no longer listed on the site and hasn't been updated since 2014, so. . . . The **Snapseed** app from Google is both powerful and popular.

Then Try...

PicsArt
Do-It-All Image Editor
picsart.com

I love Prisma for its simple interface, but **PicsArt** may be the most versatile tool. It has filters, drawing tools, collage features, creative brushes and more goodies.

Also Check Out...

VSCO

Image Editing App with a Cult Following

vsco.com

VSCO is another editing app but it has taken a cultural path that I would bet the creators hadn't expected. The app itself lets you apply beautiful filters and effects. I kept hearing about it, and I thought the cool kids loved it, so I upgraded to the paid version. But it turns out the cool kids weren't so much worshiping VSCO as they were mocking some of its biggest fans. The term "VSCO girl" refers to a young female who uses VSCO filters to give her Instagram selfies that golden glow. A VSCO girl has scrunchies to hold back her hair, a conch shell choker and a Hydro Flask. She claims to care about the sea turtles and says "and I oop" and makes a noise that must be spelled "sksksksksk."

Hot Topic:
Take Better Pictures

LightMeter
Android Light Meter for Old School Photography
In the Google Play Store

PhotoPills
Camera App to Plan Shots
photopills.com

Pocket Light Meter
Apple Light Meter for Old School Photography
In the App Store

Whether you're taking photos from your mobile device or using apps to take better pictures on real, honest-to-goodness cameras, technology can help.

My dad went through a fierce photography phase, and I remember him carrying around a separate device called a light meter to measure the light for better pictures. That was back when you had to be super sure every time you clicked the camera button because you only had 24–36 pictures on every roll of film.

More old photography math for those who were born after digital cameras:

$3–6+ for each roll of film

$12–15 to develop each roll

Total cost ~$20 for ~36 pictures, making each picture you snapped about $.50 each

Can you imagine how many fewer pictures you would snap if you had to pay fifty cents to see each one? I have snapped 6 pictures today alone!

Some photography nerds like NerdHerder Joel Heffner still enjoy the beauty and process of old school photography with a little help from today's technology. Joel uses the iOS app **Pocket Light Meter** to measure light for non-digital cameras. He says it's especially useful for pinhole photography. For Android users, **LightMeter** does the same.

Your smartphone can take a great picture, but where and when you take that picture is up to you. **PhotoPills** helps you make the best decisions about outdoor photography. Among other things, the app tells you the exact time and location of sunrises, sunsets and moon movement so you can capture the perfect shot over the mountains around your chalet while on vacation.

● ●

PHOTO / VIDEO

Edit Images on Your Computer

It's a well-known fact that if you need to crop an ex-boyfriend out of the family Christmas picture, your best option is Adobe Photoshop. The software used to be hundreds of dollars, but with Adobe's Creative Cloud monthly subscription, you can get it for a few bucks a month. But even though Adobe tools are now in the realm of affordable, free is better.

Start with...

GIMP
The Original Free Photoshop Replacement
gimp.org

Pixlr X
Online Photoshop Competitor
pixlr.com

GIMP, which stands for GNU Image Manipulation Program, was created in the mid-1990s and might be the king when it comes to open-source Adobe Photoshop competitors. Today a community of GIMP enthusiasts work together to upgrade the program, release new versions and get the word out. Download GIMP to manipulate photos with its many plug-ins and extensions, and visit the forums for lively and informative conversations about tips and bug fixes. Well, lively conversations for nerds.

Although GIMP has been around the longest, **Pixlr X** is my favorite online image editor, with a Flash-based uploader that enables you to edit from any computer without any special software. You don't have to register. You don't have to download. You just go to the site and start editing.

Pixlr Editor has many of the same features as Photoshop, but recent updates have rendered the previously puzzling tools more understandable to non-designers like me. It has also added more graphic options such as text, objects and more.

Then Try...

Adobe Photoshop Express
Adobe's Lightweight Photoshop Tool
photoshop.com/products/photoshopexpress

Krita
Free Drawing and Editing Software for Images and Animations
krita.org

Adobe Photoshop Express may be just the lightweight image editor you need. You can launch a simple online editor from the site or download the free apps. Then you can apply filters, borders and stickers, or crop, resize and fine-tune an image.

Krita is more like GIMP in that it's 100 percent free and supported by donations and volunteers. The downloadable software is primarily for illustrations, art, painting and comics, but it works wonderfully as an image editor even if you're not an artist.

Also Check Out...

Inkscape
Vector Editor
inkscape.org

Vectr
Another Vector Editor
vectr.com

For advanced printing projects, you may need a more robust tool. Most digital graphic files are sized to look great on the screen but aren't high-enough resolution to print well at a decent size. That's why your designer for a print project will often ask for vector files, which can be increased in size without loss of quality, instead of JPEGs, which can't.

Inkscape is a free open-source vector editor and is considered a worthy competitor for Adobe Illustrator. Don't even ask me how to use it—Inkscape is way beyond my humble graphic skills.

Although Inkscape is the best-known Adobe Illustrator replacement, check out **Vectr**, a tool that design experts praise for its easier interface and fast learning curve.

Print Photos and Albums

Whether you're creating a professional book with product images for work or a filling family album to treasure forever, these photo printing services make the process easy, the pricing reasonable and the product memorable.

Start with...

Felt

Accordion-Style Greeting Card from Your Phone

feltapp.com

Ever since **Felt** started offering a $5 subscription service, I've been a much better friend. For $5 a month, I can send up to three four-paneled Felt cards (including shipping). I use them for everything from a client thank-you to a husband I-love-you. They have amusing special occasions, such as Ellen DeGeneres' birthday and a lovely sentiment that says, "Dearest co-worker, sorry about my stinky lunch." The cards are beautiful, and their square shape makes them hip (as in "it's hip to be square").

Then Try...

Chatbooks
A Fancier Monthly Photo Album
chatbooks.com

FreePrints
Free Photo Prints (for Just a Small Fee)
freeprints.com

FreePrints Photobooks
Free 5 x 7" Photo Book Monthly (for Just a Small Fee)
freeprints.com

FreePrints Photo Tiles
Free 8 x 8" Stick-able Wall Tile Monthly (for Just a Small Fee)
freeprints.com

EasyTiles
Glass Photo Tile Printing
easytiles.com

My attendees have been gushing to me about **FreePrints** for years, and the 5-star reviews prove they're right. You get up to 1000 4 x 6" prints (up to 85 a month) for just the cost of shipping ($1.99–9.99). You can order other sizes as well. It's a great way to gather browsable memories of your family's best days.

But that's not all! **FreePrints Photobooks** gives you a 5 x 7" photo-book a month for another "small shipping fee." They also have **FreePrints Photo Tiles** for one of those cute little 8 x 8" stick-able wall photos a month. I ordered 20+ of them for my hallway.

The next level up in their family of printing options is **EasyTiles**. Your photos are mounted on 8 x 8" glass tiles (the same size as the Photo Tiles). I could not find the price anywhere, so I had to download the app, fearing a hefty price tag. But they're just $15 each, and they offered me a discount immediately. I hate it when they scare me like that. What's wrong with $15?

As much as I like the idea of Groovebook, I think the product is a little casual for use at the office. **Chatbooks** is more expensive but ever so much cuter. Choose 60 photos a month for a 5 x 5" book. A softcover subscription is $8, or $13 for a very impressive hardcover.

Also Check Out...

Postagram
Photo Postcards from Your Phone
sincerely.com/postagram

The Guest
Event Photo Album App
theknot.com/photo-sharing-app

You can find a whole bunch of apps that let you send real mail from your mobile device. With super-thick postcards with a picture that pops out, **Postagram** is my favorite. For about two bucks a card mailed, you can make someone smile with just a couple of clicks on your phone.

You're at a conference, a business retreat, a family reunion, and everyone is snapping fun pictures. How do you pull them all together to see all the moments? **The Guest** was created for wedding guests by The Knot, but it will work wonderfully for your family gatherings and events as well. Just create an event, invite your guests to install the app and let everyone snap away! Guests can take pictures from their regular phone camera, and everything taken during the official party time will be shared—this means no one has to stop and upload pics separately. All the photos will be organized into an album that everyone can access.

PHOTO/VIDEO

Create Videos and Multimedia

In the early days of social media, gurus proclaimed, "Video is king!" Not much has changed. If you're not making videos to share your content, you're not engaging people to see your content.

Start with...

Animoto
Multimedia Photo and Video Montage Creator
animoto.com

Magisto
Movie Maker for Video Clips
magisto.com

Animoto takes your photos and short videos and synchronizes them into a multimedia movie complete with a soundtrack. Gather 10 or more pictures and/or videos, throw in a title and choose a theme and soundtrack—then push a button. PRESTO! Animoto instantly creates a perfectly timed, perfectly professional, perfectly awesome video that can showcase your event, your boss's retirement, your kid's prom preparations, your company's products—you name it.

The most versatile paid version is just $30 a year and gives you all kinds of extra functionality. Important note: Get a membership via the app, and you can use the app and the web to create and access videos. The pricing on the web is higher. (Weird, right? Don't ask me.)

Although **Magisto** doesn't have nearly the number of options as Animoto, this app does a great job with video clips and makes a cool instant movie. Just upload one or more video clips, and the tool uses smart editing to highlight snippets and apply filters and special effects. Try it out with the free version, or get extra options starting at $30 a year. The professional level enables you to do cool things with voiceovers.

Then Try...

Adobe Spark Video
Easy Voice-Over Video Tool
spark.adobe.com

Adobe Spark Video is one of the tools Adobe released as part of a service they call Spark. Find photos or upload your own on the web app or your iOS device. Then you record voiceovers for each slide in an incredibly easy process. After you have your video, you can change the theme and add a soundtrack. If you've used the images or music that Adobe provides, the tool will add the artist credits.

The bummer about Adobe Spark Video is that you can't download the video, so you'll have to play it online.

> Why did the PowerPoint
> cross the road?
>
> To get to the other slide.

Also Check Out...

Doodly
Whiteboard, Blackboard and Glassboard Software
doodly.com

PowToon
Online Whiteboard and Explainer Video Tool
powtoon.com

VideoScribe
Downloadable Whiteboard Video Tool
videoscribe.co

PowToon is a pioneer in low-cost whiteboard generators, which can cost thousands of dollars through a design firm. The online tool lets you start with templates to create presentations and videos. It takes a little finagling to get used to the interface; but when you understand the basics, you can create a brag-worthy showstopper. You can create PowToon-branded videos and slides for free, or buy a subscription starting at $16 a month for an annual plan.

One of my clients made an incredibly impressive whiteboard video using **VideoScribe**, which you can download on your computer or use on an iOS device. The pricing is about the same as PowToon, and the animations are a little more hand-drawn. **Doodly** is another downloadable tool. I like the way it draws in (doodles) chalkboard videos, erasing sections to add more pieces. You can look like a pro with any of the three tools.

Create and Edit Audio

You've captured a wonderful video testimonial for your event or company or product, but the background noise drowns out the wonderful things the person had to say. These tools will help you edit audio and even create your own music.

Start with...

Audacity
Open-Source Audio Recorder and Editor
audacityteam.org

Perhaps one of the best free downloadable tools that I almost never use is **Audacity**. It's a fully functional, incredibly professional, easy-to-use, multilingual audio editor and recorder. It's been around for as long as I've been seeking free stuff. Audacity doesn't have an app—just download it on your computer and edit like a pro.

Then Try...

GarageBand
Apple's Music Creation Studio
apple.com/mac/garageband

Kimberly Lilley is one of the original NerdHerders. Here's why she loves Apple's **GarageBand.**

> *I often put on events that are enhanced by music or other sounds, but I need to tailor the sound to that specific moment. This free app allows me to pre-create (is that a word?) the specific fade-in or fade-out that I need (or even a cut in the middle) easily and for free! For non-Mac users, Audacity is the free sound app that seems to be the closest in capacity.*

Also Check Out...

Auphonic
Automated Online Audio Editor
auphonic.com

Hya-Wave
Super-Simple Online Audio Editor
wav.hya.io

If you have the need for an occasional audio repair, check out **Auphonic.** The site gives you two free hours a month, and generally less than a buck an hour for more. Just upload audio or video files, and Auphonic automatically detects what it thinks should happen to help your audio. You can even enhance your file with intros, outros and imported captions.

In my trials, Auphonic's automations did a pretty good job cleaning up some videos with a lot of background noise. But **Hya-Wave** did a better job, even though I didn't know what the heck I was doing.

When you upload your audio to Hya-Wave, you can choose to apply filters such as a "Biquad Allpass Filter" or "A delay with feedback and dry/wet settings." I'm sorry, what? Even though I didn't know what all the filters meant, I applied the "Biquad Peaking Filter" to the same audio I ran through Auphonic's site, and the Hya-Wave version came out much, much better! Hya-Wave doesn't have any fancy add-ins or export options. You just upload your file, apply the mystery filters and download...all without registering. And it's free. We love free.

Design

....

In This Chapter...

DESIGN

Design a Logo, Book Cover, T-Shirt, Etc.

● ●

Your marketing material is a representation of your brand and a hugely important piece of the puzzle when you create your company's identity. Professionally designed logos, book covers and other graphic elements take time, money and patience, plus lots of expertise from experienced and smart designers.

But sometimes you just don't have the money or the time. That's where online design contest services can come in handy.

Start with...

99designs
Crowdsourced Design Contests with Style Analysis
99designs.com

DesignCrowd
Crowdsourced Design Contests with Bonus Stuff
designcrowd.com

Let's say your organization has a big event every year, and you're looking for a logo that would brand the conference series. You could hire your favorite graphic designer to come up with 10 to 20 ideas for several hundred to several thousand dollars. Or you could hold a logo design contest on a crowdsourcing site like **99designs** or **DesignCrowd** for a few hundred bucks to have dozens of designers come up with ideas that you could narrow down to your top choices and share with your potential attendees for a vote. These sites design logos, flyers, t-shirts, book covers . . . almost anything that can be designed.

Crowdsourcing your design projects is not only good for your wallet. It's fun to have your community/tribe/NerdHerd—whatever you have—vote on the best ideas.

I chose two of the many players in this space to highlight. The heavyweight, **99designs,** has been around for some time. When I was playing around with a logo contest entry, 99designs asked me to choose my favorite looks from a bunch of their logos to help me find my style. **DesignCrowd** impressed me by including business card printing in its logo design.

Then Try...

Looka
AI-Based Logo Tool
looka.com

If you're short on time and need a simple logo, **Looka** (formerly Logojoy) might be the answer. The site uses artificial intelligence to meld the design elements you seek into reality. After filling out a couple of questions, you pick favorites from the generated options. Every time you show a preference, Looka evaluates your input to generate more ideas that you might like more.

After you decide on a logo, you pay $20–65 to buy everything you need to use your new logo, or for another $15 you get business card and other designs as well.

Also Check Out...

Placeit
Mockup Templates to Put Your Logo on Everything
placeit.net

As soon as I had the cover of this book, I headed over to **Placeit** to create this 3D mockup that I could share with you guys.

On Placeit, you can upload an image and—get this—place it on all kinds of things, from 3D book covers to hoodies to coffee mugs and more. The site helps you create mockups with your logo, or even helps you create a new logo. The site now includes videos and other designs for marketing and social media. You can pay for individual downloads or get an unlimited subscription for about $100 a year.

Discover New Fonts

Even after all these years of being nerdy, a new font still makes me tingle. When it comes to the look and feel of a document, changing the font can change the personality, and it's easy to find free fonts to download and use.

Start with...

Dafont
Free Font Site with Interactive Preview Feature
dafont.com

Dafont is *still* my very favorite place on the web to find fonts with pizazz to add a little something extra to a look—it has made it into every book I've written! The key to finding your perfect font on Dafont is to put sample text into the custom preview box and then search by theme (cartoon, curly, calligraphy, handwritten). Most are free for personal use, and many are just plain free. Use filters to find ones you can use commercially. Read the fine print on fonts you use for work because the guidelines for use vary greatly.

Then Try...

Font Squirrel
Free Fonts for Commercial Use
fontsquirrel.com

Google Web Fonts
Font Sets for Online Use
google.com/fonts

Font Squirrel is another great resource, though it doesn't provide a preview of your text. The cool thing about the resources on this site is that they're all free for commercial use, so you won't have the letdown of finding the perfect font and then having to give it up because it's only for personal use.

If you're looking to add a little snazziness to your website, you can find new fonts that will work on the web at **Google Web Fonts**.

Also Check Out...

Wordmark.it
Preview Site for Fonts on Your Computer
wordmark.it

Have you ever spent a half-hour in Microsoft Word scrolling through your installed fonts one by one to find the perfect look for a document? **Wordmark.it** is a clever web tool that lets you write a few words for a preview then loads (almost all) your fonts into the site so you can see them all at once. I've noticed lately that some of the stranger fonts I have don't load onscreen. But the site still makes it easy for you to choose your favorites then filter them to see your top choices together. It's 100 percent free and super easy to use.

Hot Topic:
What the Font?

Sometimes you see a font in the wild that, well, drives you wild!* If you want to identify a font, you have several options.

Fontspring Matcherator
Online Font Identifier
fontspring.com/matcherator

Identifont
Font Identifier from Descriptions
identifont.com

What Font Is
Site with a Similar Font Search Engine to Find Free Alternatives
whatfontis.com

WhatTheFont
App for Mobile Font Identification via Photo
myfonts.com/whatthefont

Snap a picture of a mystery font, and both **Fontspring Matcherator** and **WhatTheFont** will give you a hand. Matcherator is online only, but I prefer it because it'll show you both free and paid results. Even though it only returns fonts you have to purchase, WhatTheFont has two pluses. First, the mobile app will let you see a font and take a picture for real-time identification. And next, WhatTheFont has the very best name.

Identifont is different. Instead of analyzing an image, the site asks you a series of questions about the characteristics of the letters you see. Does the center bar of the uppercase "P" cross the vertical or leave a gap? Is the dot on the lowercase "i" a circle or square? As you answer questions, Identifont narrows down the possibilities and shares a list of possible fonts and where to find them. Again, the tool only returns fonts you need to purchase. But then you can visit the Similar Fonts page on **What Font Is** to find free alternatives.

* Note: I realize only font nerds like me go wild with new fonts. But you probably love them, too, since you're reading this section, right?

DESIGN

Find Royalty-Free Images and Multimedia

● ●

Envato Elements
Subscription Service for Royalty-Free Assets
elements.envato.com

Envato Marketplace
Low-Priced Images, Templates, Audio and Tons of Stuff
envato.com

When you find images or video online, you need to make sure that it's not copyright protected, and its presence on a free site is not a guarantee! I have known several bloggers who use what they thought was a free image only to receive a demand for payment from an artist (or, more often, an artist's law firm).

Thus, despite the phenomenal list of free royalty-free images and video I'm about to share, I prefer to pay for (most of) the content I use, just to be safe. And the best resource I've ever come across is a subscription to **Envato Elements**. For about $200 a year, I have access to hundreds of thousands of all kinds of content that a small business might need:

- Images
- Video footage
- Illustrations
- Presentation templates
- WordPress website templates
- WordPress plugins
- Audio files
- Sound effects
- And more, more, more

Envato Elements is the very first place I look when I am creating anything that needs a graphic element. Searching for the word "nerd" yields 244 photos, 49 graphics (including illustrations, stickers, etc.), 48 graphic templates (logos, business card templates, icons), 26 stock video files and even three 3D images. This is pretty cool because "nerd" is actually a tough search word.

The site pays its contributors for adding to the pool, so you'll find a ton of stuff. Envato also offers a marketplace where you can buy presentations, websites, templates and more individually, but with Envato Elements, your fee pays for anything you find.

The drawback is that sometimes these are the less-than-bestselling offerings from the providers, so some of the stuff is kind of, well, bad. The better resources are on **Envato Marketplace**, where each element is for sale individually for $5 to $25 and up. But most of the time I can find something I can work with, and this has saved me money on the traditional paid sites and also sparks my creativity by encouraging me to spice up all kinds of pieces with a little extra multimedia. Plus, I have peace of mind knowing that I can use what I find without fear of copyright infringement.

That being said, you can find lots of great free stuff online.

Multi-Site Image Search Engines

Everypixel
Multi-Site Image Search Engine
everypixel.com

Pexels
Curates Photos from Many Free Sites
pexels.com

One of the frustrations with finding the perfect image is that you have to search on approximately a thousand sites. **Everypixel** and **Pexels** solve that problem for you by aggregating both free and paid royalty-free image and video sites into one search engine.

Free Special-Focus Sites

These stock image and video sites are far from generic. Here's my list of the best curated sites. Most are 100 percent free for personal and commercial use, but you should read the fine print each and every time to see if an artist asks for attribution, a link back or (gasp!) money.

Burst
Shopify's Surprisingly Robust Free Image Library
burst.shopify.com

DesignersPics.com
Superb Free Images by Photographer Jeshu John
designerpics.com

Flaticon
Free Vector Icons and Icon Sets
flaticon.com

Foodiesfeed
Beautiful Images of Beautiful Food
foodiesfeed.com

Freepik
Vectors, Photos and Icons Free for Attribution
freepik.com

From Old Books
Free Images from Antique and Vintage Books
fromoldbooks.org

Kaboompics
Beautiful Images with Amazing Search Engine and Color Palette Analyses
kaboompics.com

Life of Pix
Royalty-Free Images with a Free Video Cousin
lifeofpix.com

Life of Vids
Royalty-Free Videos with a Free Image Cousin
lifeofvids.com

Mixkit
Free Art, Illustrations and Video Clips
mixkit.co

NegativeSpace
Well-Composed, Hi-Res Photos
negativespace.co

New Old Stock
Vintage Photos from Public Archives
nos.twnsnd.co

New York Public Library Public Domain Collections
Public Domain Downloads with the Coolest Visualization
Tools Ever
nypl.org/research/collections/digital-collections/public-domain

Photo Creator from Icons8
Amazing Site to Compose Your Own Stock Photos and More
photos.icons8.com

Pikwizard
High-Quality Images with Built-In Canva-Like Editor
pikwizard.com

Pixabay
Photos, Vectors and Video
pixabay.com

Reshot
Handpicked Free Stock Photos
reshot.com

Slidesgo
Free Google Slides and PowerPoint Templates
slidesgo.com

SplitShire
High-Quality Free Photos and Video
splitshire.com

StockSnap
Image Site with Robust Search Engine
stocksnap.io

Superfamous Images
Phenomenal, Texture-Rich Images by Artist Folkert Gorter
images.superfamous.com

Unsplash
Legendary Free Image Site
unsplash.com

Videvo
Mix of Free and Paid Video Clips and Stock Footage
videvo.net

Wikimedia Commons
50M+ Free Media Files in a Clunky Search Interface
commons.m.wikimedia.org

Create Flyers, Social Media Posts and Other Graphics

If you don't have an excellent graphic designer on call, and if you're graphically challenged yourself, here are tools that help you fake it.

Start with...

Canva

Design Templates for Instant Social Media Posts, Flyers, Invitations and Much More

canva.com

Non-artistic folks like me need templates and simple instructions to create professional-looking graphics, and **Canva** is just the thing. The site provides frameworks for everything from Facebook timeline images to presentation slides to business cards. It takes just a few minutes to make a badge, invitation or poster with a few clicks of the mouse—perfect for small-business folks who just need a quick graphic for a newsletter, social media post or website.

Canva is free to use for individuals. If you're working with a design team with branding guidelines, you can sign up for Canva for Work for about $10 per user per month. This gives your design team the ability to set color schemes, make their own templates, resize any graphic with a click and more. The service also makes money selling high-quality backgrounds and images for your graphics for a buck each. The images it sells are generally cheaper than you'll pay buying the graphics yourself directly from the original source. If you use your own images, you pay nothing extra.

Bring on the NerdHerd fans! Once you use Canva, you can't imagine how you ever lived without it. Candy Joyce and Shala Bible adore it. Nell Withers McCauley says she has the entire Adobe suite of products but uses the free Canva for "quick but professional social media

DESIGN

ads." Heather Smith says she learned about Canva from me ("I have participated in a couple of Beth's classes and I always read her weekly newsletters. I learn so much!" [blush]) and uses it for work and personal projects.

Kim Becking LOVES Canva with capital letters:

> *This is an awesome design program for non-designers like me. It's a great way to create beautiful branded graphics, inspirational posts and other collateral material on your own! They make it super easy to share on social media as well. LOVE IT and use it in so many ways.*

Then Try...

Adobe Spark Post
Design Templates with Animation for Instant Social Media Posts
spark.adobe.com

PosterMyWall
Flyer and Sign Templates
postermywall.com

Like Canva, **Adobe Spark Post** lets you quickly create beautiful graphics and videos for social media and marketing. With dozens and dozens of templates, you can write a few words, choose a pic, apply a theme and share. Apple device owners can download the app, and everyone can use the tool online.

Three things make Adobe Spark Post cooler than Canva:

- You can animate the text on your graphic to make your post stand out. Canva makes you pay for that feature.
- After you design a graphic, you can easily and quickly transform the image to a number of shapes, both custom and pre-set for social media.

- Adobe Spark Post is actually one of a suite of cool tools Adobe has released under the umbrella of Adobe Spark. The other tools help you create presentations, videos (Page 341) and web pages.

And one thing that makes Adobe Spark Post way more annoying than Canva: Adobe is relentless in its encouragement to sign up for the subscription service. Sure, Canva prompts you to join, but Adobe puts up notice after notice and stop sign after stop sign to "encourage" you to sign up.

Teachers turned me on to **PosterMyWall**, which specializes in templates for quick signs and flyers. With categories such as fundraising, job fair, women's day and science fair (for starters), the templates cover almost any scenario of a poster you might need. PosterMyWall has free and paid options, and the service now includes video.

Also Check Out...

Word Swag
Text-Over-Image App
wordswag.co

Oh my goodness but I love **Word Swag**! It's one of my favorite on-the-go tools to add a little somethin'-somethin' to my social media posts. The thing that makes this tool so cool is that the text comes in formatted, and you don't have to have an eye for design to create a fancy quote.

And I'm not the only one who loves it. NerdHerder Breeda Miller calls Word Swag "an easy way to appear cool and clever." And Debra Jason loves it even more.

I love sharing images and quotes. Word Swag makes it simple to take one of my photos, add text to it and create a beautiful meme. We all know the importance of catching your viewers' attention, Word Swag helps you achieve that goal—quickly and easily!

DESIGN

Create Infographics

•••

Infographics take on the job of converting big data into understandable ideas, and they're all the rage on social media. Use these template-based infographic tools to make some of your own.

Start with...

Canva (Page 94)

Easelly
Easy-to-Use Infographic Templates
easel.ly

Here we go again... listing Canva (Page 94) as a favorite for creating instant graphics. As with Canva's other graphic categories, the beauty is in the variety of templates, which let you quickly personalize an infographic to express boring facts in an exciting way. The bummer is that the templates are very limiting. They are a certain size with certain elements, and that's what you get.

Easelly is similar in that you have a structure that you can personalize. Just open a template and start changing the words, colors and layout. But Easelly has an advantage over Canva in the number of free layouts and infographic-specific elements. The Easelly upgrade is just $5 a month ... worth it if you need the extra templates and options.

Then Try...

Piktochart
Infographic Templates with Flexible Data Points
piktochart.com

Visme
Block-Layout Infographic Tool
visme.co

Although the free version has lots of limitations, I think **Visme** helps you create the most attractive infographics because of its block features. Instead of having to use an overall layout structure like Easelly, you can add sections that will make your infographic easier to personalize.

Although the templates in **Piktochart** can be a little hard to work with, this tool is best for visually representing your data. The charts and graphs are dynamic parts of the infographic, and they can be updated automatically through a connection to Google Sheets. You can choose from a large number of graph styles, including pictographs, histograms and the ever-popular pie charts.

Also Check Out...

Grafiti
Search Engine for Charts, Graphs and Data
beta.grafiti.io

If you don't have time to make an infographic or chart yourself, **Grafiti** may be the answer. The site lets you search for charts and graphs from a wide range of sources. Just put in a keyword, and graphics in that topic will load on the page, complete with links to the source so you can verify the data.

Topic Index

App Index

••

About Beth Z
Your Nerdy Best Friend

Have you ever wondered if there IS an app for that?

Beth Z has the answer.

Since her first Motorola RAZR flip phone, Beth has made a verb out of the word nerd. Beth Z filters through thousands of apps, gadgets, widgets and doodads to find the perfect free and bargain technology tools for work and home.

Although the only real trophy she ever won was for making perfect French fries at McDonald's in high school, Beth Z has been featured on Best Speaker lists by some semi-important organizations. She has written multiple books on apps and has spoken to about 100,000 people, about 99.9% of whom can't pronounce her last name.

Beth Z Helps Your Team Be More Productive

Beth Z gives live and online presentations to companies and organizations that want to be more productive, efficient and awesome. Her programs focus on solving common office challenges with easy-to-use technology.

Contact Nerd HQ for rates and availability, and visit yournerdybestfriend.com/speaking for sample videos and session topics.

For more information:
beth@yournerdybestfriend.com
619.231.9225
yournerdybestfriend.com